YALE JUDAICA SERIES

VOLUME XXIII

THE FOLK LITERATURE OF THE KURDISTANI JEWS: AN ANTHOLOGY

Major Jewish communities of Kurdistan

The Folk Literature of the Kurdistani Jews: An Anthology

TRANSLATED FROM HEBREW AND NEO-ARAMAIC SOURCES
WITH INTRODUCTION AND NOTES BY

YONA SABAR

Associate Professor of Hebrew
University of California, Los Angeles

YALE UNIVERSITY PRESS NEW HAVEN AND LONDON

This is one of a series of volumes that will be published with the support of the Judaica Series Fund established by the William P. Goldman and Brothers Foundation, Inc.

The preparation of this volume was aided by a grant from the National Endowment for the Humanities. The findings, conclusions, etc., do not necessarily represent the view of the Endowment.

Published with assistance from the foundation established in memory of Philip Hamilton McMillan of the Class of 1894, Yale College.

Set in Garamond type.
Printed in the United States of America by Edwards Brothers Inc., Ann Arbor, Mich.

Library of Congress Cataloging in Publication Data

Main entry under title:
The Folk literature of the Kurdistani Jews.
(Yale Judaica series; 23)
Bibliography: p.
Includes index.
1. Jews — Kurdistan — Folklore. 2. Folk literature, Hebrew — Kurdistan — Translations into English. 3. Folk literature, Aramaic — Kurdistan — Translations into English. 4. Folk literature, English — Translations from Hebrew. 5. Folk literature, English — Translations from Aramaic. 6. Jewish folk literature — Kurdistan — Translations into English.
I. Sabar, Yona. II. Series.

GR98.F64 398.2′09566′7 81-43605
ISBN 0-300-02698-6 AACR2

10 9 8 7 6 5 4 3 2 1

TO MY SONS, ARIEL AND ILAN,
WHO FIRST INSPIRED THE TELLING
OF THESE STORIES IN ENGLISH,
AND IN MEMORY OF
MY FATHER-IN-LAW,
CODMAN KRUGER
(1907–1981)

CONTENTS

ILLUSTRATIONS

Frontispiece

Map of the major Jewish communities of Kurdistan.

following page 100

Yona Gabbay, a well-known storyteller from Zakho. As a merchant who traveled throughout Kurdistan, he heard and told many folktales. He died in Jerusalem in 1972, when he was more than one hundred years old. Photograph by Stephanie Sabar (Jerusalem, 1967).

The author reading a Neo-Aramaic manuscript with ḥaḵam ʿAlwān Avidani. Photograph by Stephanie Sabar (Jerusalem, 1969).

Sandor, a Jewish village in Iraqi Kurdistan, ca. 1934. Courtesy Field Museum of Natural History, Chicago.

Girl wearing case amulet with pendants. Courtesy Field Museum of Natural History, Chicago.

Sandor village schoolchildren, ca. 1934. Courtesy Field Museum of Natural History, Chicago.

Man watching teapot. Courtesy Field Museum of Natural History, Chicago.

Woman at a nomadic-style loom. Courtesy Field Museum of Natural History, Chicago.

Page from a Neo-Aramaic manuscript; the last page of a Midrash on *Bĕšallaḥ* (Exodus), with a colophon, copied in Nerwa in 1669 C.E. Courtesy Jewish National and University Library, Jerusalem.

PREFACE

The Jews of Kurdistan are unique in more than one way. They are considered one of the most ancient Jewish communities, traditionally tracing their origin to the first Israelite exiles taken away by the Assyrian kings. Until their emigration to Israel they were one of the most isolated Jewish communities in the world. Scattered in about two hundred villages in the rugged and almost inaccessible mountains of Kurdistan, they had very little contact with the rest of world Jewry. Yet in spite of their isolation and other adverse factors — such as general abject poverty, small and scattered communities, constant wars among the local Kurdish chieftains — this community maintained orally a unique wealth of ancient Jewish literary traditions embellished with themes from local Kurdistani folklore and daily life.

I have made an effort to include in this volume representative selections from the various genres of this literary heritage: epic re-creations of Biblical stories, Midrashic legends, folktales about local rabbis, Jewish and general Near Eastern moralistic anecdotes, folk songs, nursery rhymes, sayings, and proverbs.

I owe many thanks to Professors Judah Goldin and Franz Rosenthal, and to Dr. Leon Nemoy, for their encouragement in the various stages of this work. I am especially grateful to Dr. Nemoy for his painstaking editorial correction of my style and for his wise advice as to the type of selections to be included in the anthology. I am also grateful to Charles Grench and Sharon Slodki, at the Yale University Press, for their kind efforts and thoughts in making this volume as attractive in form as in content.

Among others who have assisted me are Professors Dov Noy and Aliza Shenhar of the Israel Folktale Archives, who very kindly made available to me the Archives' large collection of folktales of Kurdistani Jews. I am also much indebted to Dr. Stephen Stern, who prepared the motif index, and to the editors and publishers who gave me permission to include selections from their publications.

My wife, Stephanie, read the first English draft of each selection and assisted me in other aspects of this work, in addition to providing generous moral support.

INTRODUCTION

I. Kurdistan and the Kurds

1. The word *Kurdistān* in Persian means "the land of the Kurds." It seems to have been coined by the Seljuks, the Turkish dynasty that ruled the Near East between 1038 and 1194 C.E.,[1] but terms designating the Kurds or their land appear already in ancient times, going back as far as 2000 B.C.E. The Kurds are mentioned in Sumerian and Assyrian records, as well as in classical Greek and Latin works, particularly Xenophon's *Anabasis* (401–400 B.C.E.).[2] In Aramaic the region was known as *beṯ-ḳardu,*[3] and in the Aramaic translation of Onḳelos (fourth century C.E.) the Biblical *hare ʾĂrarat* (Gen. 8:4), "the mountains of Ararat," where Noah's ark had rested, is identified as *ṭure ḳardu,* "the mountains of Kurdistan."[4] There are a few references to *ḳardu* and *ḳarduyyim* in the Talmud (sixth century C.E.) as well.[5]

1. Minorsky, pp. 1130, 1140.

2. Ibid., p. 1132. Xenophon calls the area "the country of the Carduchi"; see his *Anabasis,* bks. III–IV (pp. 97–170), which deal with the march of the Greek soldiers through Kurdistan and their fierce fights with the Kurds in the mountains. It is interesting that already Xenophon was impressed by the rugged nature of Kurdistan and the warlike character of the Kurds: "These people [the Carduchi], they said, lived in the mountains and were very warlike and not subject to the [Persian] king. Indeed, a royal army of one hundred and twenty thousand had once invaded their country, and not a man of them had got back, because of the terrible conditions of the ground they had to go through" (p. 127).

3. The spelling with *ḳ* suggests a Semitic etymology, "to be strong" (Akkadian); for this and other possible derivations (e.g., Persian *gurd,* "hero") see Minorsky, pp. 1133–34.

4. For other ancient sources of this tradition see Ginzberg, *5,* 186; *4,* 269: "On his return to Assyria, Sennacherib found a plank, which he worshipped as an idol, because it was part of the ark which had saved Noah from the deluge. He vowed that he would sacrifice his sons to this idol if he prospered in his next ventures. But his sons heard his vows, and they killed their father, and fled to Ḳardu, where they released the Jewish captives confined there in great numbers"; *6,* 479: "Haman's son Parshandatha, who was governor of Ḳardunya, where the ark 'rested.'" A local tradition referring to the presence of the remnants of Noah's ark and altar on a local mountain ("Jabal Judi") is mentioned by various travelers; cf., e.g., Benjamin II, p. 94: "At the base of the mountain stand four stone pillars, which, according to the people residing here, formerly belonged to an ancient altar. This altar is believed to be that which Noah built on coming out of the ark [Gen. 8:20]. They likewise assert that his remains are buried in the vicinity; they do not, however, specify the exact spot. I myself obtained several fragments of the ark which appeared to be covered with a kind of substance resembling tar."

5. Cf. B. BB 91a: "Our forefather Abraham was imprisoned for ten years, three in Kutha and seven in Ḳardu"; B. Yeḇ 16a: "Proselytes may be accepted from among the Ḳarduyyim." See also n. 4, above.

2. Kurdistan is a geographic-ethnic term referring to a large territory (about 600 miles long and 120 to 150 miles wide) in central Southwest Asia.[6] The Kurds are a nation without a politically recognized homeland, and before 1914 they were divided among Turkey, Persia, and Russia. At present there are about 2,200,000 Kurds in Iraq, 2,500,000 in Turkey, 2,000,000 in Iran, and smaller numbers in Syria and Russia, numbering altogether nearly 7.6 million.[7]

3. Kurdistan consists mostly of a rugged chain of mountains, with the exception of some steppe and lowland areas on the fringes. The climate is characterized by heavy snows during the winter, followed by spring rains and heavy runoff down the slopes, creating rapid torrents and swollen rivers. This combination of rugged terrain and harsh weather makes the region an inaccessible and almost impregnable fortress. Hence, day-to-day control by remote governments has always been tenuous at best.[8] Kurdistan has consequently served also as a refuge for various religiously and politically dissident groups throughout the ages.

4. The Kurds are a distinct non-Arab ethnic group, mostly Sunnī Muslim, with their own language, customs, dress, and ways of life. They speak Kurdish, an Indo-Iranian language with several regional dialects, of which the best known are Kurmanjī and Sorānī. Originally the Kurds formed a mostly rural society, with traditional tribal villages including nomadic or seminomadic groups, but an increasing number of Kurds now live also in towns and work at various urban trades. Yet most Kurds, urban and rural alike, still associate themselves with specific tribal groupings.[9] Throughout Kurdistan marriage between cousins, or at least within the tribal clan, is preferred, and marriage with the father's brother's daughter is regarded as ideal.[10] Such marriages are nevertheless accompanied by the payment of the bridal price, a substantial sum of money, to the father of the bride. Although Kurdish society is

6. Minorsky, p. 1130.

7. These are fairly conservative estimates. For various political reasons there are no accurate statistics on the Kurdish population; see Bates, p. 220.

8. Cf. Xenophon's words in n. 2, above; Minorsky, p. 1133; Bates, p. 220.

9. Minorsky, pp. 1150–54; Bates, pp. 221–22; see VI/3, below.

10. So also among the Jews; cf. Field, p. 709: "In discussing various tenets of the Mosaic Law, we were informed that everyone must marry within the village of Sandur; the limitations of the population sanctioned unions between first cousins." Cf. Feitelson, pp. 207–08; Magnarella, pp. 54–56; Patai, chap. 6, and pp. 413, 420–22.

patriarchal and the patrilineal ties are very important, Kurdish women in general enjoy more freedom and a wider participation in public life than do Arab, Persian, and Turkish women. They are also freer in their behavior toward males and rarely wear the veil which is commonly worn by women in the Muslim world.[11]

5. Kurdistan contains a great variety of sects, ethnic groups, and nationalities. Apart from the Kurdish tribes (mostly Sunnī, and the rest Shiʿite), which form most of the population, there are various Muslim Arab and Turkish tribes, Christians of various denominations (Nestorians, Jacobites, Assyrians, Armenians), as well as Yazīdīs (followers of an ancient Kurdistani religion) and Mandaeans (a Gnostic sect).[12] Until their emigration en masse to Israel in the early 1950s, there were in Kurdistan about 25,000 Jews sparsely scattered in about two hundred villages and towns. Most Christians and Jews spoke various Aramaic dialects containing many Kurdish loanwords. As a rule, the Jews lived on friendlier terms with the Kurds than with the various Christian sects.[13]

II. The Jews of Kurdistan: Origin and History

1. According to their oral tradition,[14] recorded by several travelers

11. Cf. Minorsky, p. 1151; Bates, pp. 222–23; Patai, p. 124. On Kurdish women in general see Hansen (1960, 1961). On the life of Jewish women in Kurdistan see Brauer, pp. 147–57; Feitelson, pp. 215–16. See Shai (1970), on the social life of Kurdistani Jewish immigrant women in Jerusalem.

12. See *EI*, s.v. "Yazīdī," *4*, 1163–70; "al-Ṣābiʾa" (Sabaeans-Mandaeans), *4*, 21–22.

13. See Feitelson, pp. 202–03: "These relations must have been subject to change with political upheavals. It is clear that the Jews were very much closer to their Muslim neighbors than the other religious minority group, the Nestorians. Nowadays the Jews like to exult in the memory of the social ties which existed between the two groups. It seems clear that mutual visiting took place, and while the Muslims are said to have adored the *kasher* food, the Jews also ate in Muslim houses, abstaining on these occasions from meat and sometimes preparing part of their meal themselves."

14. Cf. Rivlin, p. 11. It is interesting that various Muslim and Christian sects in Kurdistan have an oral tradition, also familiar to the travelers, that they too are the descendants of the ten lost tribes of Israel. Cf. Benjamin II, pp. 123 ff.; Ben-Jacob, pp. 11–13; Ben-Zvi (1961), pp. 197–204; Grant, *passim*, particularly pp. 176–206. Cf. also the popular legend about the origin of the Kurds: "[On] that day King Solomon called five hundred jinn and ordered them to fly after the sun towards the west and not to return until they had found the five hundred most beautiful virgins in far-distant Europe. The jinn went about their search for a long, long time, appraised and compared for a long, long time, until they had selected five hundred girls as graceful and sweet as the full moon in May. But before they came flying back with the young virgins to the royal palace, King Solomon had gone the way of all flesh. And because the virgins had found favor in the eyes of the jinn, the jinn took them unto themselves as their wives. And they begot many beautiful children, and those children bore more children. . . . And that is the way the nation of the Kurds came into being" (Zikmund and Hanzelka, p. 5). Cf. Minorsky, p. 1134.

to Kurdistan,[15] the Kurdistani Jews are the descendants of the Jews exiled from Israel and Judea by the Assyrian kings and referred to by the prophet Isaiah as *lost in the land of Assyria* (Isa. 27:13), after *the king of Assyria took Samaria, and carried Israel away unto Assyria, and placed them in Halah, and in Habor, on the river of Gozan, and in the cities of the Medes* (2 Kings 17:6). Several scholars who have studied the Jews of Kurdistan tend to consider this tradition as at least partly valid,[16] and one may safely assume that the Kurdistani Jews include, among others, some descendants of the ancient Jewish exiles. Christianity was successful in this area at least partly because it was inhabited by Jews. Also, the conversion of the royal house of Adiabene[17] to Judaism (ca. first century C.E.) seems to have induced many other non-Jews to do the same, and the Jewish settlements in the area thus received further support from the proselyte princes. By the late second century Judaism was firmly established in Adiabene. Christianity, which usually spread in existing Jewish communities, was accepted in this region without difficulty.[18]

2. It is somewhat surprising to find very few references to Kurdistan in the Talmud, even though the Babylonian Talmudic centers of Sura and Pumbeditha were situated not too far from Kurdistan. The only Kurdish town mentioned in the Talmud is Arbil (Arbela),[19] one of the oldest cities in the world. It seems that in spite of their relative proximity, the rugged northern mountains of Kurdistan proper had very little communication with the Talmudic centers in the lowlands to the south. Still, the local Aramaic dialects — closely related to the Aramaic of the Talmud — spoken by the Jews and Christians of Kurdistan offer further evidence of the antiquity of their settlement in the country. Toward the end of the Gaonic period (ca. 1000 C.E.) Aramaic ceased being the language of Jewish scholarship, although for centuries it had been the lingua franca of the Persian empire, spoken by Jews and Gentiles throughout Syria-Palestine and Babylonia. After the Arab conquest of these areas, Aramaic was gradually superseded by Arabic. Only in the

15. Cf. already Benjamin of Tudela (p. 54): "These Jews belong to the first captivity which King Shalmaneser led away; and they speak the language in which the Targum is written." Cf. D'Beth Hillel, p. 80; Benjamin II, p. 124; Field, p. 710: "According to their tradition Sennacherib took some pagans from [the village of] Sandur to Jerusalem and returned with Jews to fill their place." On this exchange of populations see 2 Kings 17:24.

16. See Brauer, p. 39; Field, p. 709; Hamilton, pp. 290 ff.

17. Whose center was the Kurdish town of Arbil; see chap. XVI, n. 1, and §2, below.

18. Cf. Brauer, p. 39; *EJ*, s.v. "Adiabene," 2, 267–68.

19. See Rivlin, p. 12, n. 12; Brauer, pp. 39–40.

isolated and rugged area of Kurdistan has Aramaic survived as a spoken language down to the present day.[20]

3. Because Kurdistan has been practically a terra incognita, its Jewish centers are rarely mentioned by Arab historians. However, occasional references to the local Jews, including one to a conquest treaty concluded by the Arabs with "the Magians and the Jews" in a certain town on the border of Armenia in the mid-seventh century, indicate a large Jewish community in that area.[21]

4. More substantial evidence about the existence of Jewish settlements in Kurdistan is found in the itineraries of two Jewish travelers to Kurdistan in the twelfth century, Benjamin of Tudela and Pethahiah of Ratisbon. Although they did not penetrate into the rugged area of central Kurdistan,[22] their accounts contain valuable information. Benjamin mentions about one hundred Jewish settlements in the area and gives the Jewish population of Amidya as 25,000, an obviously exaggerated figure[23] yet one indicating a rather large population. His most interesting account is about David Alroy, the messianic leader from Kurdistan who rebelled against the king of Persia and planned to redeem the Jews from exile and lead them to Jerusalem.[24] It seems that under Seljuk rule[25] Kurdistan enjoyed some degree of prosperity. Both travelers speak of well-established and wealthy Jewish communities, with many synagogues and rabbis. The town of Mosul,[26] the commercial and spiritual center of Kurdistan, is reported to have had a Jewish population of 6,000 (Pethahiah) or 7,000 (Benjamin). Probably as a result of persecutions and fear of the approaching Crusaders, many Jews from Syria-Palestine had fled to Babylonia and Kurdistan. The Jews of Mosul enjoyed some degree of autonomy, and the local exilarch even had his own jail; of the taxes paid by the Jews, half were given to the exilarch and half to the governor.[27]

20. Called by scholars Neo-Aramaic, on which see *EJ,* s.v. "Neo-Aramaic," *12,* 948–51, and below, VI/3.

21. See Ben-Jacob, p. 14; Brauer, p. 40; Mann, p. 477.

22. Hence some details of their information about this area should be taken with a degree of skepticism, as they seem to be based on mere hearsay; cf. Brauer, pp. 18–19; D'Beth Hillel, p. 18; Fischel (1944), p. 196.

23. See chap. XIII, nn. 4 and 17, below.

24. See chap. XIII, below.

25. Minorsky, p. 1139; Brauer, p. 40; cf. I/1, above.

26. Called by Pethahiah (p. 5) "the new Nineveh," and by Benjamin (p. 33) "Assur the Great." Before the Arab conquest it was called *Ḥesna 'Ebraya,* "Jewish [Hebrew] Castle," "a name that was retained by the Jews as late as the 13th century" (Mann, p. 477).

27. Pethahiah, pp. 5–6. On the exilarch of Mosul see the source mentioned by Brauer, p. 40, n. 6.

5. This stability and prosperity, however, did not last long. Several decades after Benjamin's visit, in about 1230, the Spanish Jewish poet Judah al-Ḥarizi came to Kurdistan. His keen and humorous observations, expressed in his *Maqāmāt* (a genre of rhythmic prose), indicate the beginning of a spiritual decline. Although he was quite impressed with the beauty of Mosul and the splendor of its synagogues, he found the congregations full of ignorant boors, and even the cantors, for all their impressive appearance, made numerous ridiculous errors while reciting the prayers: "When I came to the House of Prayer along with the congregation, I beheld it lovely as a palace and a mansion. I sat down in the midst of the throng. There were beside me two elderly gentlemen with long beards who were strong as oaks. . . . They were tall and their bellies were as heaps of wheat. They had despicable souls and their eyes were haughty."[28] And of the cantor he writes:

> Frontlets are on his forehead, and on his head there is a shining white turban, two hundred cubits high.[29] The sweep of his beard reaches down to his navel. He is covered with a prayer mantle. He drags its fringes along the ground and almost stumbles on his skirts. . . . And as he dragged out his *piyyuṭim* [hymns] to his simpletons, and the songs of his mockery to his fools, and his chants to his donkeys, some of the people remained seated and some slept in continual sleep and reclined. But some of them fled and did not return. They forsook the synagogue and scattered from the shepherd of the oxen. They fled from the cattle and the herd until there were left only four asses braying and bellowing with the *ḥazzan* [cantor]. And they thought that they were singers![30]

This and other descriptions are quite vivid but seem somewhat exaggerated for humorous and prosodic effects, which is typical in this genre.

6. For the next two hundred years — the fourteenth and fifteenth centuries — there are no reports about the Jews of Kurdistan. These "dark ages" must be attributed to the general massacres of the population and the destruction of cities and towns by the Mongol conquerors,[31] which affected the entire Near East. It is

28. al-Ḥarizi, 2, 111 (English), pp. 223–24 (Hebrew).

29. An impossible height (approximately 300 feet) for a turban, and obviously an exaggeration. The word "cubit" (Hebrew *ʾammah*) is used here for the sake of the rhyme.

30. al-Ḥarizi, 2, 112–14 (English), pp. 224–25 (Hebrew).

31. Many Kurds who escaped the sword of the Mongols fled to Syria and Egypt, and two Kurdish tribes fled as far as Algeria; the revenues of the province of Kurdistan were reduced to one-tenth of what they had been under the Seljuks; see Minorsky, pp. 1140–41.

probable that in these troubled times much of the urban population of the steppes fled deeper into the more rugged and impregnable part of Kurdistan, creating new rural communities.

7. After the Turkish victory over the Persian rulers (1534), Kurdistan came under the control of the Ottoman Turks, which lasted until the end of the First World War. Again, a certain measure of stability was restored to the area, but the constant intertribal warfare and the revolts of local chieftains against the central government continued, as they do even today.[32]

8. From the sixteenth century onward we have not only travelers' reports but also the first documents and manuscripts written by the Jews of Kurdistan proper.[33] The Yemenite Jewish traveler Zechariah (Yaḥyā) al-Ẓāhirī visited several major towns in Kurdistan — Arbil, Kirkuk, Mosul, Nisibin, and Urfa ("Ur of the Chaldees") — and found in Urfa the two columns from which, according to a local tradition, Abraham was cast into the furnace.[34] In Arbil he rented a fine attic room that had a bed, a table, and a lamp. In the city streets he met a group of young and old people whom he immediately recognized as learned individuals and with whom he discussed matters of wisdom, Jewish mysticism (Kabbalah), and poetry. He was finally invited to a great feast prepared by several persons, each one an expert in a particular area of food preparation. The occasion included also a contest in the composition of poetry on mystical subjects.[35]

9. The documents and manuscripts written by the rabbis of Kurdistan during the sixteenth and seventeenth centuries supply many details about the spiritual, economic, and social life in Kurdistan during that period.[36] Some communities lived in abject poverty, yet the rabbis, especially those of the famous Barzānī family, established many yeshivot (centers of traditional Jewish studies) throughout Kurdistan and attracted students even from as far away as Egypt and the Land of Israel. Rabbi Nathanael Barzānī had a large library of books and manuscripts, quite rare in Kurdistan, which his son Rabbi Samuel inherited. In centers of study such as

32. In addition to these troubles, "Henceforth, for about three centuries Kurdistān became the arena for the struggle between the Ottoman Sulṭāns and the Shāhs of Persia" (Minorsky, p. 1142).

33. See §9, below.

34. al-Ẓāhirī, p. 100.

35. Ibid., pp. 77 ff.

36. See VI/6, below.

Nerwa and Amidya, many Midrashim, halaḵic works, Biblical commentaries, and hymns were composed, redacted, and copied. Some were translated into the spoken Neo-Aramaic language for the use of students and laymen. The descendants of the Barzānī family, including the famous female Rabbi Asenath, the daughter of Rabbi Samuel, served as rabbis and heads of yeshivot down to our time, not only in Kurdistan proper but in the large cities of Mosul and Baghdad as well.[37]

10. During the eighteenth and nineteenth centuries Kurdistan suffered a greal deal from the constant armed conflicts between the central government in Turkey and the local aghas and tribal chieftains, resulting in a general decline in population, Muslim as well as Jewish and Christian.[38] Many localities that had earlier been reported to have large Jewish populations were reduced to a few families or none at all. Typical cases were the towns of Nerwa and Amidya: although still major Jewish centers in the seventeenth century, several decades later they were reduced almost to ruins. Amidya was besieged and destroyed in 1832 by the agha of Rawanduz. The American missionary Asahel Grant visited Amidya in 1839 and found that it had hardly any inhabitants and that out of one thousand houses only two hundred and fifty were occupied, while the rest were demolished or uninhabitable.[39] The British missionary Badger visited Amidya in 1852 and described it as being "little better than a heap of ruins, and the rest is chiefly occupied by graves."[40] Another missionary, Stern, a converted Jew, wrote in 1854 that the Jews of Amidya were treated by the agha of Rawanduz with great cruelty and that many of the survivors had fled to other towns.[41] In recent times Amidya has had only about four hundred

37. See chap. XV, introduction, and V/2, below.

38. Cf., e.g., the massacre of about 10,000 Nestorians and the devastation of their Barwārī region by the Turkish governor Nūrullāh Beg during the years 1843 to 1847; see Minorsky, p. 1147.

39. See Grant, p. 45.

40. Badger, *1*, 199.

41. Stern, p. 225: "The Jews, who formed a great part of the population, were treated with merciless cruelty and oppression; many of them migrated to other towns, and those that were not so fortunate, submitted to the yoke of the tyrant." Cf. the story told by the Jews of Amidya about this long siege and the eventual destruction of the city walls, Brauer, pp. 50–51. That Amidya was a natural fortress is evident from travelers' descriptions; cf., e.g., D'Beth Hillel, p. 79: "The town is built on the top of a high mountain surrounded with a high and strong wall built of hewn stones. They have a custom that when anyone is found guilty of death, to precipitate [*sic*] him from the top of the wall, and before he reaches the foot of the mountain he is dashed to pieces." Cf. chap. XV, legend 6, below.

Jews.[42] Nerwa's fate was not very different. Before the outbreak of the First World War, the local agha rebelled against the sheikh of Barazān who ruled over the country with great cruelty. The irate sheikh captured Nerwa and set it on fire, destroying, among other things, the synagogues and all the Torah scrolls therein. As a result all the Jews, except three families, fled the town and wandered off to other places, such as Mosul and Zakho.[43] The latter was almost the only place in our time in Kurdistan proper with a substantial Jewish population (about 5,000 in 1945).[44]

III. Occupations and Economic Conditions

1. Many of the Jews of Kurdistan were farmers, shepherds,[45] raftsmen, and loggers — occupations almost unknown in other Jewish communities in the East or in the West.[46] In past centuries more

42. See Ben-Jacob, p. 81.

43. See Rivlin, p. 79; Ben-Jacob, pp. 64–65.

44. Ben-Jacob, p. 62; cf. Sabar (1974b), p. 48. Rabbi David D'Beth Hillel, who rediscovered the Jews of Kurdistan ca. 1827, estimated the Jewish population of Zakho at that time to be 600 families (p. 76). The rediscovery of the Kurdistani Jews by D'Beth Hillel almost coincided with the rediscovery of the Nestorians by the American and British missionaries, who tried, with the help of several European converts from Judaism, to work among the Jews as well. For bibliographical details on these and other missionaries and travelers in Kurdistan, and a critical survey of their works, see Brauer, pp. 22–32. The most daring among them was Dr. Asahel Grant, a physician from Utica, New York, who was the first Westerner to penetrate deep into Kurdistan proper. He owed his survival to his useful medical skill, but he lost his young wife and twin daughters shortly after their arrival at Urmia, in Persian Kurdistan; see Laurie, pp. 97, 155–56. Dr. Grant's portrait appears as the frontispiece in Laurie's book.

45. Including some nomadic Jewish families; cf. Layard, pp. 383–84: "Three hours' ride, always rapidly ascending along the banks of the rivulet, brought us to a large encampment. The flocks had been driven down from the higher pastures, and were gathered together to be milked before the black tents. A party of women already crouched round their sheep. Their long hair was platted in tresses ending in tassels mingled with gold coins. From a high turban of gay colors, also adorned with coins, a thin white veil fell over their shoulders, and their flowing garments were of bright silk. The children ran to and fro with wooden bowls, and a girl standing near sang a plaintive air, beating the measure on a tambourine. The features of the women and of the men, who came out of their tents as we rode up, as well as the tongue in which they addressed one another, showed at once that they were not Kurds. They were Jews, shepherds and wanderers. . . There were many other families, keepers of sheep like themselves, scattered over the mountains; they were shepherds again, as they had been when they were an abomination to the Egyptians." (cf. Gen. 43:32).

46. See Brauer, p. 172; Ben-Zvi (1961), p. 37; cf. Benjamin II's description (p. 130) of the Jewish farmers: "A portion of the higher classes devote themselves to the culture of the soil; one sees them going in the morning with their wives and children into fields and vineyards, from which they return in the evening. . . . I was much gratified to find that a spirit of industry and enterprise seemed to have taken possession of my coreligionists here; they seemed to vie with each other as to who should be most industrious."

villages were populated entirely by Jews than later on,[47] and some — e.g., Sandor — were so until the emigration of the Kurdistani Jews to Israel. Rabbi David D'Beth Hillel, who visited the village around 1827, describes it as follows: "It is a large village. There are about a hundred families of Israelites, farmers. . . . They have an abundance of cattle, and most of them are very rich. . . . This place is indeed a land flowing with milk and honey. The climate is wholesome, and there are both good water and excellent wines."[48] In larger centers Jews traded in grain, cotton, wool, cattle, gum and gallnuts, sesame, and tobacco. Many had vineyards and orchards. The artisans included weavers, dyers, shoemakers, and a few silversmiths and goldsmiths.[49] In the twentieth century, for security reasons and owing to the improvement of transportation by the use of motorized vehicles, many Jews (as well as Kurds and Assyrians) gradually left the villages and the hardships of farming and moved to urban centers, looking for an easier life as shopkeepers, merchants, and butchers. The towns, with their large synagogues and numerous religious functionaries, were more suited to Jewish life and provided greater security against attacks by nomadic tribes and brigands as well as relief from the natural calamities of the rugged areas.[50]

2. A common group among the poor in the larger towns, such as Zakho, were the peddlers who traveled in companies of two or more, riding donkeys and mules and selling certain groceries (such as tea and sugar) and notions (such as needles, buttons, and thread). This

47. Brauer, p. 172, Benjamin II, pp. 89–90: "Tselma — the village of the Jews. . . . According to ancient Biblical custom . . . the village bears the name of its founder, a Jew, celebrated and universally respected in the neighborhood for his riches, noble character, and his tried warlike bravery. This person was so munificent that he expended the greater portion of his fortune in dispensing charity. . . . Tselma, when attacked by plundering hordes, repulsed them by his own personal courage and thereby continued to rise more and more in the respect of the inhabitants of his village. . . . According to eastern custom, he has two wives, who have borne him seven children. I remained two days in this truly patriarchal family, and enjoyed many proofs of attention and sympathy."

48. D'Beth Hillel, p. 79. Cf. also his description of Sukho (pp. 80–81): "This village contains about 30 families of Israelites who have a little synagogue. . . . They are very kind people. They are all farmers and rich, having an abundance of flocks. They have also a multitude of fine white cedar trees, which are planted round about the village. . . . Indeed, it is a very rich and pleasant place; no other nations reside there." On the village of Sandor, see Field (including photographs of the village and its Jews, some reproduced here and in Feldman and Miller).

49. D'Beth Hillel, p. 76; Brauer, pp. 181–84.

50. Cf. Brauer, pp. 170–71, 176 ff.

occupation was extremely dangerous, as their routes were often infested with robbers, and many lives were lost at the hands of Kurdish brigands.[51] Of the peddlers of Zakho it was said that they never died in their homes but rather found natural or violent death on the road.[52]

3. Another interesting and unique occupation, especially among the Jews of Zakho, was rafting and logging. Situated on a large island formed by the two branches of the Khābūr River, the main route for the transport of materials from central Kurdistan to the Tigris steppe, Zakho became an important shipping center. About seventy Jewish families in the town were loggers and raftsmen. The rafts were square or rectangular, made of logs tied together alone or over inflated sheepskins.[53]

4. Other skills common among Jews were spinning (done mostly by women), weaving of light rugs and clothing, and dyeing of woolens. Weaving was common in the rural areas as well as in the urban centers. Many farmers worked in weaving, especially during the winter, when they had little farming to do. It is interesting that in the towns some ḥaḵamim (rabbis) worked at home as part-time weavers in order to earn additional income.[54] The Jewish weavers were recognized in their communities as superior workmen and were greatly esteemed by the Kurdish aghas as well. Shemuel Eliyahu, a weaver from Dohok, used to weave fine prayer rugs for his agha,

so that he would be favorably remembered when the agha knelt to pray. This same agha used to invite the weaver to his house in the mountains, sending his armed retainers to escort him. The sheikhs of the surrounding villages, who were dependent on him, were also present on these occasions. The agha seated the weaver in the place of honor at his right hand, and in clear and unambiguous language declared, 'This is my Jew,' and if anyone harmed him, 'his blood shall be upon his own head.' He also saw to it that 'his Jew' got kosher dairy food, and he bought new utensils for him to use.[55]

51. Cf. chap. XVII, tale 2, and nn. 61–62, below.

52. Brauer, p. 178, n. 8; Ben-Jacob, p. 17. Cf. Feitelson, p.202: "Jews were often peddlers traveling among the remote Kurdish villages. As non-participants in the recurrent hostilities between rival Kurdish tribes and villages, they seem to have been especially suited to this profession."

53. Brauer, pp. 183–84.

54. Ibid., p. 182; cf. chap. XV, legend 2, below, about Rabbi Samuel as a weaver.

55. Schwartz, p. 77. This article includes also several illustrations of weaving patterns and color photographs of the rugs.

According to Benjamin II, the woolen rugs made by the Kurdistani Jews were so fine that they were exported abroad as well.[56]

5. In general, the occupations of the Kurdistani Jews were typical of a rural or small-town society, and therefore few wealthy merchants or bankers were found among them, unlike, for example, the Jews of Baghdad, who commonly practiced such occupations.[57] Money in general was scarce in Kurdistan, and so were items of luxury. Much of the trading was by way of barter, for example, shoes could be exchanged for chickens, notions for farm produce, "a hanging [rug] . . . for its equivalent in farm produce, such as eggs, milk, honey, fruit, tobacco, wheat, etc. In other cases payment was partly in kind and partly in cash."[58]

6. Some Kurdistani Jews, after their emigration to Israel, continued to work as farmers, establishing rural settlements in the Jerusalem mountains and elsewhere.[59] Of those who settled in cities, mostly in Jerusalem, some worked first at hard manual labor, as porters, masons, and stonecutters, and a few who started as common laborers in the building trade are now among the wealthiest people in Israel, owning luxurious hotels and restaurants. Much of the construction business in Jerusalem was and still is dominated by Kurdistani Jews.[60]

56. Benjamin II, pp. 129–30.

57. See ibid., pp. 140–41.

58. Schwartz, p. 77. The Jews were regarded by the Kurds as successful and shrewd merchants, as the following anecdote illustrates: "Once, so they tell, a Jew came to the house of an agha. The agha said to the Jew, 'The Jews are swindlers — teach me the art of swindling.' The Jew was frightened and did not know what to do. He said to the agha, 'Bring me a large ball of fine woolen yarn.' When that was brought to him, he tied the end of the yarn to the agha's finger and said, 'Hold it until I come back.' The agha held the yarn, and the Jew left the house and kept unwinding the ball. After he had gone some distance, he cut the yarn and tied it to a tree. Then he went to the marketplace and sold the rest of the ball of which only a little was used up. The agha meanwhile was sitting and waiting. He waited one hour, and still the Jew did not come back. He waited two hours, and still the Jew did not come back. Finally, he went out to look for him and realized that the Jew had taught him a practical lesson in swindling" (Brauer, p. 180, as told by an informant from Amidya).

59. Where they became a subject for a literary work in Hebrew by Joseph Ehrlich. For a list of villages settled by Kurdistani Jews in Israel see Ben-Jacob, p. 26.

60. Cf. V/3, below. In more recent years some Kurdistani Jews in Israel have become prominent in the Israeli army as well as in the academic world. Cf. Magnarella, p. 53: "It is estimated that about 70 percent of the working Jewish Kurds of Sanandaj [Persian Kurdistan] are employed in private family business, for example, in retail shops, peddling, or as rug dealers, cloth merchants, or doctors in private practice. Most of the remaining 30 percent are employed in positions associated with the government, for instance, as pharmacists, doctors, officials, teachers, engineers, and clerks. On the average, the standard of living of Jewish Kurds is better than that of Muslim Kurds in the city." I found a similar situation in Urmia when I visited there in the summer of 1975; see Sabar (1975a), p. 294. Cf. n. 65, below.

IV. Religious and Spiritual Life

1. The level of spiritual life in any society depends largely upon its physical security, economic conditions, population size, and communication and contact with other societies. In the case of the Jews of Kurdistan all these factors were negative. The security of life in the area was always precarious.[61] It was common for population remnants to migrate from place to place because of destruction or devastation by one tribal chieftain or another. The Jewish population in any one locality would often dwindle from several hundreds or even thousands to a few families, if that. Yet during some short, less troubled periods of relative security a few centers of learning did flourish. Because of the difficult economic conditions, people had to work hard and long just to sustain themselves. Many suffered from hunger, physical ailments, and as a result of natural calamities.[62] As in any farming society, very little time was left for study or for developing a spiritual life. The Jewish community was also one of the smallest in the world. The entire population of Jews in Kurdistan, before their almost total emigration to Israel, amounted to about 25,000, scattered over a large area in about two hundred villages and small towns. Owing to the rugged nature of the area and the constant danger on the highways, these small communities were often quite isolated even from each other, and certainly from Jewish communities outside Kurdistan, including even the relatively near metropolitan communities of Baghdad, Damascus, and Istanbul.

2. It is no wonder, therefore, that the few daring Jewish travelers who visited Kurdistan generally found the Jews there at a low

61. The dangers have been mentioned by every traveler to Kurdistan, beginning with Xenophon (see n. 2, above); cf., e.g., Benjamin II, pp. 105–06: "No caravans pass through the recesses of the mountains I wished to explore. The locality is the most desolate and dismal that can be imagined; it is, so to say, the very heart of the desert, little known even to the dwellers of the country and but seldom visited. Rocky mountains and deep hollows in which enormous hordes of robbers conceal themselves are the principal features of this wilderness. The traveler is very frequently attacked when he least expects it, as the robbers are very expert and cunning and hide themselves so systematically that the wayfarer cannot dream of any danger until he is suddenly and unawares pounced upon. It was only with the greatest trouble that we could advance, and we were always compelled to be on our guard, as we were not safe for a moment." Cf. III/2, and n. 51, above.

62. See, e.g., the natural disasters described in chap. XVI, below. In 1892 a terrible river flood in Zakho devastated about 150 Jewish homes and the two synagogues and caused several persons to drown. This calamity came on top of several others, such as the murder of seven Jews by Kurdish brigands and a severe drought and famine; see Ben-Jacob, pp. 209–10.

spiritual level. The travelers were impressed by the Aramaic tongue spoken by the Kurdistani Jews[63] but were appalled by their shallow knowledge of Judaism and Jewish law. Benjamin II writes that "the ignorance of our Jewish brethren here is so great that they are not even capable of reciting a prayer; and nowhere, I must confess with pain, did I find them in such a debased state and sunk in moral turpitude as here."[64] This and similar statements, however, are true for the most part only about remote rural areas but far from true about larger urban centers.[65] The travelers' statements were often based on hearsay, on misunderstanding due to unfamiliarity with the local customs and lack of knowledge of the local languages, or just on fleeting impressions, as they stayed only a very short time in each place.

3. The Jews of Kurdistan, as in any traditional rural society, were deeply religious and observed what they knew of Jewish law quite strictly. To be sure, their religion expressed itself in the daily practice of religious customs derived from ancient oral traditions and transmitted from generation to generation, rather than in learned abstract precepts.[66] Although many could not read the

63. Cf., e.g., Benjamin of Tudela (p. 54): "They speak the language in which the Targum is written"; Pethahiah (p. 27): "Whoever stays there for a while begins to understand their language, because it is close to our [Aramaic] tongue or the Targum"; Ben-Jacob, pp. 21–22.

64. Benjamin II, p. 106; cf. also Benjamin II, pp. 132–33; Rivlin, pp. 23–24; Ben-Jacob, pp. 20–21; al-Ḥarizi's description, II/5, above. This was not true, however, in other periods; cf. n. 65, below.

65. Cf. Ben-Jacob, p. 21; Pethahiah–Gruenhut (p. 8): "There is no illiterate person [*'am ha-'areṣ*] in all the land of Babylonia and Assyria and the land of Media and Persia that does not know all the twenty-four books [of the Bible] . . . for the *ḥazzan* [cantor-reader] does not read the Torah [during public prayer], rather whosoever is called up to the Torah reads it himself"; Benjamin of Tudela (p. 54): "Amongst them are learned men." Cf. also the following account (ca. 1969) of the Jews of Sanandaj, a large town (pop. 40,000) in Persian Kurdistan: "Owing to their superior economic condition and the great stress which they place on education, the average Jewish Kurd attains a higher level of education than does the average Muslim in the area. Many of the Jewish Kurds who are in their twenties and thirties have had the advantage of education past class 12, and the proportion of this minority community which enjoys professional standing is great; illiteracy is probably nonexistent" (Magnarella, pp. 52–53); cf. n. 60, above.

66. Cf. Rivlin, pp. 38 ff. For a list of ancient Biblical and Talmudic customs retained by Kurdistani Jews but forgotten or radically changed in other Jewish communities, see Rivlin, pp.47–56; Benjamin II, pp. 130–31, e.g.: "Wherever I went during vintage and harvest time, I found a custom strictly observed by the Jews and Kurds, which brought to my mind the precepts of the Bible. Neither the ears of corn, nor the grapes, nor fruits are wholly collected, but the portion of the widows and orphans is always left; it is even allowed to go into a ripe cornfield, to break the sheaves, and there and then to boil the corn in water, but the ears of corn must not be cut, neither may they be carried away. In the same way grapes are

Hebrew prayers, almost everyone attended services in the synagogue, not only on the Sabbath and Jewish holidays but also on weekdays. I remember that in Zakho, my hometown, there were several *minyanim* (prayer quorums) every morning, beginning at 5:30, for woodcutters, butchers, and others who had to be at work early. A Jew desecrating the Sabbath or a Jewish holiday was almost unheard of.[67] All Jewish holidays were observed most strictly and with great joy and celebration.[68] In every house there was usually at least one person who knew how to read the Hebrew blessings, and the more common ones were memorized even by the illiterates. Moreover, in times of relative prosperity many yeshivot were established by the rabbis of Kurdistan, some of whom had students even from outside the country[69] who in turn later served as rabbis in large urban centers, such as Mosul and Baghdad.[70] Some rabbis were pious mystics who wrote or edited Hebrew and Aramaic Midrashic and halakhic works, liturgical hymns, and mystic poems.[71] Rising at midnight to recite devotional prayers, fasting twice weekly or oftener, and other ascetic practices were common among these pious men.

4. The religious practices of the Kurdistani Jews included, in common with other Near Eastern and North African Jewish and non-Jewish communities, the visitation and veneration of local shrines. These pilgrimages were undertaken by individuals, or more commonly by entire groups, during the Jewish Festival of Weeks (Pentecost), which was appropriately called *ʾeḏ-zyara,* "Festival of Pilgrimage." These traditional shrines included famous places, such as the tombs of the Biblical prophets Nahum in Alqosh, Jonah in Nineveh, and Daniel in Kirkuk, as well as several local caves supposedly visited by Elijah.[72] In addition to these there were shrines of illustrious local rabbis, for example, the *be-ḥazzane,*

---

allowed to be gathered in the vineyards, and to be eaten there." Cf. Lev. 19:9–10; Deut. 23:25–26.

67. This strict observance was recognized by the Gentiles of Kurdistan as well; cf. chap. XX, proverb 55 and chap. XV, legend 4, §3, below. Cf. Feitelson, pp. 204–05: "Religion formed an integral and indivisible part of everyday life. . . . The laws of Sabbath, kashrut, and Purity were observed most strictly by everyone." On the strict observance of the Jewish law of cleanness by the Jewish women of Kurdistan see chap. X, n. 25, below.

68. Cf. Rivlin, pp. 33–38; Brauer, pp. 217–94; Feitelson, pp. 205–06.

69. See chap. XV, introduction, p. 107, below.

70. Ibid., p. 105.

71. See chap. VI, below.

72. Cf. chap. IX, below.

"house of the cantors," and the tombs of Rabbis Nathanael and Samuel Barzānī-Adoni, all in Amidya.[73] Benjamin II was present in Alqosh during the Festival of Weeks and describes the celebration thus:

At break of day morning prayer is recited; after which the men, bearing the Pentateuch [Scroll of the Law] before them, go armed with guns, pistols, and daggers to a mountain in the vicinity, when, in remembrance of the Law, which on this day was announced to them from Mount Sinai, they read in the Torah and recite the Mousaph prayer. With the same warlike procession they descend the mountain. The whole community breaks up at the foot, and in an Arabic fantasy, a war performance, begins. The picturesque confusion, the combatants, their war cries heard through the clouds of smoke, the clashing of weapons, and the whole mimic tumult presents a fantastic spectacle, which is not without a certain dignity, and makes a strange impression on the spectator. This performance . . . is not practiced by the Jews in any other parts of the globe. This war performance is said to be a representation of the great combat, which according to the belief in those parts, the Jews, at the coming of the Messiah, will have to maintain against those nations who oppose their entrance into the promised land and their forming themselves into a free and independent kingdom. The women who remained behind in the town come, singing and dancing to the accompaniment of a tambourine to meet the men, and they all return together. Even the professors of other creeds take a part in this jubilee festival of their guests, which moreover is to them a matter of pecuniary advantage.[74]

This detailed description is quite realistic and fits well with what I myself remember of this celebration.

5. In spite of the general preoccupation with daily routine practices, such as prayers and keeping the Jewish holidays, as described above, the moral principles of Judaism were learned as well. Just as Jewish law was transmitted orally from generation to generation, so the moral principles of Judaism were inculcated orally through the sermons in the synagogue.[75] The sermon (Neo-Aramaic *draša* or *daruš*, Hebrew *dĕrašah*) played a most important role in the religious and national edification of isolated communities such as

73. Cf. chap. XV, introduction, p. 105; chap. XIII, n. 8, below. For more details on these and other shrines see A. Ben-Jacob, *Ḳĕḇarim Ḳĕḏošim bĕ-Ḇaḇel* [Holy tombs in Babylonia] (Jerusalem, 1973); Benjamin II, pp. 76–79, 83–84, 88–89, 97–103, 114, 137–38, 147–48, 152–53.

74. Benjamin II, pp. 99–100. On local messianic movements see chap. XIII.

75. Cf. chap. XIV, and chap. XV, tale 4, §7, below.

Kurdistan, where the rate of illiteracy was high. The ancient custom of having a sermon in the synagogue on Sabbath afternoon, following the *Minḥah* prayer, was in force in the large centers of Kurdistan down to my own time. The ḥak̲amim of Zakho in recent times used to deliver a free oral translation into the spoken Neo-Aramaic language of selections from homiletic and didactic works, such as *Pirḳe ʾAb̲ot̲* ("The Sayings of the Fathers"),[76] Midrash Tanḥuma,[77] and *ʿOd̲ Yosef Ḥay,* a collection of tales and homilies by the famous Rabbenu Joseph Ḥayyim of Baghdad.[78] However, the Neo-Aramaic homilies preserved in manuscripts from the seventeenth century indicate that in the past the ḥak̲amim prepared their own collections of homilies for the weekly sermon,[79] which included tales and legends of the life and deeds of the patriarchs, ancient kings and heroes, prophets and rabbis, mystics, and ordinary pious men and women, all carefully selected to fit their particular audience.[80] These legends not only were fascinating in themselves but also directly taught ethical principles, repentance for misconduct, and steadfast devotion to the faith of the fathers. The miracles and salvations so often mentioned in these sermons gave the Jewish community much comfort, as well as strength to endure the hardships of daily life in exile and to keep up the hope for redemption and for the coming of the Messiah.[81]

V. Relationship to the Land of Israel

1. Another indication of the religious and national sentiments of the Kurdistani Jews is their strong and continuous relationship to the Land of Israel. As already mentioned, the Jewish communities of Kurdistan maintained a tradition tracing their origin to the exiled tribes of Israel.[82] This tradition was kept alive in various ways. Several localities in Kurdistan either had the same names as places in the Land of Israel (e.g., Alqosh, Arbil) or were given Biblical names by the local Jews (e.g., Ekron for ʿAḳra, Kelaḥ (Calah) for

76. For an English translation and commentary see Judah Goldin, *The Living Talmud: The Wisdom of the Fathers* (New Haven, 1955; reissued as a Mentor Book, New York, 1957).

77. Edited by S. Buber (reprinted New York, 1946).

78. On this and his other works see *EJ,* s.v. "Joseph Ḥayyim ben Elijah al-Ḥakam," 10, 242–43.

79. See VI/4, below.

80. For examples see especially chaps. II, III, V, XI, XII, below.

81. For other details see VI/4, below; Sabar (1976a), pp. xxi–xxv.

82. See II/1, above.

Kirkuk, Asshur for Mosul, Mount Sinai for a mountain near Alqosh).[83] Zakho was known as "the Jerusalem of Kurdistan."[84] Even the letters of the Hebrew alphabet were taught by association with towns in the Land of Israel, for example, *ḥeṯ* for Hebron, *ṭeṯ* for Tiberias, *yoḏ* for Jerusalem.[85] We have already mentioned the veneration of shrines associated with various Biblical prophets.[86]

2. The messianic movements in the twelfth century led by David Alroy and Menahem were basically courageous efforts to return the local Jews to the Land of Israel.[87] As a result of the persecution by the Crusaders, many Jews from the Land of Israel had fled to Iraq and Kurdistan. The ties with the Holy Land had been disconnected for a few centuries, but with the reestablishment of Jewish settlement there the ties with the Jewry of Kurdistan were renewed. A yeshiva in Safed at the end of the sixteenth century had students from Kurdistan,[88] while a rabbi in Kurdistan around that same time boasted of having at his yeshiva students from the Land of Israel.[89] In the following centuries several *šaddarim,* rabbinic messengers from the Land of Israel, visited various localities in Kurdistan[90] and were joyously welcomed and almost worshiped, as Benjamin II describes: "When a Chacham [ḥaḵam] from Jerusalem comes into these parts, which occurs but very seldom, they go out solemnly to meet him, kiss his shoulders, his beard, and even his feet, according to the rank of him by whom he is saluted; they then carry him in triumph to the house of the Nassi [community leader], bare his feet and wash them, and the water used for that purpose is collected for drinking."[91] It

83. See Rivlin, pp. 56–57.
84. Ben-Jacob, p. 61.
85. Brauer, pp. 201–02.
86. See IV/4, above. That the Kurdistani Jews saw Kurdistan as in many ways an extension of the Land of Israel in Biblical times is indicated also by their views on various natural phenomena; for example, the sweet dew common in the area was identified with the Biblical manna; cf. Benjamin II, p. 136: "Another extraordinary appearance [in addition to the abundance of quails in Kurdistan] which reminds us of the journey of the Jews through the wilderness, is the manna which here, in the form of grain, descends with the dew. It has now been ascertained by travelers in the east, beyond the slightest shadow of doubt, that the manna is a distillation from trees which falls on the ground every morning. It is collected in vases at the break of day, and placed in the sun, in the warmth of which it melts and becomes a cheesy kind of substance, in which state it is eaten with bread at breakfast [cf. chap. XVIII, Feeding Rhyme *1,* below]. I found it sweet like honey and of an agreeable smell. . . . At Kirkuk all the fields and meadows are covered with it." Cf. Exod. 16:13 ff.
87. See II/4, above, and chap. XIII, below.
88. Rivlin, pp. 57–58.
89. See chap. XV, introduction, p. 107, below.
90. For details see Rivlin, pp. 58–62.
91. Benjamin II, p. 128.

was also customary to buy from these messengers at a high price "a grave of four cubits in the Land of Israel." The messenger would give the buyer a signed document, stating that he was fortunate enough to own a grave in the Land of Israel, and the buyer would treasure it until his death, when his relatives would bury it with him in his grave in Kurdistan.[92] All Jewish dead were placed in their graves with their feet facing in the direction of Jerusalem,[93] probably in order to hasten their arrival there on the Day of Resurrection. The messengers were regarded also as the connecting link with Jewish law, and were therefore consulted on various aspects of *kašruṯ* (Jewish dietary law), matrimony, and other matters, and their decisions were often followed.[94]

3. With the reestablishment of Jewish settlement in the Land of Israel in modern times the Jews of Kurdistan were the first among the Near Eastern Jewish communities to move there. Some emigrated as early as 1812.[95] Jews from Urmia (in Persian Kurdistan) settled in the new quarters of Jerusalem before the First World War. Afterward, between 1920 and 1926, many Kurdistani Jews emigrated to the Land of Israel in spite of the great dangers on the way resulting from the collapse of Turkish rule and the total anarchy prevailing in the area. Some Jewish communities in Kurdistan, such as that of the ancient village of Barashe, emigrated en masse. Because of their strong sentiment for Jerusalem, most of them settled in the new quarters of the city, especially in the quarter known as Maḥăneh Yĕhuḏah, which is now inhabited almost

92. Brauer, p. 164. The importance of this document is indicated also by the following story (Brauer, p. 164): "People say that in [the village of] Jalla [near Arbil] a certain man stretched out his arm and extended his hand after his death. After the [customary] washing [of the corpse], the members of the burial society tried to lower his arm but could not do so, for the arm was as stiff as if made of iron. Then the thought occurred to the deceased man's wife that he wanted the writ, and she hurried to fetch it. At the very moment that they put the writ in the deceased man's hand, his fingers closed [over it] and his arm became as pliable as wax."

93. Ibid., p. 166.

94. For details of actual cases see Rivlin, p. 62. Sometimes, however, the messengers' decisions were not accepted by the local rabbis; cf. chap. XV, legend 6, below; Benjamin II, pp. 92–93 (regarding the remarriage of a woman whose peddler husband disappeared); p. 100: "It was explained to me that these customs [described above, IV/4, which Benjamin suggested should be discarded as "doubtless of foreign origin"] have been held in respect since ancient times, and that they must be kept until the coming of the Messiah"; pp. 108–09 (after a long discussion the local rabbi accepted Benjamin's opinion regarding the remarriage of a woman whose husband had been converted to Islam); pp. 111–12 (Benjamin dismissed an impostor rabbi appointed by a local Kurdish chieftain).

95. For this and the following details see Ben-Jacob, p. 24; Rivlin, p. 63.

exclusively by Kurdistani Jews. Others settled in rural areas, such as the village Alroy, near Haifa. After the State of Israel was established, practically all the Jews of Kurdistan emigrated there (during 1950 and 1951)[96] and settled in the city of Jerusalem as well as in several rural localities in the Jerusalem mountains and elsewhere in the country.[97]

VI. The Literature of the Kurdistani Jews[98]

1. The Kurdistani Jews, being mostly a rural society, developed a rich oral folk literature, just as their religion was maintained mostly by oral tradition.[99] Even the written literature recorded in manuscripts from Kurdistan had originated in oral tradition. Likewise, the translation of the Bible into various Neo-Aramaic dialects was transmitted orally from generation to generation with little change in style and vocabulary, and was only recently written down by the ḥakamim at the request and with the encouragement of scholars in Israel.[100] Reading and — much less — writing were not common. Usually only the ḥakamim were literate, and most of the written literature, especially in Hebrew, was recorded by them for their own use. The Neo-Aramaic translations of Midrashim and liturgical texts were at times written down in order to be read by the ḥakamim in public for the benefit of the mostly illiterate men in the synagogue and women at home.[101]

2. However, certain general distinctions may be discerned between orally preserved and written literature, which differ in their character, contents, and form. The oral folk literature is predominantly secular and its contents and sources are Kurdish or general Near Eastern.[102] The folktales are usually told in Neo-Aramaic, but most of the folk songs, especially those that are part of the folktales,

96. This is especially true of Iraqi Kurdistan. In the summer of 1975, when I traveled in Persian Kurdistan, I found about thirty Jewish families in Urmia, and a few others were reported to be living in the nearby towns as well as in Tehran; cf. n. 65, above.

97. Cf. III/6, above. The yearning of the Kurdistani Jews for the Land of Israel is also well expressed in their folk literature; cf. chap. XVII, tales 4, 23, below.

98. This chapter is an updated summary of my "Survey" (Sabar [1976a], pp. 161–78).

99. See IV/3, 5, above.

100. See §§4, 10, below.

101. For details see Sabar (1980).

102. Cf. the old Yiddish literature, in which "the didactic literature is based on traditional elements; the recreational works drew on the German heroic epic, chivalric tales, European folk songs and folk plays" (Y. Mark, "Yiddish Literature," in *The Jews: Their History, Culture, and Religion,* ed. L. Finkelstein [Philadelphia, 1966], p. 1193).

and some rhymes and proverbs are in Kurdish and occasionally in Arabic, Persian, or Turkish — a clear indication of their non-Jewish source.[103] On the other hand, the preserved written literature is mainly religious, and its contents and sources are specifically Jewish, except for local embellishment or recomposition. A great part of it was written and preserved in Hebrew, and the rest of it represents Neo-Aramaic translations from the Hebrew, and in some cases perhaps from Judeo-Arabic.[104]

3. Neo-Aramaic, a descendant of older Aramaic, is divided into dialects and subdialects according not only to the place where they were spoken but usually also to the religion of the speakers, Jewish or Christian.[105] The Muslims spoke Kurdish, a non-Semitic Iranian language. This too has various dialects, the most widespread being Kurmanjī, the spoken language of some Jews and Christians (Armenians) as well.[106] A few Jewish communities that probably spoke Neo-Aramaic at an earlier date had Arabic, Turkish, or Persian (according to the region) as their spoken language.[107] The Jewish Neo-Aramaic dialects may be divided as follows, according to their major centers:

a. Nerwa-Amidya,[108] in Northern Iraqi Kurdistan, near the Turkish border;

b. Zakho,[109] slightly northwest of Amidya;

c. Kirkuk-Rawanduz,[110] southeast of Iraqi Kurdistan, near the Iranian border;

d. Urmia, in Azerbaijan,[111] near the Iranian-Turkish border.

The second is a subgroup of the first, and the third is a subgroup of the fourth. The majority of the manuscripts originating in Kurdistan are in the Nerwa-Amidya dialect, and are the oldest known (seventeenth century).[112] Most of the others are in the Zakho and Urmia dialects and are more recent. All are written in Hebrew

103. For details see Sabar (1978a).

104. See n. 114, below; Sabar (1976a), p. xxv.

105. The western Neo-Aramaic dialect of Maʿlūla, Syria, is spoken by Christians and Muslims as well. For this and other details on Neo-Aramaic see *EJ*, s.v. "Neo-Aramaic," *12*, 948–51; Sabar (1976a), introduction.

106. See I/4, above; Minorsky, pp. 1151–54.

107. Cf. *EJ*, s.v. "Neo-Aramaic," *12*, 949.

108. On which, see II/9, 10, above.

109. Ibid., and above, III/2, 3.

110. Including Arbil; see Ben-Jacob, pp. 88 ff., 106 ff., 117 ff.

111. Ibid., p. 171.

112. See §4, below.

characters.[113] Neo-Aramaic has of course much in common with older Aramaic dialects, such as that of the Talmud, but as one might expect, it underwent many changes in phonology, morphology, and especially vocabulary, which now includes numerous borrowings from neighboring languages — Arabic, Kurdish, Persian, and Turkish.[114]

4. The traditional religious literature, much of it preserved in manuscript, includes the following types:

a. Homilies on the Pentateuchal lessons. The available manuscripts include large homilies on *Wayḥi* (Gen. 47:28–50:26), *Bĕšallaḥ* (Exod. 13:17–15:26), and *Yiṯro* (Exod. 18:1–20:23), all in the Jewish Neo-Aramaic dialect of Nerwa-Amidya.[115] Most of these homilies are derived from older Midrashim and commentaries on the Bible, but their redactors did a remarkable job in reworking and extending the material and welding it into a single organic whole. It is fascinating to see how the homilist could bring together many threads from diverse sources in order to weave his literary fabric. The homilies are an excellent example of continued creativity in a remote corner of Jewish settlement.

b. Expositions of the *hafṭaroṯ* (lessons from the prophets). The available manuscripts include the following lessons read on special holidays: the Book of Jonah, read on the Day of Atonement during the afternoon service; Isa. 10:32–12:6, read on the eighth day of Passover;[116] Hab. 2:20–3:19, read on the second day of the Festival of Weeks;[117] Jer. 8:13–9:23, read on the Ninth of Ab. These expositions differ from the homilies in being mainly a rather free Neo-Aramaic translation of the Biblical Hebrew text, with occasional Midrashic commentary derived from the Targum Jonathan[118] and Rashi's[119] and Ḳimḥi's[120] commentaries.

113. The Jews have never used the Syriac characters common among the Neo-Aramaic-speaking Christians; see Sabar (1976a), p. 162, n. 7.

114. See n. 105, above. On the Hebrew and Arabic loanwords in Jewish Neo-Aramaic see Sabar (1974a, 1975a, 1975b, and "The Arabic Elements" [forthcoming]).

115. All three have been published; see Sabar (1976a), the selections in chaps. II, III, V, XI, XII, below, and Sabar, *Midrašim* (forthcoming).

116. See Sabar, "Peruš Dĕraši" and "Tafsir lĕ-Hafṭarah" (forthcoming).

117. Published in Sabar (1966), pp. 381–90.

118. A Midrashic Aramaic translation of the Prophetical Books; see *EJ*, s.v. "Jonathan ben Uzziel," *10*, 188.

119. Acronym of Rabbi Solomon ben Isaac, d. 1105, the leading popular commentator on the Bible; see *EJ*, s.v. "Rashi," *13*, 1558–66.

120. Rabbi David Ḳimḥi, d. ca. 1235; see *EJ*, s.v. "Ḳimḥi, David," *10*, 1001 ff.

c. Expositions of three Biblical "scroll books" (*mĕḡillot̲*), similar in character to the expositions of the *hafṭarot̲*. The exposition of the Song of Solomon (read on Passover) is almost a literal translation of its allegorical old Aramaic translation (Targum). The others are expositions of the Book of Esther (read on Purim, for women) and of the Book of Lamentations.[121]

d. Literal Neo-Aramaic translations of the Bible. As already mentioned, traditional Neo-Aramaic translations of the Bible (except Psalms and Song of Solomon) were transmitted orally from generation to generation. The Hebrew text of the Bible was studied side by side with an oral Neo-Aramaic translation in every Jewish school in Kurdistan.[122] The translation was usually quite literal but was often based on the traditional commentaries, such as Rashi and the old Aramaic Targums. However, in certain cases, where a literal translation might seem blasphemous, a more homiletic or allegorical translation was preferred, as for the Song of Solomon and the Psalms.[123]

e. Liturgical and paraliturgical literature. Singing and chanting are a common pastime among the Kurdistani Jews. Beside their secular Kurdish musical heritage of folk songs and ballads they have a rich corpus of liturgical (synagogue) and paraliturgical (home) literature in Hebrew and Neo-Aramaic. This corpus includes many songs and hymns sung on the Sabbath, festivals, and mourning days (such as the Ninth of Ab), as well as at weddings, circumcisions, and Bar Mitzvahs, and when visiting shrines of prophets and holy men.[124] They may be divided into four main types according to the nature of their contents:

Ḳinot̲, lamentations intended to arouse religious and national sentiments, such as the dirges for the Ninth of Ab, recited in mournful recitativo[125] and expressive of the sorrows of life in exile and of the longing for redemption and return to the Land of Israel.

121. See Sabar (1976a), pp. 168–69.

122. Beginning, in line with an old tradition, with the Book of Leviticus; cf. Lev. Rabbah, 7:3; Rivlin, p. 48; Brauer, pp. 202–03.

123. Cf. Rivlin, p. 28, Brauer, p. 203. Three Neo-Aramaic translations of the Bible were committed to writing by Rivlin; see Sabar (1976a), p. 169, n. 52, and Sabar, *Sefer Bĕrešit̲* (forthcoming); Rivlin, pp. 69–70, 79–80.

124. See IV/4, above. Many of these hymns were published; see Ben-Jacob, pp. 151–202, and below, §5. For a list of Neo-Aramaic hymns in manuscript see Sabar (1966), pp. 345–47; cf. chap. IX, below.

125. See chap. X, below, and Sabar (1981).

Pizmonim, Hebrew songs of miscellaneous contents, sung at home on the Sabbath and on festivals for the sheer pleasure of singing.

ʾAzharot, versified expositions of the 613 commandments in brief Neo-Aramaic rhymes, such as the one by Ibn Gabirol[126] recited on the Festival of Weeks and the one on the rules governing Passover.[127] Their purpose was to convey knowledge of the laws and rules to Jews who could not read.

Tafsirim, Neo-Aramaic rhymed legends, loosely based on Biblical and Midrashic sources, with much additional recomposition and embellishment,[128] meant both to entertain and to instruct the audience. They may be regarded as the foremost literary product of the ḥakamim of Kurdistan and include such titles as "Adam and Eve," "Moses and the Daughter of Pharaoh," "Samson's Story," "David and Goliath," and "Solomon and the Queen of Sheba."[129]

5. The paraliturgical literature includes also songs and poems in Hebrew written by native poets of Kurdistan. A. Ben-Jacob mentions twenty-eight such poets who wrote over 170 poems and songs in Hebrew and Aramaic.[130] The most prominent among them were Phinehas ben Isaac Ḥarīrī, his father, and his son Ḥayyim, who lived in Ḥarīr, near Arbil, and in the neighboring towns in the seventeenth and eighteenth centuries. Another well-known poet is Samuel ben Nathanael Barzānī-Adoni.[131] An interesting Hebrew poem was written by his daughter Asenath, in which she laments the lack of community support for the yeshiva that she headed and the general absence of learned men in the community. Among the more recent poets is Moses ben Isaac Bajulnaya, of Zakho, who wrote Hebrew poems retelling the religious folklore of the community.[132]

6. Other types of literature in Hebrew are Midrashim, folktales (*maʿăsiyyot*), and works dealing with rules of conduct and ritual, mysticism, and practical Kabbalah (incantations against demons, the evil eye, misfortunes, and ailments; pleas to ministering

126. Spanish Hebrew poet, d. ca. 1058.
127. Published in Sabar (1966), pp. 390–411.
128. For more details see Sabar (1980).
129. See chaps. I, IV, VI-IX, below.
130. See n. 124, above.
131. Chap. XV, below.
132. For more details see Sabar (1976a), pp. 171–72, n. 63.

angels and divine guardians; and folk cures and interpretations of dreams).[133] Some ḥaḵamim busied themselves writing amulets as a means of making a living.[134] Finally, important sources for the history of the communal and private life of the Jews in Kurdistan are the numerous Hebrew epistles of diverse contents and times; lists of names (usually of deceased ḥaḵamim); descriptions of, or casual remarks on, historical or unusual phenomena;[135] and last but not least, colophons, usually written in flowery and witty Hebrew rhymes.[136] While the ḥaḵamim made Neo-Aramaic translations from Hebrew in order to instruct the illiterate public, they composed in Hebrew for themselves.

7. In addition to the written, basically religious, literature in Neo-Aramaic and Hebrew described so far, there were also several types of secular oral literature. The rich oral folk literature of the Kurds[137] provided the most popular pastime for the Kurdistani Jews.[138] Some of the best tellers of these Kurdish tales were Jews, and they were sought after by Jews and Muslims alike. One such teller, the late Yona Gabbay (better known as Mamo Yona, "Uncle Jonah"), of Zakho, was well known throughout Iraqi Kurdistan and was considered a major representative of this tradition. He was illiterate, but he could tell his stories with equal ease in Neo-Aramaic, Kurdish, or colloquial Arabic, to suit his audience. The Neo-Aramaic style and much of the vocabulary of these narratives are markedly different from the daily Neo-Aramaic speech and show clear features of an old tradition. The style is literary, often vivid and humorous. The vocabulary is very rich and includes many archaic Neo-Aramaic and foreign words and expressions referring to Near Eastern cultural life, as well as onomatopoeia, imitative expressions, and other vocal effects. Some of these stories, such as *Zīn-u-Mámē,* the well-known tragic Kurdish love story,[139] include songs and dirges that are always chanted in Kurdish, even when the rest of the story is told in Neo-Aramaic. The contents,

133. Ibid., p. 173; cf. chap. XV, introduction, pp. 109–10, below.

134. Cf. chap. XVII, tale 24, below.

135. Cf. chap. XVI, below. Many of these epistles were published; see Mann; Sabar (1976a), p. 174, n. 78.

136. See examples in Sabar (1976a), pp. xliii–xliv.

137. See Minorsky, pp. 1154–55.

138. Cf. the popular saying, "Two things are necessary in winter, fire and folktale: fire, to warm the body, and folktale, to warm the heart."

139. See Minorsky, p. 1154; Sabar (1976a), p. 163, n. 10.

generally speaking, go from heroic adventures or misfortunes, tragic love affairs that are often mildly erotic, and imaginative moralistic exempla to humorous and entertaining anecdotes about popular characters, such as the cycle of tales about Bahlūl, the celebrated wise and witty Persian dervish.[140] The general theme of the tale may well be familiar to the audience, but a skillful teller can still captivate his listeners with it again and again. The tales vary in length from an hour's telling to installments filling several long winter nights.[141]

8. Jewish folktales derived from various popular Jewish sources, such as *'Ośeh Pele'* ("Book of Amazing Wonders"), were quite common. These are similar in content and character to Hebrew and Yiddish collections of folktales on ethical subjects, and were derived from Midrashic and aggadic sources directly or through popular Islamic oral traditions, with many additional native embellishments. This type includes also miraculous stories and legends about the local rabbis.[142]

9. The Kurdistani Jews have a rich stock of folk songs, rhymes, and proverbs, aside from the liturgical songs mentioned above. According to Professor Edith Gerson-Kiwi, who has been studying their music for many years, "the rich [Kurdish] unwritten literature of folk epics, ballads, and dance tunes . . . has been widely accepted by the Jews and integrated into the rest of their singing styles. In many cases Jewish bards and ballad singers may even be considered the true representatives of this type of musician."[143] Professor Gerson-Kiwi makes the following distinctions regarding the language distribution of the musical heritage of the Kurdistani Jews:

a. Hebrew, for liturgy (synagogue or home, on Jewish festivals);

b. Neo-Aramaic, for paraliturgical songs (weddings and other celebrations);

c. Kurdish, for genuine Kurdish folklore;

d. Arabic, for the social type of secular songs, with popular and artistic town music (a recent phenomenon).[144]

140. See chap. XX, proverb 156, below.

141. Unfortunately, none of these tales is short enough to be included in this anthology.

142. See particularly chap. XV, below. The Israel Folktale Archives (IFA) has collected so far 579 folktales from Kurdistani Jewish informants in Israel (332 from Iraqi Kurdistan, 222 from Persian Kurdistan, and 25 from Turkish Kurdistan); see Dov Noy, ed., *Ḥodeš Ḥodeš wĕ-Sippuro, 1974–1975* [A tale for each month] (Jerusalem, 1978), p. 265. Many of these were published in Hebrew, with comparative notes by folklorists; see the list in Noy, p. 225. More than 20 of these tales are included here in chap. XVII.

143. Gerson-Kiwi, p. 61.

144. Ibid., p. 62.

Most short rhymes relating to local folklore and ethnic festivities, as well as greetings and curses, are in Neo-Aramaic, but some are in Kurdish, Arabic, or Hebrew.[145] Even in the casual daily speech of the Kurdistani Jews one is likely to hear many proverbs and sayings.[146]

10. Practically all the Kurdistani Jews are now in Israel. Because modern Israeli Hebrew is a national language, it is having a strong impact on Neo-Aramaic, and like the other Jewish dialects in Israel, Neo-Aramaic is gradually being replaced by it.[147] For this reason and because of the drastic change in the life-style of Kurdistani Jews in Israel,[148] very little new literary activity continues in Neo-Aramaic. Most of the Neo-Aramaic material collected by scholars in Israel originated in Kurdistan. One exception is the work of the late ḥaḵam ʿAlwān Avidani, a native of Amidya who settled in Jerusalem in 1931.[149] This venerated ḥaḵam reworked some old Neo-Aramaic manuscript texts into an "all-dialectal Jerusalemite Neo-Aramaic," which he hoped would be understood by speakers of all Jewish Neo-Aramaic dialects. This "last Mohican" in the tradition of the great ḥaḵamim of Kurdistan tenaciously tried in his own way to attract the younger generation to the tradition of their fathers. In his semiapologetic introduction to his Hebrew collection of tales and homilies, *Sefer Maʿăśeh hag-Gĕḏolim,*[150] he states his purpose thus: "All the people are asleep, leaving religion and the Torah in a remote corner, as it is said, *But Jonah was gone down . . . and was fast asleep* [Jonah 1:5]. So is this generation, which follows football, cinema, and nightclubs. . . . Therefore, I thought perhaps these tales will attract their attention and cry out to them 'Repent, repent!', as it is said, *Ask thy father, and he will declare unto thee, thine elders, and they will tell thee* [Deut. 32:7]." His hope may never be completely realized; nevertheless, there seems to be some sporadically renewed interest among the younger generation in their

145. See Sabar (1974a), pp. 215–17; (1975a), pp. 290–91; (1978a), p. 232 (index); "The Arabic Elements" (forthcoming), chap. 8; Brauer, *passim*; Garbell, pp. 273–79.

146. See selections in chaps. XVIII–XX, below.

147. See Sabar (1975b). The number of Christian Neo-Aramaic speakers is also gradually diminishing owing to frequent emigration from the rural areas to various urban centers in the Middle East as well as in Europe and the United States; see Sabar (1978b).

148. For various aspects of the social and cultural changes in the life of Kurdistani Jews in Israel see Cohen; Sabar (1975b); Shai (1970, 1974); Weintraub et al., pp. 164–75.

149. See chap. XV, introduction, p. 111, below.

150. See the selections in chap. XV, legends 1, 4, 7, below.

fathers' heritage. One indication of this is, among other cultural activities, a Hebrew periodical entitled *Hiṯḥaddĕšuṯ* ("Renaissance"), published by the National Organization of Kurdistani Jews in Israel.[151] However, the most important work now being conducted in Israel on the heritage of the Kurdistani Jews is the scholarly personal and institutional collection and preservation of their oral and written traditions. The Ben-Zvi Institute in Jerusalem has a good collection of Hebrew and Neo-Aramaic manuscripts (original and photocopies); the National and University Library in Jerusalem has several manuscripts, including two Neo-Aramaic translations of the Bible, commissioned to be copied for Professor J. J. Rivlin;[152] and Professor Gerson-Kiwi has collected many samples of musical-liturgical heritage.[153] Literary collections have been made and published by Rivlin, Garbell, and Sabar.[154] Much recorded material, including folktales, liturgies, and other traditions, has been collected by the Hebrew University Institute for the Study of Folklore and the Institute for the Study of the Traditions of Jewish Communities (directed by Professor Shelomo Morag), by the Ethnological Museum and Folklore Archives of Haifa (under Professor Dov Noy and others),[155] and by the Israel Academy of Sciences and Humanities in Jerusalem (under Professor H. J. Polotsky).[156]

151. So far four issues have appeared (1972, 1975, 1978, 1981).
152. See n. 123, above.
153. Cf. §9, above.
154. See Bibliography, under Garbell, Rivlin, and Sabar.
155. See n. 142, above.
156. For more details see Sabar (1976a), pp. 175–76.

NOTE ON THE ENGLISH TRANSLATION

I have translated the texts as literally as possible; however, the word order of the original is not always preserved. A more literal translation of the word or phrase in question, when necessary, is enclosed in angle brackets ⟨ ⟩. Words in parentheses clarify the text. The rhyming in the original Neo-Aramaic texts of epics, nursery rhymes, folk songs, and proverbs has usually not been retained in the translation. Most Biblical quotations are according to the first edition (1917) of the Jewish Publication Society of America's version of the Bible.

THE FOLK LITERATURE OF THE KURDISTANI JEWS: AN ANTHOLOGY

I

Adam and Eve

Synopsis and General Character

This epic is an amalgamation of the Biblical narrative and various legends, yet it is unique for several reasons. In contrast to the story of Adam and Eve in the Bible and in the Midrash, in which the main motif is the fall of man from grace because of his sin, the leading motif here is man's rise and salvation following his repentance and prayer. Moreover, the conclusion of the story in this epic is totally different from the tragic end — the banishment from the Garden of Eden — in the Biblical and Midrashic sources. In this version Adam, after his duly stressed repentance, is returned by God Himself to the Garden of Eden, where he is granted divine favor and mercy and lives on in comfort, praising the Lord for His grace. This motif of man's repentance and his salvation by the merciful God, rather than of his sin and punishment, is indicated already in the opening verse and is repeated throughout the epic (vv. 1, 8, 15–27).

While Adam is the prototype of all human beings, Eve appears here only as a minor character. Yet she is Adam's female counterpart in her submissiveness and repentance. In contrast to her evil character in the Biblical story, she admits here that she has caused Adam to sin, she does not say a word about her seduction by the Serpent, and she is willing to accept her well-deserved punishment. It is interesting that Adam, too, avoids specifying Eve's guilt and instead blames the Serpent (cf. below, and vv. 8, 17). However, Eve's reward for her repentance seems to be much more modest and earthly than Adam's. Nothing is said clearly about her return to the Garden of Eden. Instead, God "remembered" her and granted her two sons (v. 27). This again is in marked contrast to the Biblical and Midrashic sources (see below, n. 38) but conforms to Kurdistani ideas, according to which sons are considered a rich reward from God.

The characterization of the Serpent is also unique. He is personified and described as a "young, good-looking man" (v. 9). Furthermore, the Serpent's desire seems to have been to seduce not Eve but Adam, and for that purpose he often visited the Garden of Eden even before the creation of Eve (vv. 9, 10). This is supported also by Adam's accusation of the Serpent, while Eve remains silent about him. Finally, it is said that there will be enmity in the future between the Serpent's offspring and Adam's, whereas in the Bible it is said that the enmity will be between the Serpent's offspring and Eve's (v. 21).

The sequence of events is often different from that in the Biblical account and is at times inconsistent, repetitious, and even contradictory, as is typical of oral tradition and amalgamated legends. Thus the woman is mentioned before her creation (see vv. 8, 10), and the enmity between the offspring of Adam and that of the Serpent is mentioned in verse 21, although one would have expected it to follow verse 12.

BIBLIOGRAPHY

Neo-Aramaic text: Rivlin, pp. 111–22.
Gen. 1:26–4:2.
Ginzberg, *1*, 47–107 (synopsis); *5*, 63–135 (notes).

1

The great exalted God,
(Who) has created all souls and beings,
Will redeem us from hell-fire.

2

When God was about
To create man,
He consulted the Torah.

3

The Torah said:
"I want Thee to create man,
For Thou shalt not leave me in heaven (forever).
To man shalt Thou give me;
Comfort shalt Thou find in me."[1]

1. This positive advice given by the Torah is in contrast to the reservations about, or even objections to, the creation of man expressed by the angels and the Torah in the Midrashic sources; see Ginzberg, *1*, 3, 52–55.

4

Thereupon the Holy One
Brought dust from the four corners of the world.[2]
The first hour, He kneaded it.
The second hour, He made it (into) a soulless lump.[3]
The third hour, He put in it veins (and) bones.
The fourth hour, He laid over it flesh (and) skin.
The fifth hour, He placed in it a soul.
The sixth hour, He placed him on his feet.
The seventh hour, He made him walk.
The eighth hour, He settled him in the Garden of Eden.
The ninth hour, he ate from the tree.
The tenth hour, God drove Adam out.[4]

5

Adam was (worthy of his name) Adam.[5]
His eyes, like (those of) angels, were in his head —
(That is), before he sinned
His eyes were located in his forehead.[6]

6

Adam looked at himself,[7]
(And lo), Adam was naked.
Adam came running,
In a fig (tree)[8] he hid himself;
He sewed (together) fig leaves.
(With them) Adam covered himself.

2. According to Ginzberg, *1*, 54–55, God ordered the angel Gabriel (or Michael, n. 14, ad loc.) to bring the dust for Adam's body.

3. The Hebrew word *golem* is used in the Neo-Aramaic text. For its meaning here see Ginzberg, *5*, 79.

4. The Midrashic sources mention twelve hours. The activities, as well as their order, are somewhat different, e.g., the dust is kneaded only in this epic; see Ginzberg, *1*, 82; Rivlin, p. 112, n. 12.

5. This formula is repeated several times with regard to Adam, Eve, and the Serpent (vv. 7, 11, 13, 14). Cf. Gen. 5:2. It expresses the old notion that one's name indicates one's nature, for better or for worse (e.g., 1 Sam. 25:25). Here it seems to have a positive sense, but in the following verses it may be negative or sarcastic.

6. Lines 2 and 4 seem identical in meaning. On Adam's resemblance to the angels in the gaze of his eyes, or in his having a celestial light by which he could survey the world from end to end, see Ginzburg, *1*, 50, 86; *5*, 65–66, 103; Rivlin, p. 113, n. 15.

7. Literally, "put his face (mind) to his front." Rivlin's translation, "turned (the matter) over in his mind," is unwarranted.

8. Gen. 3:8 simply says, *amongst the trees of the Garden,* without further specification.

7

God said:
"O Adam, Thou art Adam.[9]
Did I not say: From all (the trees in) the Garden thou mayest eat,
(But) from this tree[10] thou mayest not eat,
(For) thou wilt bring death into the world?"[11]

8

Adam said:
"O my Master, my Lord,
Many are my sins (and) iniquities.
(But) the woman whom Thou hast given me,
She has increased my sins (and) iniquities (even more)."[12]

9

The Serpent was a young, good-looking man.[13]
To the Garden of Eden he used to come;
To make Adam sin was his desire.[14]

10

Adam was the work of God's hands.[15]
(Then) sleep and slumber on Adam's eyes He laid.
A rib from him He removed;
From it He created Eve.[16]

11

O Adam, you are Adam.
A hoe for yourself you shall find;
All your life you shall dig (in) the earth;
Wheat (and) barley you shall sow,

9. Probably with a negative implication. See n. 5, above.

10. The tree is not specified here, and the whole act of eating from the tree of knowledge, the main sin and theme of the Biblical narrative, is indicated only indirectly (vv. 5, 18); the stress in this epic is on repentance and salvation rather than sin and punishment.

11. See n. 28, below.

12. In Gen. 3:12, unlike here, Adam lays the entire blame upon Eve. Cf. below, v. 17, where Adam omits Eve's part in the sin altogether.

13. The Serpent is introduced here, probably for the purpose of personification, by the Hebrew noun *naḥaš*, but elsewhere the Neo-Aramaic noun *xuwwe* is retained. On the manly character of the Serpent see Ginzberg, *1*, 71. Rivlin's translation of *jwanḳa* as "sly" (Hebrew *'arum*), instead of "young, good-looking man" (as also indicated in his own n. 24), is unwarranted and merely an imposition of the Biblical text (Gen. 3:1) upon this epic.

14. Cf. v. 17.

15. Cf. Ginzberg, *1*, 49: "he is the only one who was created by the hand of God; the rest sprang from the word of God"; *5*, 63, n. 3; Rivlin, p. 115, n. 27.

16. Cf. Gen. 2:21. A contrast seems to be implied here between the primary creation of Adam and the secondary creation of Eve; cf. n. 15, above.

(But) instead of wheat (and) barley
You shall reap thorns and thistles.[17]

12

O Adam, by the sweat of your brow you shall live.[18]
Always wandering (and) dispersed you shall be.[19]
Always racked with pain and suffering[20] you shall be,
(For) you have caused death in this world.

13

O Serpent, you are Serpent.[21]
All your life you shall eat dust;
Your hands (and) feet you shall draw inside you;[22]
On your belly you shall crawl;
(Every) seven years you shall give birth (only) once.[23]

14

O Eve, you are Eve.
Always racked with pain and suffering you shall be;
Under the rule of your husband you shall be.
Whenever you give birth, you shall feel deathlike pangs.[24]

15

When Adam heard (all this),
Adam sat down and wept,
The dry earth he wetted (with tears).
Thereupon God showed him mercy.[25]

16

Adam said:
"O Lord, what shall I do?[26]

17. Cf. Gen. 3:17–18; Rivlin, p. 115, n. 36; Ginzberg, *1*, 79–80, 97–98.

18. Gen. 3:19.

19. Gen. 4:12, applied to Cain. Cf. v. 8, line 3 with Gen. 4:13.

20. Literally, "(you will be sighing) *ach, och*" (exclamations of ache and pain); probably based on Gen. 3:17. Cf. Ginzberg, *1*, 97–98.

21. See n. 5, above.

22. Gen. 3:14. Cf. Ginzberg, *1*, 77–78; *5*, 101, n. 84; Rivlin, p. 116, n. 43. All sources speak of cutting off his limbs, rather than pushing them inside his body. Interestingly enough, this notion is preserved in a modern Neo-Aramaic proverb as well. See chap. XX, proverb 158.

23. Ginzberg, *1*, 77: "the pregnancy of the female serpent lasts seven years"; Rivlin, p. 116, n. 45.

24. Gen. 3:16. Rivlin's translation of *šanet* as "affair," derived from the Arabic *ša'n*, is erroneous. Read *žanet*, Kurdish for "birth pangs."

25. Cf. below, vv. 18, 19; Rivlin, p. 117, n. 52; Ginzberg, *1*, 86 ff. The theme of God showing immediate mercy to people weeping in prayer is common in Neo-Aramaic literature. It is based on B. Ber 32b. Cf. chap. XV, legend 1, §3; chap. XVII, tale 20.

26. An expression of helplessness; cf. vv. 23, 26.

I said, From this tree I shall not eat,
(For) I may cause death in this world."

17

He said (further):
"O Lord, the Serpent said:
If from this tree you will eat,
Like angels you will be,
You will know (the difference between) evil and good."[27]

18

Adam said (further):
"O Lord, I pray Thee, have mercy upon me!
From the tree of knowledge I did eat,
Great evil did I do;
I have caused death in this world.[28]
My God, I pray Thee, have mercy upon me!"

19

God, merciful as He is,
Thereupon showed him mercy.
Adam being naked,
God brought a suit of clothing from the Garden of Eden;[29]
(With it) He clothed Adam;
God covered Adam's nakedness.

20

God showed (further) mercy unto Adam.
He put garments of light on him.
He led Adam along;
He placed him again in the Garden of Eden.[30]

27. Eve's role is ignored. Cf. v. 9, above. Perhaps a play on the words *ḥawwah,* "Eve," and *ḥiwya,* "serpent"; cf. Gen. Rabbah 20: "The Serpent is thy [Eve's] serpent [seducer], and thou art Adam's Serpent."

28. Cf. vv. 7, 12, 16; Ginzberg, *1,* 102; but see n. 34, below.

29. The sources speak of garments of light (*'or*) before the fall, and garments of skin (*'or*) after the fall. Cf. Gen. 3:31; Ginzberg, *1,* 74–75, 80–81; *5,* 97, 103, 112–13; Rivlin, p. 119, n. 66. It is not clear whether these garments are identical with the garments of light mentioned in the following verse.

30. See n. 29, above. This version of the return to the Garden of Eden is unique. However, the sources do mention that "God was full of pity for Adam and his wife . . . and He would have permitted them to remain in Paradise, if only they had been penitent. But they refused to repent" (Ginzberg, *1,* 80). However, according to this epic and other sources (see n. 25, above) Adam did repent, but this epic alone carries this logic a step further by placing Adam back in the Garden. Some sources suggest that Adam was buried in paradise or near it; but see Ginzberg, *5,* 125–26.

21

God said:
"O Adam, between thee and the Serpent there shall be enmity.
On roads he shall lie (in wait) for thee;
He shall sting thy heels.
Thou shalt crush his (offspring's) heads."[31]

22

Adam prayed unto God.
God accepted Adam's prayer.
Inside the Garden of Eden He placed him.
God loved Adam.[32]

23

He said:
"O Lord, what shall I do?
I did not intend to sin;
I do want to repent,
(For) I am the father of the world."

24

The Holy One said:[33]
"For thee I shall work wonders.
For the sake of the three Fathers[34]
I shall revive the dead from their graves."[35]

25

Adam (now) dwelt (again) in the Garden of Eden.
For him God made it pleasant.
God blessed Adam.
For the sake of Moses, God pardoned him.[36]

31. This verse seems to be misplaced and should perhaps follow v. 12. In Gen. 3:14–15 God addresses the Serpent, not Adam, and the enmity is to be between the offspring of the Serpent and that of the woman, indicating their common guilt. In this epic, however, Adam is consistently the antagonist of the Serpent.

32. Adam is the object of God's love, blessing, and glory; cf. vv. 25, 27.

33. Rivlin combines this verse with the preceding one, but the different rhymes as well as the pattern clearly indicate that they are meant to be separate.

34. This is perhaps related to the view that "the three patriarchs [Abraham, Isaac, and Jacob] are designated as mortals who never sinned," i.e., Adam is not to be held responsible for men's death, as they were created mortal in the first place (Ginzberg, *5*, 129–30). Cf. n. 36, below.

35. Cf. Ginzberg, *1*, 101; Rivlin, p. 121, n. 80.

36. Perhaps related to the view that Moses was a reincarnation of Adam; see Rivlin, p. 121, n. 82. It is also possible that the patriarchs (cf. n. 34, above) and Moses are mentioned here as a hint that Adam himself was not righteous enough to deserve such a great reward, but God showed him mercy for the sake of his righteous descendants. On the view that Adam's sin was the cause of Moses' death, see Ginzberg, *6*, 148, n. 888.

26

Eve said:
"What shall I do?
I caused Adam to sin;
I want to repent;
I shall accept punishment upon myself."[37]

27

God glorified Adam,
(And) He remembered Eve.
Two sons He granted her.
(Thus) Adam lived on in comfort,
(And) he praised God.[38]

37. Contrast this with her answer in Gen. 3:13. Cf. Ginzberg, *1*, 87: Eve asks Adam to slay her, "for the Lord God became wroth with thee only on account of me"; cf. Ginzberg, *1*, 101–02.

38. This happy ending is contrary to all the other sources, and the rewarding of Eve with two sons is unique. Moreover, in the Midrashic sources Eve's pregnancy is associated with the Serpent and Satan; cf. Ginzberg, *1*, 105; *5*, 133–34. In Gen. 4:1–2 nothing is said about God "remembering" Eve; the notion, however, is Biblical (e.g., Gen. 30:22; 1 Sam. 1:19). On Eve in Islamic literature, see Schwarzbaum, pp. 205–11.

II

Joseph and Zulikhaye

Synopsis and General Character

This legend about Joseph's struggle between passion and virtue appears as a homiletic comment on the difficult verse Gen. 49:24. It is a combination of old and late Midrashim on Gen. 39, yet it differs from other treatments of this theme in its elaboration and ordering of details, as well as in its embellishments from local folklore.

After having failed to seduce Joseph by passionate overtures, Zulikhaye,[1] Joseph's master's wife, resorts to various devices such as lavishing gifts upon him, feigning illness, and plying him with wine. When Joseph is about to succumb to her passion and his own desire, God appears to him in the image of his father, Jacob, to remind him of the dire consequences of transgression, whereupon Joseph's desire subsides (§§1–3). When he is "overcome by Satan" once more, God threatens to destroy the world, whereupon Joseph gets rid of his semen through his fingernails (§4). His desperate mistress prepares a banquet for her female friends, hoping to hear some useful advice on how to seduce Joseph. The friends, amazed at his beauty and overwhelmed by their own desire, advise her to get rid of him altogether by accusing him of dallying with her, so that he may be slain by his master (§§5–6). As a final desperate step, she informs Joseph of this scheme, begging him to comply with her wishes, or else she will torment him and destroy him (§7). Seeing that Joseph remains steadfast, she proceeds with her scheme. Upon hearing her accusation, Joseph's enraged master imprisons him and plans to slay him. But when Asenath, the master's adopted daughter, tells him of his wife's plot against Joseph, he releases him from prison (§8). As an epilogue, Asenath is rewarded for her deed of kindness (§§9–10).

1. The name Zuleikha, attributed to the wife of Joseph's master in Islamic and late Jewish sources (Ginzberg, 5, 339, n. 113), appears in these Neo-Aramaic manuscripts with the Kurdish ending *-ye*; cf. Sabar (1976a), p. 42, n. 53.

BIBLIOGRAPHY

Neo-Aramaic text: Sabar, *Midrašim* (forthcoming).
Ginzberg, 2, 44–58 (synopsis); 5, 339–41 (notes).
Gen. 39.

---

(1) As soon as Joseph was sold (as a slave) to Potiphar, Zulikhaye, his mistress, attacked him like a crazy bear.[2] To mislead him (into committing a sin), she would seize him, kiss him, and say to him, *Lie with me!* (Gen. 39:7).[3] Also, every day she would dress him in two kinds of turban, one in the morning and one at the end of the day, yet he would not raise his eyes at all (to look) at her.[4]

(2) She waited until the day of their festival ⟨snare⟩,[5] (on which) it was their custom to make a pilgrimage to the shrine of their idols. On that day, say our sages, all the people in the house of Joseph's master went off (to the shrine), except that wicked woman, who remained alone in the house. She feigned illness in order not to go (there), as it is said, *When he went into the house to do his work, and there was none of the men of the house there within* (Gen. 39:11). Did it happen that the house of that wicked man was ever empty of people? (No), except when they all went to their altar.[6]

(3) Now she made Joseph drink so much wine that he lost his head ⟨steadfastness⟩ and was about to obey her.[7] Right then the Holy One, blessed be He, made His Shekinah appear in the image of Joseph's father in front of him, saying to him, "O Joseph, my son, in time to come the names of thy brothers will be written on the stones of the ephod (together) with the Ineffable Name, to be worn by the priests over their hearts, so that when they are asked (to divine), they may (be able to) give the (right) answer. However, if thou commitest this transgression, know that thou wilt set thyself apart from them. Is it not a pity that thy name should be erased

2. See Sabar, *Midrašim* (forthcoming), n. 152, ad loc.

3. This manifest passion right in the beginning is in contrast to her carefully disguised love in other Midrashic sources; cf. Ginzberg, 2, 44–58.

4. Cf. Ginzberg, 2, 48; 5, 339, n. 112.

5. A derisive term for a Gentile holiday; see Sabar, *Midrašim* (forthcoming), n. 154, ad loc.

6. Cf. Ginzberg, 2, 53; 5, 340, end of n. 118, and 341, n. 132.

7. The intoxication of Joseph with wine seems to occur only in this version. The Midrashic sources mention other means of seduction, such as adorning herself with precious stones and perfumes; cf. Ginzberg, 2, 54.

from among theirs?" At that moment his desire subsided ⟨his evil inclination broke⟩ and he did not approach her, as it is said, *By the hands of the Mighty One of Jacob* (Gen. 49:24).[8]

(4) (However), once more Satan overcame him and he was about to approach her again. The Holy One took the foundation stone[9] and said to him, "If thou wilt touch her, I shall throw this stone right now and destroy the world," as it is said, *From thence, from the Shepherd, the Stone of Israel* (Gen. 49:24). Thereupon Joseph stuck his fingernails in the ground while standing up on his feet. Thus his semen turned back and came out from under the nails of his fingers, as it is said, *But his bow abode firm, and the arms of his hands were made supple* (ibid.). Thereupon he quickly ran outside.[10]

(5) When the people returned from the shrine of idolatry, wives and daughters of governors came to visit her. Thereupon she prepared a banquet and put before them many apples,[11] giving each of them a knife to cut the apples before eating. Then she brought Joseph and placed him in front of them. They were now confused and amazed at his beauty. Hence, while they meant to cut the apples to eat (them), they touched the knives to their hands and cut them (instead), yet they did not notice it because of their desire for him.[12]

(6) Then she revealed her secret and told them that she had been unable to undress him.[13] "What advice do you have for me? Here you have seen him for only one hour, yet you have become so confused because of your desire for him; now I, in whose house he is all the time, how much more so!" They replied, "Hatch a plot against him, saying, 'He came to dally with me, but I did not let him.' Then hand him over to your husband to be slain, and you will be rid of him (altogether)."[14]

(7) Thereupon she called him again and said to him, "Either obey me or else I will hand you over to your master and hatch a plot against you and vanquish you." He replied, *The Lord executeth justice*

8. Cf. Ginzberg, 2, 53–54.

9. The rock that is the focal point of the world, cf. *EJ*, s.v. "Even Shetiyyah," 6, 985–86.

10. Cf. Ginzberg, 2, 54; B. Soṭ 36b.

11. Other sources (Jewish and Islamic) mention citrons instead of apples; cf. Ginzberg, 5, 339, n. 118; Sabar, *Midrašim* (forthcoming), n. 157, ad loc. This replacement seems to be dictated by local realities, as apples are common in Kurdistan but citrons are rare.

12. Cf. Koran 12:31.

13. Euphemism for "to seduce him."

14. Cf. Ginzberg, 2, 50–51, 55, with a few variant details.

for the oppressed (Ps. 146:7 ff.) She said, "I will prevent you from having any food ⟨bread⟩, so that you will starve to death." He replied, *The Lord giveth bread to the hungry*. She said, "I will put you in chains until you die." He replied, *The Lord looseth the prisoners*. She said, "Either look at me or else I will blind your eyes." He replied, *The Lord openeth the eyes of the blind*. She said, "I will break your back and disjoint it." He replied, *The Lord raiseth up them that are bowed down*. She said, "I will make you hateful to your master." He replied, *The Lord loveth the righteous*. She said, "I will drive you out to wander about in the world." He replied, *The Lord preserveth the stranger*.[15]

(8) When she saw that nothing would avail against him, she brought a rod of iron and placed it under his chin, in order to raise his head (and force him) to look at her, yet he did not look at her.[16] She then waited until his master came home and said to him, "You have brought us a Hebrew slave to dally with us!"[17] When Potiphar heard this, he became very angry at Joseph and put him in prison for twelve years. Furthermore, he wanted to slay him, but Asenath went secretly and swore to Potiphar, her master, (saying), "Zulikhaye has hatched a plot against Joseph your servant." Thereupon he believed her and freed him from prison.[18]

(9) The Holy One said, "O Asenath, because of thee Joseph was freed; therefore his destiny shall be bound ⟨made⟩ with thine. By My Glory, I shall make (him) marry thee and I shall raise out of thee two tribes that shall be equal to the tribes of the sons of Jacob." As it is said, *And he gave him to wife Asenath the daughter of Potiphera, priest of On* (Gen. 41:45).

(10) However, she was not his daughter but an orphan child whom he had raised in his home.[19] Why then does (Scripture) say here that she was his daughter? Because, say the sages, whosoever raises an orphan child in his home is (considered the same as) his

15. Cf. Ginzberg, 2, 48.

16. Ginzberg, 2, 52, in a different context; Sabar, *Midrašim* (forthcoming), n. 158, ad loc.

17. Cf. Gen. 39:14, 17.

18. Other sources usually mention an anonymous baby telling Potiphar of Joseph's innocence; cf. Ginzberg, 2, 57; 5, 341, n. 134; but according to Ginzberg, 2, 76 that baby was Asenath. Also, the freeing of Joseph from prison at this point is quite in contrast to most other sources; cf. Gen. 39:19–23; Ginzberg, 2, 57–58, 76; Koran 12:35. However, even in our version it is not clear whether Joseph was freed at the end of the twelve years or at the beginning. Cf. §9.

19. Cf. Ginzberg, 2, 76–77.

(natural) parent. Whence do we know ⟨have⟩ this? From Bithiah the daughter of Pharaoh, who raised Moses and provided food for him, wherefore Torah called him her son, as it is said, *And he became her son* (Exod. 2:10). By that act of kindness she[20] went to paradise on foot and did not taste death.

20. Referring to Bithiah (see chap. IV, below); cf. Ginzberg, *2*, 271; B. Sanh 19b. However, some sources grant paradise to Asenath as well; cf. Ginzberg, *2*, 173, 175.

III

Joseph and His Brothers in Egypt

Synopsis and General Character

The Biblical drama of Joseph and his brothers[1] has been a favorite subject of the aggaḏah and Jewish folk literature in general. The legend fills the scriptural frame of the story with many fresh details that are only loosely related to the Biblical text and are mostly a creation of the popular imagination. This version is mainly an oration by Judah and a heated discussion between him and Joseph after the seizure of Benjamin. It includes mutual recriminations as well as threats, which almost end in the total destruction of Egypt. While similar in many details to other Midrashic sources, this version is distinctive for its elaboration of details and its embellishments.

The threat by the brothers to destroy Egypt in retaliation for the seizure of Benjamin by Joseph is followed by an oration by Judah, who acts as spokesman for the brothers, in which he reviews their past mistreatment by Joseph (§§2–5). Then, as proof of their familial loyalty and their determination to protect Benjamin, Judah mentions their war with Shechem in behalf of their sister, Dinah, and threatens that Egypt may come to the same disastrous end (§§6–8). The following discussion consists mostly of charges and countercharges regarding their past iniquities. They also try to outdo each other in threats (§§9–13). Finally Judah, realizing that he cannot overcome Joseph by threats or by strength, appeals to his reason and emotions (§§14–19). But seeing that Joseph remains intransigent, Judah resorts to a mixture of blasphemies and expressions of resignation, pointing especially to the sorrow that will afflict their aged father upon hearing of any additional harm to his family (§§20–29). At this point Joseph's intransigence turns to compassion and he reveals his identity (§30). When the brothers return to Canaan they meet Serah, the daughter of Asher, and ask

1. The title in the manuscripts is simply Tafsir Way-yiggaš ("Commentary on Gen. 44:18–47:27").

her to bring the good tidings to Jacob as gently as possible. She does so by singing a lullaby to a child lying in a crib (§31). The story ends with the arrival of the brothers and the return of Jacob's entire family to Egypt, where a happy reunion with Joseph takes place.

BIBLIOGRAPHY

Neo-Aramaic text: MS 2030 of the Ben-Zvi Institute in Jerusalem, copied in the 17th century. The Neo-Aramaic text appears in two other late manuscripts, Ben-Zvi MS 18 and the National Library (Jerusalem) MS 8° 2950. The textual differences are mostly dialectal,[2] except that in MS 18 the story continues until Jacob's reunion with Joseph.[3] A short epic version, entitled "The War of Judah and Joseph," appears in Rivlin, pp. 140–52 (Neo-Aramaic with Hebrew translation). All these Neo-Aramaic versions seem to be based on an old Aramaic version found in MS 2030.

Ginzberg, *2*, 99–124 (synopsis); *5*, 352–60 (notes).

Gen. 44:18–46:30.

---

(1) When Joseph saw his brothers in Egypt, he wanted to take his brother Benjamin (away from them) by some sort of ruse. However, each one of them struck his chest, saying, "I shall destroy Egypt and leave neither man or beast in it (alive). Moreover, I shall leave in it not (even) one stone on top of another. (Not only that), but I shall turn it topsy-turvy."[4]

(2) Now Judah was their king,[5] and his strength was equal to that of all of them. He therefore proceeded ahead of all of them toward Joseph, like a young lion in the prime of his youth and strength.[6] "With this tremendous (strength)," he said, "I shall perform wondrous acts amidst the Egyptians."

(3) (Then) he said, "O ruler of Egypt, listen to what I say to you and let no one hurt us. Indeed, the first time we came to you, you said to us, 'It is Pharaoh whom I fear,' but last time you said to us, 'It is God whom I fear.'[7] From this (inconsistent) talk of yours we

2. For details on these manuscripts see Sabar (1966), pp. 345–46 (*dalet̲, zayin, ṭet̲*).

3. See n. 30, below.

4. Cf. Ginzberg, *2*, 101, 106–07.

5. Cf. Rivlin, p. 140: "Just as you [Joseph] are king in your place, so am I king in the Land of Canaan," and n. 130, ad loc.; Ginzberg, *5*, 350, n. 234; §14 and n. 19, below.

6. Cf. Ginzberg, *2*, 105 on the war between Joseph the bull and Judah the lion, based on Gen. 49:9, 22; Deut. 33:17.

7. In Gen. 42:15, 16 Joseph simply swears by Pharaoh, whereas in Gen. 42:18, three

realize that you are plotting against us and are falsely accusing us, (saying), 'You are spying on the country.'"

(4) "You spoke to us rudely, yet we put up with you. Moreover, you put us in prison for three days, yet at the end of the three days you told us, 'Let one of you remain with me in prison (as) a hostage, until you bring Benjamin your brother to me.' Thus you took Simeon away from us and put him in prison before our eyes, yet we put up with you."

(5) "We also, in all sincerity, brought our brother Benjamin to you, so that you would stop telling us, 'You are spies.' But then you employed sorcery against us and turned us falsely into thieves. Just as the sorcerer who himself swallows a coin and afterward takes it out of the mouth of another person, so did you do.[8] You made your silver cup disappear, and then you took it out of the load of our brother Benjamin, in order to make him a slave to yourself because of his alleged stealing."

(6) "Now you may have heard about my two brothers. If not, listen, and I will tell you what my two brothers, Simeon and Levi, did when they conquered the fortress and town of Shechem and of his father, Hamor. They drew their swords and slew all the males that were in it, young and old, and did not leave even one (alive). Also, Shechem and his father were finally slain on account of our sister Dinah, because they had set an eye on her and drew her away from us. Now she is not even counted among the twelve tribes, and has no portion with us in the Land of Israel."

(7) "Now how much more so our brother Benjamin, who is counted among the twelve tribes and does have a part and portion with us in the Land of Israel. Moreover, it is in his portion (of land) that the Shekinah will dwell and Jerusalem will be situated, and in Jerusalem the Temple will be built as God's residence."[9]

(8) "Now you listen to me: let no one harm us, lest we do to you as my brothers did to Hamor and Shechem, the king of the Hiwites. Now my strength, with God's help, is much greater than that of my two brothers (together).[10] By the glory of God, the God of my

---

days later but still during the brothers' first visit, he declares that he is a God-fearing man. Cf. Ginzberg, 2, 103: "Thou who didst say 'I fear God,' thou showest thyself to be like unto Pharaoh, who hath no fear of God."

8. This seems to be an addition from local realia.

9. Cf. Ginzberg, 2, 101, 104.

10. Cf. §2, above.

father, Israel, if I draw my sword out of its sheath, I shall not so easily put it back in its place until I have annihilated all the Egyptians with it. I shall begin the killing with you and finish with your master, Pharaoh."[11]

(9) Joseph said to him, "Be careful, (for) if you draw your sword out of its sheath, I shall tie it around your neck." Judah replied, "Right now I shall open my mouth and swallow you." Joseph retorted, "Take care, (for) as soon as you open your mouth, I shall stuff it with a marble ballista ball."[12]

(10) Judah replied, "Know that the (same) fire (that burned) against Shechem and his father is being kindled in my heart." Joseph retorted, "I shall extinguish that fire in your heart with the fire of your daughter-in-law Tamar."[13]

(11) Judah replied, "I shall now drench all of your Egypt with blood, until you all drown (in it)." Joseph retorted, "Drenching is your business, (just) as you drenched the shirt of your brother Joseph with blood and brought it to your father, saying, 'Look at this, is it your son's or not?' "[14]

(12) Judah replied, "If I call now my brother Simeon, he will destroy your Egypt utterly." Joseph retorted, "You are (indeed) expert callers to each other, just as you had called to each other, (saying), 'Let everyone know that (Joseph) the dreamer of good dreams for himself has come — let us kill him.' "

(13) Then Judah, enraged, shouted (with) such a fearful voice that all the Egyptians trembled, half the walls in Egypt collapsed and were destroyed, and all pregnant women who were there miscarried.[15] Now Joseph, astonished and apprehensive, motioned to his firstborn son, Manasseh, to pat Judah's shoulders with his hand, so that his rage might cool off.[16] Then Joseph struck with his fist at the pillar of his chamber, which was made of marble, and crushed it.[17]

(14) When Judah saw these supernatural acts ⟨secrets⟩, he said (to himself), "These wonders undoubtedly belong to my father's house." After his rage had cooled off and his anger calmed down, he

11. Cf. Rivlin, p. 140; Ginzberg, 2, 104.

12. Cf. Rivlin, p. 141.

13. Cf. §27, below; Ginzberg, 2, 108: "Surely the fire kindled to burn Tamar . . . will extinguish the fire of Shechem" (cf. Gen. 38:24).

14. See n. 30, below; cf. Rivlin, p. 142; Ginzberg, 2, 108.

15. Cf. Rivlin, pp. 143–44; Ginzberg, 2, 106; 5, 354, n. 275.

16. Cf. Ginzberg, 2, 110, in a different context.

17. Ginzberg, 2, 107.

began to speak courteously with soft words to (Joseph) the ruler of Egypt.[18] He begged him gently, saying, "O king, my master, I plead with you to allow me to speak to you as would a servant of yours. Please do not be angry with your servant, as there is none greater than you in Egypt except one — Pharaoh.[19] Please let us converse together in justice and treat each other with truth, O Egyptian." (Thus) Judah spoke to him.

(15) "Well, then, have your say as you wish, and use your weapons carefully and well prepared," replied Joseph to them. "Well, now, choose which law and which rule you wish us to use (in the discussion) with you, O Egyptian," said Judah. "I wish (to use) the same law as the one you used against Joseph, and the same rule you employed against him in Dothan,"[20] said Joseph.

(16) "If you (still) claim that we stole your silver cup, we will repay you as much as you wish, O Egyptian," said Judah. "From your old days until this day you have been thieves," said Joseph. "See what is the value of your silver cup, and we will repay you as much as you wish," said Judah. "The same value as that which you placed on your brother Joseph, whom you pushed away out of your sight for a pair of shoes which each one of you put on his feet," said Joseph.[21]

(17) "Had we been lovers of what is forbidden, we would not have returned to you from the land of Canaan your ten money belts which we found in our loads, O Egyptian," said Judah. "Do you think that good and honest deed was yours? It was nothing but mine," said Joseph.[22]

(18) "How amazing that concealed facts are revealed to you as well as open ones, O Egyptian," said Judah. "My knowledge is (derived) from the cup which you stole, for it tells me everything you have done," said Joseph.[23]

(19) "You cast at us your hard words like arrows that come out of the hands of a mighty man, and slay us with them, O Egyptian," said Judah. "You have been since your (old) days the ones who cast hard words and stir up strife," said Joseph.

18. Ginzberg, 2, 103 ff.

19. Judah is implying that since they are equal in rank and strength, they should also argue as equals; cf. n. 5, above.

20. Cf. Gen. 37:17.

21. Cf. Ginzberg, 2, 17–18, and §20, below; Amos 2:6, 8:5–6.

22. Hinting that he purposely placed the money in their bags as an act of generosity; cf. Gen. 42:25.

23. Cf. Gen. 44:15.

(20) "We have seen many kings more strict than you, but we have not seen a shameful king like you, O Egyptian," said Judah. "Did you (not) see your shame when you weighed the price of your brother Joseph on the scales, so that none of you would get so much as a penny more than another?" said Joseph.[24]

(21) "I am (morally) much better than you, and my father than your master, Pharaoh, O Egyptian," said Judah. "One fingernail of my aged father is worth more than I, than you, and (even) than Pharaoh and all the Egyptians (together)," said Joseph.[25]

(22) "It would be better for us as well as for you if you do not separate Benjamin from us, so that we remain eleven brothers (all together), O Egyptian," said Judah. "It would be (even) better if you had remained twelve brothers and had not let Joseph disappear out of your hands," said Joseph.

(23) "We are all children of a prophet and a very pious man in the land of Canaan, O Egyptian," said Judah. "You are (indeed) all children of a prophet and a pious man, but you all became united ⟨one back⟩ in (planning) an evil scheme to sell Joseph to the Arabs," said Joseph.

(24) "Would that no grain crops were sold in the land of Egypt, so that we would not have to come to you and fall into bondage to you, O Egyptian," said Judah. "Would that you had not sold your brother Joseph to the Arabs, so that you would not have to come to me," said Joseph.

(25) "Has no (other) stranger (besides us) descended to Egypt to buy grain crops?[26] May you be punished by God for maltreating us ⟨our iniquity be upon your neck⟩, O Egyptian," said Judah. "Maltreating has been your business, as when you maltreated Joseph, bound him to the back of the Arabs' camel, and let him go forth as a prisoner, showing no mercy to him," said Joseph.[27]

(26) "How ⟨in which face⟩ can we go (back) to our father, and what answer shall we give him regarding our brother Benjamin, O Egyptian?" said Judah. "This should be your answer, go and tell it to him: 'Benjamin has followed his brother Joseph,'" said Joseph.[28]

24. Cf. Ginzberg, 2, 107–08. Weighing on the scales seems to be an addition from local realia. Cf. §16, and n. 21, above.

25. Joseph begins to hint at their common origin by his reverence for his and their father; cf. below, §§23, 28.

26. Cf. Ginzberg, 2, 105.

27. Ginzberg, 2, 19.

28. Cf. Ginzberg, 2, 102: "Tell your father, 'The rope follows after the water bucket.'" This proverb is current in Neo-Aramaic as well; see chap. XX, proverb 4, below.

(27) "The fire that was kindled by Shechem and his father is glowing (again) in my heart, O Egyptian," said Judah. "The fire that is glowing in your heart will be put out by the tears of your aged father," said Joseph.[29]

(28) "Our father is old, and you have caused him (even greater) anxiety by taking Benjamin away from him" said Judah. "Your father is (indeed) an aged and old man, and it is you who have distressed him and embittered his life by selling your brother Joseph," said Joseph.

(29) "Our father's eye is fixed upon the road, watching for our arrival home, so that he may see us (all again)," said Judah. "Your father's eye is looking to the gate of heaven, (expecting) the coming of the good tidings that Joseph is well," said Joseph . . .[30]

(30) At that moment Joseph's voice gave way and he sobbed and wept, saying to his brothers, "I am your brother Joseph! Is my father still alive?" (But) his brothers could not answer him, for they felt embarrassed in front of him.[31] Joseph then said to his brothers, "Now do not be embarrassed and sad because of your having sold me. Moreover, I was sold four times[32] before I reached Egypt. For God has sent me here to supply you with food, so that you may become a great nation. Now hurry and go up to my father and tell him, 'Thus said your son Joseph: God has made me the ruler over all of Egypt. Come down to me and do not wait . . .' "[33]

(31) All eleven brothers then went up from Egypt and came to their father Jacob in the land of Canaan. On the way (home) they met Serah the daughter of Asher and told her, "You go on, before we arrive, and tell the good tidings to our father, 'Joseph is still alive.'" She came home running and announced (the news) to our father Jacob with wisdom, intelligence, and understanding, not suddenly, so that his soul should not fly away: she sat near a child's cradle and

29. Cf. this mild answer with the one in §10, which is much harsher.

30. All three manuscripts repeat here almost verbatim the contents of §§9, 11, 12, the main difference being that in the section parallel to §11 Judah threatens to drown Egypt in blood by plucking a hair from over his heart; cf. the sources in n. 14, above. However, after this repetition the text in MSS 2030 and 2950 ends with Joseph making himself known, whereas in MS 18 it continues until the reunion of Jacob with Joseph, which we have followed in our translation. This extended end, with a few changes, appers in Rivlin's version as well.

31. Gen. 45:1–3.

32. Probably referring to the Midianites, the Ishmaelites, the Medanites, and Potiphar; cf. Ginzberg, 2, 15–23, 39 ff.

33. I have omitted here the next portion of the text in the manuscript, which is almost a literal translation of Gen. 45:10–24.

began singing like this: "Go to sleep, go to sleep, Joseph is the ruler of Egypt."[34] (When) Jacob heard these words from Serah, he said to her, "My daughter, let us hear ⟨see⟩ this once more. Repeat your words, as these good tidings about Joseph are very pleasant. If this be true, as you say, I will pray to God of heaven to prolong your life, and you shall not die. Moreover, at the end of your days (on earth) you shall walk on your feet to paradise."

(32) At that moment the sons of Jacob arrived and announced to their father, saying, "Joseph is still alive and is the ruler of Egypt. These are presents, clothing and wagons, that Joseph has sent for you." They then gave him Joseph's letter, and he read it.[35] Thereupon the holy spirit descended upon him and his soul was revived.[36] Right then Jacob and his household went down to Egypt with great pomp. There he appeared before Joseph and hugged him and kissed him and rejoiced greatly, just as if he had seen the resurrection of the dead. Mayest Thou, (O Lord), show all Israel the King Messiah and the resurrection. Amen, so be Thy will![37]

34. Cf. Ginzberg, *2*, 115–16. The rocking of a cradle and the singing of a lullaby occur only in the Neo-Aramaic versions and reflect local realia. Cf. Rivlin, p. 150; Garbell, p. 117, n. 1; below, chap. X, I(A), §15. The fullest version of the lullaby, rhyming in the original Neo-Aramaic, appears to be Garbell's: "Hushabye, hushabye, my child, Joseph is in Egypt; he has two sons, one Manasseh, the other Ephraim." On the popularity of the name Serah (Śeraḥ) among Kurdistani Jews, see Sabar (1980), p. 295, n. 1.

35. Cf. Gen. 45:26–27; Ginzberg, *2*, 116–17; Rivlin, p. 151. The letter, presented as proof that they are telling the truth, is not mentioned in these sources and seems to reflect local realia and a literary theme; cf. chap. X, I(A), §5, below.

36. Cf. Ginzberg, *2*, 116, in a somewhat different context.

37. In Rivlin, p. 152, the story ends with all the sons of Jacob becoming viziers and pashas in the land of Egypt, based on Gen. 47:6.

IV

Moses and Bithiah, the Daughter of Pharaoh

Synopsis and General Character

This epic about the infancy of Moses is a combination of the Biblical narrative, various legends, and embellishments from local realia and folklore. In it Bithiah[1] is characterized not only as a devoted and compassionate foster mother but also as a powerful woman who heroically protects the child Moses from the evil schemes of her father and his counselors. This unique image of Bithiah has made the epic a favorite among Kurdistani Jews, and the name Bithiah (Bathyah) popular among the Jewish women of Kurdistan.

The epic begins with Miriam's dream about the forthcoming birth of Moses and his supernatural qualities as a child and as a future leader and lawgiver (vv. 1–3). His father, Amram, fearful of the decree of Pharaoh against male Israelite children, at first hides Moses and then sets him adrift in a box upon the river (vv. 4–6). The floating box, watched anxiously by Miriam, is observed by Pharaoh's daughter and her forty maidens, who struggle to catch it but fail to do so, and all except Bithiah drown in the river. Bithiah finally succeeds in taking hold of the box when a westerly wind pushes it nearer to her (vv. 7–9). When she finds the infant in the box, she calls all the Egyptian wet nurses to nurse him, but Moses refuses to be nursed by any of them. Miriam, standing nearby, offers her help and brings his mother, Jochebed, to nurse him. Bithiah, pleased with Jochebed, invites her to come to her palace as a permanent wet nurse for Moses (vv. 10–16). While Moses is being raised in the palace, the court magicians warn Pharaoh of the threat that awaits Egypt from Moses and advise putting him to death. Pharaoh sends his army to bring Moses to his court, but his army is confronted by his daughter's army. She agrees to bring Moses to her father only on condition that he be accompanied by her own army to protect him (vv. 17–20). When the child Moses is seated in Phar-

1. Pronounced by the Jews of Kurdistan *Batya, Basya,* or *Basso*; see Sabar (1974b), p. 46, n. 16; (1980), p. 295, n. 1; and below, n. 11.

aoh's lap, he pulls his beard and removes his crown. The death sentence issued against him for this action is foiled by Bithiah's threat to destroy Egypt and by the angel Gabriel's wise counsel. Finally, Bithiah returns with Moses to her palace, where she treats him as a beloved prince (vv. 21–28). The last four verses (vv. 29–32) form an epilogue recounting incidents that hint at Moses' future role as the redeemer of Israel from Egyptian bondage.

BIBLIOGRAPHY

Neo-Aramaic text: Rivlin, pp. 153–64.
Exod. 2:1–15.
Ginzberg, 2, 258–89 (synopsis); 5, 394–410 (notes).

1

Miriam had a dream.[2]
She told (it) to her mother and father.
Her mother was (then) pregnant.[3]
She said: "O mother,
You will have a son."
O Moses dear!

2

She said (further): "O mother,
(What) a son he will be!
Circumcised he will be!
Savior of Israel he will be!
A messenger of God he will be!
He will bring down the Torah to the Jews."[4]
O Moses dear!

3

(When in) the ninth month the child was born,[5]
The whole house became filled (with) light.
He did not need any circumcision.

2. Cf. Ginzberg, 2, 264–65: "prophetic dream"; Rivlin, p. 153, n. 1: "prophecy," "God's spirit."

3. Cf. B. Soṭ 12a; she had been pregnant for three months. See n. 5, below.

4. Other sources do not include the circumcision (cf. v. 3, below) and the giving of the Torah in Miriam's prophecy; cf. Ginzberg, 2, 264; Rivlin, p. 153, nn. 5–8. For the different views about Moses' circumcision see Ginzberg, 5, 399, n. 51.

5. All other Midrashic sources say that Moses was born in the seventh (or sixth) month of pregnancy; cf. Ginzberg, 2, 264; 5, 397, n. 44; Rivlin, p. 153, n. 3.

With his parents he immediately had a conversation.[6]
O Moses dear!

4

His father Amram was much afraid.
He thereupon concealed the child in cotton wool.
(Thus) hidden he remained (for) three months,
(For) Amram was much afraid of Pharaoh's decree.[7]
O Moses dear!

5

(For) Pharaoh had issued a strict decree:
"Any Jew who has a son,
(His son) shall be thrown into the river.[8]
Only a daughter may be left alive."
O Moses dear!

6

Thereupon Amram brought a box.
He put the child into the box.
He put some sugar in his mouth.
He set the child's box adrift upon the river.[9]
O Moses dear!

7

Miriam walked down along the river (bank).
She watched the box of Moses like a shepherdess.[10]
Then Bithiah[11] the daughter of Pharaoh appeared,

6. Cf. Ginzberg, 2, 264; 5, 397.

7. Cf. Ginzberg, 2, 265; Amram feared that both he and his son would be slain if the secret of his hiding the baby should leak out. The hiding of the child in cotton wool is unique, perhaps borrowed from Josh. 2:6 or from local folktales; see Rivlin, p. 154, n. 14. Cf. v. 6 and n. 9, below.

8. Exod. 1:22. Throughout the epic the Neo-Aramaic word *baḥḥar* (Arabic *baḥr*, "sea, large body of water") is used for any body of water (cf. n. 39, below), perhaps influenced by the common use of the Red Sea in relation to the exodus. However, I have used "river" throughout the translation. The common word for "river" in Neo-Aramaic is *xawora* (originally the proper name of a river in Kurdistan; cf. 2 Kings 17:6 [*Ḥabor*; Arabic *Khābūr*]·

9. Cf. n. 4, above. According to Exod. 2:2–3 and Ginzberg, 2, 265, it is his mother, not his father, who hides him and sends him away. Another unique detail is the placing of sugar in the child's mouth, probably to keep him quiet, which is a borrowing from local realia; cf. Rivlin, p. 155, n. 18. Also, according to this verse and the following ones, the box was pushed far into the river, whereas according to Exod. 2:3 it was placed in the flags by the (Nile) river's brink; cf. the discussion of the rabbis in B. Soṭ 12a (Ginzberg, 5, 398, n. 46) regarding the meaning of *suf* in this verse. According to one rabbi it is the same as *yam suf*, "the Red Sea," while according to the other rabbi it means *ʾaḡam*, "swamp." See n. 8, above.

10. Cf. Exod. 2:4; Ginzberg, 2, 265.

11. Meaning "daughter of God." In Exod. 2:5 she is introduced merely as "the daughter

With forty[12] maidens she descended to the river.
(When) she beheld the child's box in the river,
She called to her maidens (for help),
(But) in no way could she catch hold of the box.
O Moses dear!

8

All forty maidens stretched their hands to the box,
(But) all drowned in the sea,[13]
(For) they could not catch hold of the box.
O Moses dear!

9

(Then) a wind came up from the west,
(And) struck the box.
The box floated ⟨went⟩ toward Bithiah.
Bithiah stretched her hand,
(Behold, the box) came within reach of her hands.[14]
O Moses dear!

10

Bithiah immediately opened the box,
(And) found in it that sweet child.[15]
She gathered all the wet nurses of Egypt,
(But) the child would not take the breast of any woman,
(And) would not taste ⟨eat⟩ the milk of any woman.[16]
O Moses dear!

11

Miriam, standing by, said,
"O Princess, I shall go,
I shall bring you a wet nurse."
O Moses dear!

12

Bithiah said, "Please go.

---

of Pharaoh"; but her name Bithiah is stated in 1 Chron. 4:18. On her various names see Ginzberg, 2, 270; 5, 398, n. 48; 401, n. 60. See n. 1, above.

12. This number, unknown to other Midrashic sources (cf. Rivlin, p. 155, n. 22), seems to be borrowed from local folktales; cf. chap. VII, n. 22, below.

13. According to Ginzberg, 2, 266–67, the maidens refused to obey her because of her father's edict, and all except one were smitten and buried by the angel Gabriel.

14. This, too, is unique; cf. Ginzberg, 2, 267: "She succeeded in grasping it because her arm was lengthened miraculously"; Rivlin, p. 156, n. 26.

15. According to Exod. 2:6 she found the boy crying and took pity on him; but cf. Ginzberg, 2, 267: "She beheld an exquisitely beautiful boy."

16. Cf. Ginzberg, 2, 267.

I shall give you many gifts.[17]
(From now on) I shall act as protector ⟨stone wall⟩ for this boy.[18]
O Moses dear!

13

Miriam quickly returned home
(And) told (this) to her parents.
Thereupon her mother went (to Bithiah).
When she saw her child,
She sat down and wept.[19]
O Moses dear!

14

Bithiah put Moses in Jochebed's lap.
When the child saw his mother,
He laughed (and) wept.[20]
The child took the breast of his mother,
The child sucked his mother's milk.[21]
O Moses dear!

15

Bithiah said to Jochebed,
"You shall be a wet nurse for me;
You shall dwell in my palace.
You shall have many rewards from me,
If you just nurse this child for me."
O Moses dear!

16

Thereupon Bithiah led the child and his mother with her,
(And) placed (them) in her palace.[22]
She called ⟨put⟩ his name Moses,
(For) she took him[23] from the river.
O Moses dear!

17. No source mentions gifts to Miriam; cf. Exod. 2:8; Ginzberg, *2*, 268; probably influenced by the rewards granted to Jochebed, her mother; see below, v. 15.

18. Cf. v. 20, below.

19. Local embellishment; cf. v. 14, below; Rivlin, pp. 109 and 157, n. 36.

20. Local embellishment suggesting his simultaneous joy and sorrow.

21. Cf. Ginzberg, *2*, 268.

22. According to Exod. 2:9–10 and Ginzberg, *2*, 268 ff., Jochebed took Moses back to her own home and brought him to the palace only at the end of two years. However, cf. Ginzberg, *2*, 271: "That Moses might receive the treatment at court usually accorded to a prince, Bithiah pretended that she was with child for some time before she had him fetched away from his parents' house."

23. No wordplay in the Neo-Aramaic text, but see Exod. 2:10; Ginzberg, *2*, 270.

17

The magicians came to Pharaoh,
(And) advised (him) about Moses.
They counseled evil counsels,
(But) could not overcome Moses.
O Moses dear!

18

They said to Pharaoh,
"The man who might destroy Egypt
Is (dwelling) with Bithiah your daughter.
Rise up forthwith, fetch him, seize him,
Slay him before our eyes,
Else you will not be able to overcome him."[24]
O Moses dear!

19

Thereupon Pharaoh sent soldiers
To go and fetch Moses.
Pharaoh (also) stationed an army on the road,
(Yet) the soldiers were not able to fetch Moses because of Bithiah.
O Moses dear!

20

(For) Bithiah had mustered her own army,
(Since) she had become the protector of Moses.
She refused to come (to her father alone).
(Therefore) Bithiah brought Moses along with her own army
(And) stood (ready for battle) against her father.[25]
O Moses dear!

21

When Pharaoh saw Moses,
He was filled with great awe.
(When) Pharaoh seated Moses in his lap,

24. The appearance of the magicians on their own initiative before Pharaoh and their advice to him at this point to kill Moses are unknown elsewhere. According to Ginzberg, 2, 268–69, the astrologers, who had previously informed Pharaoh of an impending danger when Moses was conceived, erroneously told him that the danger had been averted when Moses was set adrift in the little ark. A death sentence was issued against Moses by Pharaoh's court only later, when Moses removed his crown; cf. below, v. 21. According to Rivlin, p. 159, n. 59, the Neo-Aramaic version may have been influenced by the legend about Jesus, Matt. 2:1–6.

25. Cf. vv. 12, 22. The military confrontation between Bithiah and her father occurs only here. All that is said in Ginzberg, 2, 270 is that "she stood up against her father's wicked counsels." Cf. Rivlin, pp. 159–60, nn. 61, 65.

Moses put his hand on Pharaoh's beard;
He pulled Pharaoh's beard[26]
(And) removed his crown from his head.
Immediately a death sentence was issued against him.[27]
O Moses dear!

22

Bithiah said,
"I am Bithiah,[28]
I am the mother of Moses.[29]
I shall destroy Egypt,
(But) I shall not deliver Moses into your hand."[30]
O Moses dear!

23

Right then the angel Gabriel appeared
(And) stood up as an officer in (Pharaoh's) court ⟨dīwān⟩.[31]
He said, "He is (only) a little child,
(Therefore) no death sentence is (permitted) against him."
O Moses dear!

24

Jethro (too) said, "He is (only) a little child."
(But) Job kept silent, said nothing.
(However), Balaam said, "His (only) cure is death,
(Even though) Moses is (only) a little child."[32]
O Moses dear!

25

(Then) the angel Gabriel said:
"(If) you will heed ⟨do⟩ my advice,
You will bring one tray of gold pieces and another tray of burning coals.[33]

26. A local jocose embellishment; cf. Rivlin, p. 160, n. 69.

27. Cf. Ginzberg, 2, 272.

28. Cf. chap. I, n. 5, above.

29. See Exod. 2:10; chap. II, §10, above.

30. See n. 25, above.

31. According to Ginzberg, 2, 274 (Rivlin, p. 161, n. 74), he was disguised as one of the wise men of Egypt who were summoned by Pharaoh.

32. Cf. Ginzberg, 2, 272 ff.; 5, 402, n. 65; Rivlin, p. 161, n. 78. According to Rivlin (n. 79), the last line is an addition by the narrator-singer spoken out of mercy for Moses, rather than a quotation from Balaam. However, Balaam's point is that Moses deserves death in spite of his tender age, for "although he is yet a child . . . with wisdom has he done this and chosen unto himself the kingdom of Egypt" (Ginzberg, 2, 272).

33. Ginzberg, 2, 274: "an onyx stone . . . a coal of fire," both in the singular, and no tray is mentioned.

You will place these before the child,
Then you will know (his true nature)."
O Moses dear!

26

One tray of burning coals and another tray of gold pieces
Were placed before Moses.
Moses stretched out his hand to the gold pieces,
(But) the angel[34] pushed his hand away from the gold pieces
(And) put (it) into the burning coals.
O Moses dear!

27

(As) the hand of Moses was burning,
He put his hand into his mouth.
(Now) his tongue was burned.
(Therefore) everyone said, "He is (only) a little child."
(However), Yumblum[35] was torn apart with anger.
O Moses dear!

28

Bithiah took Moses (and) brought him (home).
She seated him on a throne of gold.
She maintained a hundred servants for him.
She loved him very much.[36]
O Moses dear!

29

One day Moses was walking in Egypt.
He saw an Egyptian and a Hebrew.
The Egyptian was striking the Hebrew.
Moses pronounced ⟨brought⟩ the Ineffable Name.[37]
He slew the Egyptian
(And) hid him in the sand.
O Moses dear!

34. Apparently Gabriel (cf. Ginzberg, 2, 274); but other sources have "an angel"; see Rivlin, p. 162, n. 81.

35. Perhaps identical with Jambres, a son of Balaam; see Ginzberg, 2, 283; 5, 402, n. 65; Rivlin (p. 162, n. 84) translates it "Satan," deriving it from *Iblīs* or *Armilos*.

36. This "happy ending" is basically local embellishment; cf. the endings of chaps. I, II, III, above. According to Ginzberg, 2, 275, "his foster mother snatched him away, and she had him educated with great care." The following verses seem to be an epilogue or an extraneous addition.

37. Literally, "the name of *Šem Mĕforaš*," the Hebrew expression left untranslated in Neo-Aramaic. Cf. Ginzberg, 2, 280; Exod. 2:12.

30

The next day, (when) Moses was walking,
He saw two Hebrews fighting.
Moses said, "Why are you fighting?
You are (both) Hebrews,
You are (both) under the yoke of the bricks.
Why (then) are you fighting?"
O Moses dear!

31

They said to him,
"Go away, you, what are you?
Just yesterday you slew an Egyptian
(And) hid him in the sand.
Are you perchance our master?"
O Moses dear!

32

Moses was very frightened.
Soon Pharaoh heard (of all this).
Moses left hurriedly.[38]
He arrived at the river bank.[39]
Moses escaped to Midian.
O Moses dear!

38. Cf. Exod. 2:13–15, with modifications.

39. According to Exod. 2:15, "he sat down beside a well." Perhaps the Neo-Aramaic version hints at his joining the Ethiopian army across the river; cf. Ginzberg, 2, 284–85; Rivlin, p. 164, n. 92, but see above, n. 8. Or perhaps a local motif; cf. p. 119, below.

V

The Death of Moses

Synopsis and General Character

The inevitable death of even the most righteous person, such as Moses, is the main motif of this Midrash. The original Neo-Aramaic text appears in a discussion of the approaching death of Jacob in the Midrash to the Biblical lesson *Wayḥi* (Gen. 47:28–50:26), which also includes a Midrash about the death of King David; all three are characterized in the Midrashic literature as very pious men. The moral lesson of this Midrash is clearly stated: "So that all people will know that even though these (pious men) always practiced the word of God and His precepts, and there was not even one idle day in their life, yet they died. People should learn from this not to be haughty in their life."[1]

The general content of this Midrash is similar to that of the various Midrashic stories about Moses' death.[2]. Yet it differs in its omission of many digressive details and in the sequence of the sections of the narrative.[3]

The Neo-Aramaic Midrash on *Wayḥi,* from which this text is taken, begins with general comments about the mysteries of life and death, which are revealed only to God; the deaths of great and righteous people, such as Jacob, Moses, and David, which have a calamitous impact on the world, are particularly puzzling and incomprehensible. Our text follows, beginning with the theme of the fleeting quality of life. Even when one's life is long, on the day of one's death it is like the passing shadow of a flying bird. Various calamities are then mentioned from which one may ordinarily have some hope of relief, whereas from mortality there is no hope of escape at all (§§1–2).

Thus, even Moses' numerous prayers to avert his death remain unanswered. Moses then mournfully begs God to keep him alive at

1. Sabar, *Midrašim* (forthcoming). Cf. Ginzberg, *3,* 435–36.
2. On which, see Bibliography, below.
3. See nn. 8, 12, 14, 27, below.

least in the form of a lower creature, such as a bird, a sheep, or a fish, but God refuses to grant him this wish (§§3–5). Moses finally accepts God's judgment but appeals to the primeval creations of the world, such as heaven and earth, to beg for mercy for him; however, they all remind him of their own perishability in time to come. Moses' persistent efforts to remain alive are eagerly watched by Sammael, the angel of death (§§6–9). On the last day of his life Moses occupies himself with writing thirteen scrolls of Torah and teaching it to Israel. When he is finally ready to die, God commands in succession the angels Gabriel, Michael, and Zagzagel to go and take Moses' soul, but all three give reasons for their inability to do so (§§10–11). When God finally imposes this task on Sammael, who has been gloating while awaiting this moment, the latter shamefully fails to fulfill his charge and ends up being blinded in one eye by Moses (§§12–18). Finally God Himself, accompanied by the angels Gabriel, Michael, and Zagzagel, descends to earth to take Moses' soul, but now the soul refuses to leave Moses' body. God then takes the soul with a kiss of His mouth. God, angels, and all creation mourn the death of Moses (§§19–24).

Bibliography

Neo-Aramaic text: Sabar, *Midrašim* (forthcoming).
Rivlin, pp. 191–95; 301–05 (very short epic versions).
Jellinek, A., ed. "Midraš Pěṭiraṯ Mošeh." In *Beṯ ham-Midraš, 1,* pp. 115–29. Leipzig, 1853.
Eisenstein, J. D., ed. *ʾOṣar Midrašim,* pp. 356–85. New York, 1915.
Ginzberg, *3,* 417–81 (synopsis); *6,* 146–68 (notes).[4]
Deut. 34.

---

(1) *And the time drew near that Israel (Jacob) must die* (Gen. 47:29). Jacob saw by means of prophecy that the time had approached for him to die. Scripture should have said, "his time was completed" or "reached (its limit)." Why (then) does it say *drew near*? Because it is reasonable (to think) that even if a person lives a thousand years, it seems (to him) on the day of his death that he has lived (but) one day

4. For other Jewish and non-Jewish sources on the death of Moses see Leslau, pp. 103–11; 180–82; Schwarzbaum, pp. 33–57.

and has not benefited from this world at all. His days fly by like the shadow of a bird: its shadow, as long as it flies, does not rest on the ground even for one moment but constantly moves with it, as it is said, *Because our days upon earth are a shadow and there is no abiding* (Job 8:9; 1 Chron. 29:15).[5]

(2) Hence this means that in all the trials of this world there is some reason to have hope: if a man is in prison, he may be freed; if he is poor, he may become rich; if he is weak, he may wax strong; if he is ignorant, he may grow wise. However, no person can have any hope for himself against future death, (or expect) that he may live forever. Even if he is equal to our master Moses, may he rest in peace, he will not be forever saved from death. Thus his fasts and prayers to save himself from inevitable death are not accepted (by heaven).[6]

(3) How do we know this? From (the case of) our master Moses. When his time arrived to depart from this world, he stood up and offered five hundred and fifteen prayers to the Holy One, blessed be He, as indicated by the numerical value of (the word) *w'tḥnn,*[7] so that he might not die, as it is said, *I shall not die, but live, and declare the works of the Lord* (Ps. 118:17). Nevertheless the Holy One, blessed be He, did not accept his prayers,[8] as it is said, *Let it suffice thee; speak no more unto Me of this matter* (Deut. 3:26). At that moment the Holy One, blessed be He, called the angel in charge of proclamations, whose name is Akraziel,[9] to proclaim unto all the angels that they are to lock all the gates of the high heavens, so that Moses' prayers should not reach Him.[10]

(4) Thereupon Moses stood up, put on blue[11] (mourning) sack-

5. See Sabar, *Midrašim* (forthcoming), n. 17, ad loc.; cf. Rivlin, p. 302: life in this world is as transient as a caravan.

6. I could not find any source for this statement, which may be a local addition.

7. *And I besought* (Deut. 3:23); 6 + 1 + 400 + 8 + 50 + 50 = 515.

8. According to Ginzberg, 6, 147, n. 876, at the end of these prayers "God heard him and granted him the privilege to look at the Promised Land." Cf. Jellinek, *1*, 121; Eisenstein, p. 376. This and all similar allusions, common in the Midrashic sources, regarding Moses' desire to see the Promised Land, are ignored altogether in this version, as its main theme is the death of Moses alone. Cf. nn. 12, 27, below.

9. Meaning "Herald of God"; cf. Ginzberg, 6, 147, n. 875.

10. Cf. Ginzberg, *3*, 418–19.

11. This is obviously a local addition; no color is mentioned in the other sources; cf. Jellinek, *1*, 120; Eisenstein, p. 376. The Neo-Aramaic word *milana* usually means "(dark) blue," but in some dialects it means "green" as well. Cf. old Aramaic *milla,* a species of oak whose gallnut was used for tanning material or ink (Jastrow, p. 773). However, clothes dyed in both colors were commonly used by mourners throughout Kurdistan.

cloth, and rolled himself in ashes. He beseeched God and prayed to Him, saying, "Master of the world, turn me into a bird, which flies to the four corners of the world to pick up its food from the ground, (seizing) each grain from a different direction and eating it, drinking water from streams and mountain brooks until eventide, when it returns and collapses ⟨falls on its mouth⟩ in its nest (from fatigue). Let me, too, be like it, just so I do not die." God replied, *Behold, thy days approach that thou must die* (Deut. 31:14).

(5) Moses said, "Make me, then, a sheep, to feed on grass on mountains and in fields, or make me a fish with fins and scales, to swim in the sea, and I will not wish to eat or drink, just so I may not taste death." God replied, *Dust thou art, and unto dust shalt thou return* (Gen. 3:19). Moses said, "Decree, then, to turn my eye into a socket, and let a door pivot in it thrice daily, but do not let me die." God replied, Enough! *What man is he that liveth and shall not see death?* (Ps. 89:49). Enough of so much beseeching, because thou must die."[12]

(6) When Moses saw that no escape was left from this decree, he accepted the divine judgment as true regarding himself, and said, "*The Rock, His work is perfect, for all His ways are justice; God of faithfulness and without iniquity, just and right is He* (Deut. 32:4). Blessed be He, for He shows no injustice, no oversight, no partiality, no deceit, and no venality." Then Moses raised his voice in a bitter cry to all creation upon earth, saying, "O heaven and earth, ask mercy for me, so that I may not die!" They replied, "O righteous one, what have we ourselves benefited, that we might now benefit you? Did not God decree that we too shall perish, as it is said, *The earth shall wax old like a garment, and the heavens shall vanish away like smoke* (Isa. 51:6)?"

(7) Moses (then) raised his eyes to the mountains and hills, saying, "Ask mercy for me, as it is said, *I will lift up mine eyes unto the mountains; from whence shall my help come?* (Ps. 121:1)." They replied, "O righteous one, Moses, the true shepherd, who is going to plead mercy for us? For God has decreed that we are to vanish, as it is said, *For the mountains may depart, and the hills be removed* (Isa. 54:10)."

(8) Moses (now) turned his face to the sun, the moon, the stars, and the constellations, the lights of the world, saying, "Speak well

12. Cf. Ginzberg, *3*, 442, 450–51; Jellinek, *1*, 124–25; Eisenstein, p. 368; with many variations of content, context, and sequences, and all in relation to Moses' wish to see the Promised Land. Cf. n. 8, above.

of me to the Holy One, blessed be He, for He certainly will accept your recommendation not to let me die." They replied, "O beloved prophet, (if) our recommendation is not good for ourselves, how can it be good for anyone else? For in the days to come God will darken our light and obliterate us from the skies, as it is said, *Then the moon shall be confounded, and the sun ashamed* (Isa. 24:23). And it is also said, *All the host of heaven and their constellations shall molder away* (Isa. 34:4; 13:10)."[13]

(9) Now wicked Sammael, the patron of the evil spirits, was watching like a person awaiting a great celebration and looking forward to (seeing) the death of Moses, when the time came to take away his soul, as it is said, *The wicked watcheth the righteous, and seeketh to slay him* (Ps. 37:32)."[14]

(10) When Moses saw that there was no advocate to avert the decree of death against him, he wrote, on that same day when he was to die, thirteen scrolls of Torah. He gave twelve of them to the twelve tribes, to each tribe its own scroll of Torah. He also enjoined them to occupy themselves with it and to practice its precepts. The remaining scroll he concealed in God's ark of the covenant for the days to come, as it is said, *Take this book of the Torah and put it by the side of the Ark of the Covenant of the Lord, your God, that it may be there for a witness* (Deut. 31:26).[15]

(11) Then, (as he was about to) deliver his soul to the Holy One, blessed be He, he said, "O Lord of the world, *Into Thy hand I commit my spirit; Thou hast redeemed me, O Lord, Thou God of truth* (Ps. 31:6)." Right then God said to Gabriel, "Go and bring me Moses' soul." Gabriel replied, "O my Lord and Master, Moses is equal to sixty myriad Israelites —how can I go and tell him, 'Give me your soul?'" Then God said to Michael, "Go and bring me his soul." Michael, too, wept, saying, "O Lord of the world, I dare not go and approach him, for his virtue is great — who else except Thee will dare to take his soul?" God (then) said to Zagzagel,[16] "Go and take his soul and bring it (here)." Zagzagel replied, "Lord of the world,

13. Cf. Ginzberg, *3*, 431 ff., 450–51; *6*, 149, n. 895; Jellinek, *1*, 125–26; Eisenstein, pp. 379–80.

14. This section on Sammael seems to be out of place, or is an introductory remark, as his main involvement is later on (§§12–18). Cf. Ginzberg, *3*, 449 (in a different context); Eisenstein, p. 369.

15. Cf. Ginzberg, *3*, 439; Jellinek, *1*, 122; Eisenstein, p. 378; Rivlin, p. 192: "I am the messenger of God, I am the scribe of God's Scroll of Torah."

16. For a possible etymology of his name, see Ginzberg, *6*, 150, n. 898; cf. n. 26, below.

he is my disciple and I am his teacher[17] — how dare I touch him? Can a person slay his beloved with his own hands?"

(12) God then said to Sammael, "You go, then." Thereupon Sammael rejoiced greatly, saying, "How good it is! How good it is! The time has come (at last) for Moses to turn (his soul) over to my hands." He immediately girded on his sword, wrapped himself in wrath, and went to stand over Moses. He saw that Moses was writing the Ineffable Name, divine illumination was playing on his forehead, and words were coming out of his mouth like pearls.[18] As Sammael hesitated to approach him, Moses lifted up his eyes and saw him standing over him.

(13) (When) Sammael looked at Moses' face, his eyes immediately darkened, his mouth became twisted, and he was unable to say a word, out of fear of the divine (illumination) resting on Moses' face. Moses then said to him, "Sammael, Sammael, *There is no peace, saith the Lord, concerning the wicked* (Isa. 48:22). What are you doing standing near me?" Sammael replied, "I have come on a mission from God. Your time has come to depart from this world. Give me your soul, so that I may take it up to God. For all souls created from the six days of creation to the destruction of the world, God has entrusted them to me, that is, I am to take them and bring them up to Him."

(14) Moses said, "You are powerless against me, for I have as many virtues as all the creatures of the world (together). I shall not therefore deliver my soul into your hands. (Furthermore), when I came out of my mother's womb, I was (already) circumcised. I never sucked the breast of any other, unrelated woman but only my mother's. I was three years old (when I began) to prophesy, and I knew that I would receive the Torah for Israel. I (then) took the crown off Pharaoh's head and put it on my own head."[19]

(15) "At the age of eighty I (still) performed miracles and wonders, took sixty myriad Israelites out of Egypt, split the sea for them into twelve roadways, turned bitter water into sweet, hewed the tablets out of precious stone, and thrice ascended to heaven. I remained there one hundred and twenty days without eating or drinking, and like the holy angels spoke face to face with the

17. Cf. Ginzberg, *3*, 419: "Moses had learned from his teacher Zagzagel, the teacher and scribe of the celestial beings."

18. Cf. chap. IV, v. 3, above; Rivlin, p. 191.

19. Cf. chap. IV, vv. 2, 3, 10, 21, above, and the notes ad loc.

Shekinah, the Creator of the world. I overwhelmed the angels and snatched the Torah away from them, and none of them could say one word (against this)."

(16) "In battle I overwhelmed and slew Sihon and Og, the son of Anak, the mighty man of the Anakim (giants), who were so tall that water did not reach even to their ankles at the time of the flood. Thus no person can do wonders (such as) I have performed. Yet you come and tell me, 'Give me your soul.' Get you away from me, you wicked one!"

(17) So Sammael, full of shame, returned to the Holy One, blessed be He, without the soul of Moses. God scolded him, saying, "O wicked one, hast thou not gone to bring Moses' soul?" He replied, "Lord of the world, hadst Thou charged me ⟨put on my neck⟩ to turn Hell upside down, I would have been able (to do so). But I beg of Thee, I cannot stand up against the son of Amram." God said to him, "O wicked one, when I first told thee, 'Go and bring me his soul,' thou wast quite happy and couldst hardly believe that (the time had come for) thee to go (for it). How canst thou now say, 'I am powerless against him'? Go again at once and bring it!"

(18) Then Sammael wrapped himself in great wrath, drew his sword from its sheath, and went to stand over Moses. When Moses saw that Sammael had come again before him, he took God's staff, which was in his hand (and) on which the Ineffable Name was written, and pursued him until he struck (him with) it in his eye. He thus blinded one of Sammael's eyes, so that Sammael could no longer overpower Moses.

(19) Thereupon Moses prayed before God, saying, "Lord of the world, Thou art merciful and gracious, Thou hast revealed Thyself to me and hast spoken with me face to face. How (then) canst Thou deliver me into the hand of the wicked Sammael, the angel of death? *Let us fall now into the hand of the Lord, for His mercies are great; and let me not fall into the hand of man* (2 Sam. 24:14)." The Holy One, blessed be He, replied, "O Moses, prepare thyself. By My Glory, I Myself shall descend and take thy soul."[20]

(20) At this Moses prepared himself with (great) sanctity and purity, whereupon God descended in His own glory, He together with three[21] angels, Gabriel, Michael, and Zagzagel. Gabriel spread

20. Cf. Ginzberg, *3*, 466–71; 6, 160, n. 947; Jellinek, *1*, 127 ff.; Rivlin, p. 193.

21. According to Rivlin, p. 195, God descended with "myriad myriads of angels" to take Moses' soul.

a silk mat under Moses, Michael placed a silk sheet over him, and Zagzagel put a silk pillow under his head. Now Zagzagel stood at Moses' feet, Gabriel stood on one side, and Michael on the other, and the Lord, exalted be He, praised be His Name, and preeminent be His glory, stood at his head. Then He said to Moses, "Fold thy hands over thy chest," and Moses did so; "stretch out thy feet together," and Moses did so; "close thine eyes," and Moses did so.[22]

(21) Then God said to the soul (of Moses): "O My daughter, I have made it thy fate to be in the body of this righteous man one hundred and twenty years, and that is all. Now these years have come to an end. Please come out of this body and do not delay." Moses' soul sat down and wept, saying, "O Lord of the world, Thou art the Lord of souls, and in Thy hand are the souls of all creatures. With Thy graciousness Thou hast favored me by creating me and placing me in the body of this righteous, innocent, holy, and pure man. And all his life even a fly did not rest upon it. How canst Thou deprive me of it and take me out of it? What other refuge and dwelling like it can I find?"

(22) God said to her, "O soul, please come out, and I shall take thee up with Me and place thee on[23] the throne of My glory, among the holy angels." She replied, "O Lord of the world, I find more joy in being in the body of this righteous man than in being among angels; for while the angels Azza and Azzael[24] descended from heaven and sinned, this righteous man, although flesh and blood, never sinned. Moreover, he did not even approach his own lawful wife since Thou has revealed Thyself to him in the bush."

(23) When the Holy One, blessed be He, saw that the soul did not wish to come out, He bent (over Moses) and took his soul away with a kiss of His mouth, as it is said, *So Moses the servant of the Lord died there by the mouth*[25] of the Lord (Deut. 34:5). Then God sat down, wept, and lamented over Moses, saying, "Woe, woe! *Who will rise up for Me against the evildoers? Who will stand up for Me against the workers of iniquity?* (Ps. 94:16)." Angels, too, lamented, saying, "What a pity, and how evil it is that wisdom has (now) disappeared

22. Cf. Ginzberg, *3*, 471–72; 6, 161, n. 948; Jellinek, *1*, 128.

23. Ginzberg, *3*, 472: "under"; Jellinek, *1*, 129, and Eisenstein, p. 368: "in."

24. On these two fallen angels and their various names (Azza/Uzza, Azzael/Azazel) see Ginzberg, *5*, 152.

25. The Hebrew expression *ʿal pi*, usually translated "according to the word," is here taken literally.

from the world, as it is said, *But wisdom, where shall it be found?* (Job 28:12)." Sun and moon, stars and heavenly spheres lamented and wept, saying, "Whence will arise another prophet like Moses? As it is said, *And there hath not arisen a prophet since in Israel like unto Moses* (Deut. 34:10)."

(24) Then the angel Metatron,[26] peace be upon him, appeared to console God and to offer Him condolences, saying, "O Lord of the world, Moses is Thine whether dead or alive, and his soul remains with Thee. Why, then, dost Thou grieve so much?"[27]

26. According to Ginzberg, *6*, 150, n. 898, he is no other than Zagzagel; see n. 16, above.

27. The Midrashic sources continue beyond this somewhat abrupt ending by quoting God's reply to Metatron to the effect that with the death of Moses the Israelites have lost the intermediary between them and God, as well as giving several other details; see Ginzberg, *3*, 474 ff.; Jellinek, *1*, 129; Eisenstein, p. 368. Cf. n. 8, above. For other stories about Moses, see chap. XVII, tales 18, 23, below.

VI

The Duel of David and Goliath

Synopsis and General Character

Dueling stories, such as the one about David's duel with Goliath, while common in Greek[1] and Near Eastern literature in general, are rare in Jewish literature. It is no wonder, therefore, that the Biblical narrative of this duel, embellished with additional Midrashic[2] and local[3] motifs, became a very popular religious epic among the Kurdistani Jews, and indeed such stories are common also in their secular folk literature. One indication of the story's popularity is that it is still sung by men as well as by women,[4] whereas almost all the other oral literature originating in Kurdistan has become obsolete since the emigration of the Kurdistani Jews to Israel. Another indication is that Rivlin has included in his book *Širaṯ Yĕhuḏe hat-Targum* several versions of this epic, collected from various informants and composed in different Neo-Aramaic dialects, whereas for most of the other epics he has only one version.[5]

The Neo-Aramaic versions differ from the others in many details.[6] The mournful refrain and the sad melody in which the entire epic is chanted turn it into a lamentation for King David, who like Moses could not escape death notwithstanding his heroic deeds. The refrain, sternly repeated at the end of each verse, serves as a constant reminder that even David, the victorious hero who performed mighty deeds of valor and subdued giants and beasts, succumbed in the end to the angel of death.

The general outline of the story is similar to that of the Biblical

1. For some parallels cf. nn. 20, 37, 41, below.

2. See, e.g., vv. 2, 5, 9, 24, 27, 29, and corresponding notes.

3. See, e.g., vv. 1, 3, 14, 16, 17, 21, 23, 25, 26 (n. 48), 28, 31, and corresponding notes.

4. See Bibliography, below. Religious epic songs, excluding lamentations such as this one and *Lel Huza* (chap. X, below), were rarely sung by women; for details see Sabar (1980), pp. 288–90.

5. See Bibliography, below, Cf. Rivlin, p. 83: "In any case, it is clear that this epic (of David and Goliath) was among the most widespread and favorite in the community."

6. See. n. 3, above.

narrative, with several repetitions and variations of the themes.[7] The epic begins with an invitation to the audience to listen to the story of David's duel with Goliath at Megiddo (v. 1). The Philistines, with Goliath as their champion, declare war against the Israelites in order to prevent them from practicing their religion. King Saul, dismayed by this threat, promises to give his daughter as well as a share in his kingship to anyone who will volunteer to defeat Goliath (vv. 2–3). When David brings food to his brother Eliab in the camp, he hears about Goliath's threat and Israel's fear (vv. 4–6). A detailed description of Goliath's armor is followed by his bragging about his past victories, and his challenge and insults to Israel (vv. 7–11). The following verse (v. 12) stresses the nobility of Jesse, David's father, and the participation of David's brothers in the war. When Eliab tells David about Goliath's challenge and Saul's promised reward for Israel's champion, David expresses his wish to fight Goliath, but Eliab scorns David's bravery and voices his fear that David will be easily defeated. In contrast, David's slaying of wild beasts while acting as a shepherd is mentioned as evidence of his might (vv. 13–17). When Saul clothes David with his own armor to equip him for combat with Goliath, David finds it too heavy and chooses five stones instead. Upon seeing who his rival is to be, Goliath concludes that Saul must be out of his mind to choose little David to challenge him, but David assures Goliath that he will, with God's help, prevail over him, and he generously grants him the right to strike first (vv. 18–23). Goliath, gravely insulted, uproots a mountain and throws it at David, but the latter, very agile as he is, evades it and jumps over it. Meanwhile the five stones have become one, and with them David strikes Goliath's forehead. Having no sword, David asks Uriah the Hittite to lend him his sword to cut off Goliath's head. Uriah is willing to do so, but only on condition that he be given a Jewish woman as a reward (vv. 24–27). When the victorious David dances holding Goliath's head in his hand, Saul becomes apprehensive that David might now take over his kingship entirely. Word is spread that David is a descendant of Ruth the Moabite and should therefore be excommunicated, but the excommunication is thwarted by Amasa. Following Goliath's death, the Israelites defeat and despoil the

7. Cf., e.g., vv. 2 and 5; 3 and 14; 4 and 13; 19 and 24; 28 and 30.

Philistines. All the nations wonder at the greatness of Israel's God (vv. 28–31).

BIBLIOGRAPHY

This translation is based on the Neo-Aramaic text in the dialect of Zakho (Iraq) published by Rivlin, pp. 228–52. In the apparatus to this text, Rivlin quotes several parallel verses (to vv. 1–4, 14–16, 19) from a version recorded by Dr. Benjamin Klar in Kurdistan.[8] Another version, in the Neo-Aramaic dialect of Urmia (Iran), is found in Rivlin, pp. 289–300, as is still another short version, in Hebrew, by ḥaḵam Benjamin of Rustaḳa (Iraq), pp. 306–09. Another Neo-Aramaic epic, entitled "The Duel of David and Goliath," Rivlin, pp. 253–61, devotes only two verses (1–2) to this duel, and the rest of the verses (3–23) deal with the conflict between David and Saul.

Jacqueline Allon recently recorded in Israel two other versions, one by ḥaḵam Samuel Baruch and the other by Mrs. Zilpah Ḥakham, which she kindly placed at my disposal.[9]

1 Sam. 17:1–58.

Ginzberg, *4*, 85–89 (synopsis); *6*, 250–53 (notes).

I

Hearken, all my friends,
Listen, all my dears,
To this battle of David and Goliath the Philistine,
Who fought in the field of Megiddo.[10]
  Oh what a pity, oh what a great loss, is (the death of) King David![11]

8. See Rivlin, pp. 68, 83.

9. A detailed comparison of all these versions, as important as it may be for a thorough study of oral transmission, is beyond the scope of this book. While the general content is more or less the same in all versions, they differ in many particulars of language, prosody, form, and content, such as the sequence of events, omission or inclusion of details, and variation of themes. Some of the significant variations will be mentioned in the notes; see, e.g., nn. 10–12, 37, 41, 44, 46, 51.

10. The location given in 1 Sam. 17:1–2 is *between Socoh and Azekah . . . in the vale of Elah*. See *The MacMillan Bible Atlas* (1968), map. 91. However, all the Neo-Aramaic versions that specify the location give it as Megiddo (cf. Klar's version in Rivlin, p. 230), perhaps influenced by the battle of Pharaoh Nechoh with Josiah (2 Kings 23:29; 2 Chron. 35:22). When Mrs. Allon asked ḥakam Baruch about this inconsistency, he replied that David slew Goliath at Megiddo and that the valley of Elah was the scene of another battle; "There were several battles with the Philistines," he added.

11. Literally, "Oh what a pity, a hundred (times) what a pity, oh what a pity and loss for David the king!" This refrain is repeated with some variations in all the versions.

2

As all the Philistines gathered,
With them came Goliath the Gittite.
He proclaimed, "I shall prevent ⟨acquit⟩ the Israelites
From (practicing their) religious rules and prayers."[12]
    Oh what a pity, etc.

3

Then King Saul cried and wept.[13]
He said, "Whosoever goes forth to slay Goliath,
I shall surely give him Michal my daughter,
Also a share of my kingship shall be for him."[14]
    Oh what a pity, etc.

4

David was a herder of sheep.
He brought food for Eliab his brother.[15]
Then David said to Eliab his brother,
"Tell me, where is this (crying) voice coming from?"[16]
    Oh what a pity, etc.

5

Saul and Israel were weeping because of the Philistines,
Who would go forth every day and occupy the gates of their synagogues;
(For) forty days they prevented Israel from reciting the Shemaʿ.[17]
They kept telling Israel, "Come and fight with us (instead)!"[18]
    Oh what a pity, etc.

6

All the Israelites gathered together
(And) walked back and forth in great confusion,
(Yet) they could not give Goliath an answer.[19]
    Oh what a pity, etc.

12. Cf. v. 5, below; Ginzberg, *4*, 86; *6*, 250, nn. 31–32. The parallel verse in Klar's version (Rivlin, pp. 230–31) is: "(As) all the Philistines gathered on the top of the mountain, Goliath the Philistine snorted like a pig / Saying, 'I shall spread death and poison in Israel.'" Cf. 1 Sam. 17:3.

13. Cf. 1 Sam. 17:11, *Saul and all Israel . . . were dismayed and greatly afraid.*

14. Cf. the variation in v. 14, below. Sharing the kingship is not specified in 1 Sam. 17:25 (cf., however, 1 Sam. 18:5) but is perhaps influenced by Esther 5:3 or Dan. 5:7.

15. Cf. the variation in v. 13, below. According to 1 Sam. 17:17, his father told him to take corn and loaves to all his brothers in the camp.

16. Cf. 1 Sam. 17:23, 26, with modifications.

17. Cf. v. 2, and the references in n. 12, above. The legend is based on 1 Sam. 17:16.

18. Cf. 1 Sam. 17:8.

19. Probably based on 1 Sam. 17:11.

7

The height of Goliath the Philistine was six Philistine[20] cubits and one span.
He was clad in a coat of mail which weighed five thousand shekels of brass,
And the blade of his lance weighed six hundred shekels of iron.
(Also) a bearer of weapons went before him.
Oh what a pity, etc.

8

Goliath the Philistine stood on a mountain.
He cried unto Israel and said,
"Why do you midgets come out to fight with me?
Am I not (just) one single Philistine?"[21]
Oh what a pity, etc.

9

"Already in years and times past
I attacked the sons of Eli your priest.
I slew them and destroyed their house,
And seized the ark of your Torah.
It remained seven months in my house,
Yet I treated it with respect and honor.[22]
I have performed so many honorable deeds for my nation,
Whereas Saul, your king, has not performed for you even one honorable deed,
Although you like him so much.[23]
Well, then, go and tell him to choose a strong man,
To come and stand up against me,
So that I may see who he is."[24]
Oh what a pity, etc.

10

(After a while) Goliath said to them,
"Where is that strong man whom I have mentioned to you?
Let him come.

20. Instead of "Philistine cubits" the original text has "their cubits," to indicate their giant size compared with the normal size of the Israelites. For the rest of the verse see 1 Sam. 17:4–7. Cf. the detailed descriptions of the hero's armor in Greek and Yugoslav epics in A. B. Lord, *The Singer of Tales* (Cambridge, Mass., 1960), pp. 86–91.

21. Cf. Klar's version in n. 12, above; 1 Sam. 17:8.

22. Cf. Ginzberg, *4*, 86; *6*, 223, n. 33; Rivlin, p. 234, nn. 55, 58; 1 Sam. 4:11; 6:1–5.

23. Perhaps based on 1 Sam. 11:15.

24. Cf. 1 Sam. 17:10.

If he prevails over me, smites me, and slays me,
Then we and all our people, young and old,
Shall become slaves to you and serve you (forever).
But if I prevail over him and slay him,
Then from you we shall take
The vengeance[25] of seven generations, of seven ancestors.
We shall make you our servants and we shall be your masters (forever)."[26]

Oh what a pity, etc.

11

When Saul heard these words,
Fear entered his heart.[27]
He said to Israel, "My fellows,[28]
This Goliath — no one in the world can prevail over him."[29]

Oh what a pity, etc.

12

At that moment a noble man from Bethlehem (in) Judea came in.
His name was Jesse.
He had eight sons.
This man dwelt among the nobles and magnates of Israel.[30]
He had also sent three of his sons with Saul to the battle.
The names of the three (were)
Eliab, the firstborn, Abinadab, and Shammah.
David was the youngest of them all.[31]

Oh what a pity, etc.

13

David was a herder of sheep.
Now (when) he brought a present (of food)[32] for Eliab his brother,
He heard the sound of Saul's weeping rising upward.

25. Rivlin erroneously translates the Neo-Aramaic *ḥefi* by the Hebrew *ḥăḇal,* "what a pity," deriving it from the Arabic *ḥēf* (*ḥayf*), "injustice, shame." However, the homonym here is related to the Aramaic-Syriac *ḥefa,* "attack, passion, vehemence," hence "vengeance" in Neo-Aramaic. As for the seven generations, see the reference in Rivlin, p. 236, n. 67.

26. Cf. 1 Sam. 17:9.

27. Cf. 1 Sam. 17:11.

28. Rivlin erroneously translates *walokun,* an informal figure of speech meaning "you fellows," as "you know."

29. Cf. Saul's words to David in 1 Sam. 17:33.

30. On the aristocratic origin of Jesse cf. Ginzberg, *4,* 81; Rivlin, p. 289 (Urmia version): "Jesse the scion of a high-ranking family."

31. Cf. 1 Sam. 17:12–14.

32. Cf. v. 4 and nn. 15–16, above.

He said to his brother,
"O brother, tell me, whose voice is this?"
Oh what a pity, etc.

14

Eliab said to his brother,
"O brother David, this is the voice of King Saul.
He has been saying, 'Whosoever goes forth against Goliath the Philistine and slays him,
I shall give him Michal my daughter
And appoint him my right-hand vizier.'"[33]
Oh what a pity, etc.

15

David said to his brother,
"I shall go.
In the God of Israel I put my trust.
Today I shall wage a war against the Philistines
And glorify the name of God among them.
I shall cut off the head of Goliath
And take it to Saul, my master."[34]
Oh what a pity, etc.

16

Eliab became enraged and angry at David his brother[35]
And (mockingly) slapped David's head, saying,
"O father, O mother,[36] (listen to what) this little David is saying:
'I shall go forth against Goliath, a strong, mighty, and tall man,
And slay him'
But I am afraid that Goliath will strike him down with (just) one blow."
Oh what a pity, etc.

17

Yet (when) David was a herder of sheep,
Lions together with bears once came
And were about to pull his kidneys

33. Namely, the most important official in his court; this title is common in Kurdish folktales; cf. Persian *dast-i rāst,* "the right hand, prime minister" (F. Steingass, *Persian-English Dictionary,* London, 1963, p. 521a); Rivlin, p. 238, n. 91. See also v. 3, and n. 14, above.

34. Cf. 1 Sam. 17:37, 45–46.

35. Cf. 1 Sam. 17:28, but the rest of Eliab's words here are quite different.

36. This expression, similar to the English "Dear me!", is used when one is mildly surprised, concerned, or perplexed; cf. vv. 18, 31 (line 8).

Out of his fat, from his belly ⟨heart⟩.[37]
He stood up against them
And killed both of them with blows (of his bare hands).
    Oh what a pity, etc.

18

Now Saul clothed David with his own coat of mail
And girded his sword around his loins.
But David said, "O father, they are so heavy.
I cannot (bear them). It is impossible."[38]
    Oh what a pity, etc.

19

Thereupon David ran to the river.
There he selected five stones
And placed them in his bag.
Then he hung it upon his shoulder
And approached Goliath the Philistine.
    Oh what a pity, etc.

20

When Goliath the Philistine came (close)
To see who was to fight with him —
Lo, he sees that David is the one.
When he saw that he was a ruddy little youngster,
He scorned him, saying,
"Am I Saul's dog that he is jesting with me?
Is it not a disgrace for me to stand up against this one?
Yet what am I to do with Saul?
He is (certainly) confused
Because he cannot prevail over me,
And he does not know what (else) to do.
He must be at a loss,
If he puts against me a little youngster
Who cannot discern between his right and his left.[39]
    Oh what a pity, etc.

37. According to this version, as well as the recorded versions, the beasts attacked David himself, in contrast to 1 Sam. 17:34–37; Ginzberg, 4, 83; 6, 238, n. 15; Rivlin, p. 294 (Urmia version). This version was perhaps influenced by a similar theme in Samson's story, Judg. 14:5–6; cf. the epic of Samson in Rivlin, p. 212, v. 6. Cf. Lord (op. cit., n. 20, above), p. 89: "The young Basil has proved his strength by killing wild beasts."

38. For this and the following two verses (19–20) cf. 1 Sam. 17:38–43, with modifications.

39. Rivlin, relying on the partly confused vocalization, translates lines 9–10 as "I am

21

Then Goliath said to David,
"Say not, 'He is powerless (against me),'
Or that (you are stronger because) you are a scion of nobility.[40]
Nay, I am (so much) stronger than you
(That) with one finger I (can) turn around
One thousand five hundred and seventy seven persons like you.[41]
If you do not believe me,
Soon you will see my might.
Come on, so that I may give your flesh
Unto the beasts of the earth and the fowls of the sky."[42]
Oh what a pity, etc.

22

David answered Goliath, saying,
"You are bragging about your might,
About your sword, shields, and spears,
But I put my trust in the God of Israel.
God will deliver you into my hands.
I shall cut off your head
And destroy the camp of the Philistines.
Then all the people will see this deed,
Which no other man, however strong or mighty, can accomplish."[43]
Oh what a pity, etc.

23

David said further,
"O Goliath, strike your blow (first),[44]

---

confused because I cannot prevail over him," which does not make sense. The last line is a local addition, probably borrowed from Jonah 4:11.

40. Cf. v. 12 and n. 30, above. Rivlin's translation of the Neo-Aramaic *bir-maʿḳule* as the Hebrew *bar-daʿaṯ,* "sensible person," is erroneous because while *maʿḳul* (Arabic *maʿqūl,* "sensible") means in Neo-Aramaic both "sensible" and "noble," *bir-maʿḳule* means only "noble, scion of nobility."

41. Boastful proclamations and exaggerated numbers such as these are common in the speech of braggarts and legendary giants in many Kurdish folktales. In the recorded version of Mrs. Ḥakham, Goliath boasts that he will turn little David into a pinch of snuff that will hardly be sufficient for one of his nostrils. According to Rivlin, p. 244, n. 145, such expressions in dueling scenes are common in Arabic and Greek literature as well. For a Philistine champion (possibly related to Goliath) who had six fingers on each hand and six toes on each foot, see 2 Sam. 21:19–20; Rivlin, p. 244, n. 141.

42. Cf. 1 Sam. 17:44.

43. Cf. 1 Sam. 17:45–47.

44. This is in contrast to 1 Sam. 17:48 and seems to be a local addition; see n. 41, above. According to Mrs. Ḥakham's version, each one insisted that the other act first.

For (only) one hour is left of your life.
Afterward you shall be removed ⟨excommunicated⟩ from among your people."
Oh what a pity, etc.

24

David had selected five stones
And put them in his bag.[45]
(But) after one hour had passed by,
(All) became one stone.[46]
Therefore he planned carefully and wisely.
Oh what a pity, etc.

25

Goliath was now saying,
"It is a disgrace for me to fight
With weapons against this youngster."
He therefore took a mountain,
Pulled it up by its roots,
And hurled it at David.
But David, being very quick,
Instantly flew up and jumped on top of the mountain.[47]
Oh what a pity, etc.

26

Then David reached quickly for that stone,
Put it into his sling,
Swung it around three times,[48] and threw it.
Now the stone flew away (from David),
Penetrated the Philistine's forehead, and was stuck (there).

45. Cf. v. 19 and n. 38, above.

46. Or "only one stone was left"; but cf. Ginzberg, *4*, 87: "When he touched them, they all turned into one pebble" (Zohar, III, 272a). Rivlin, p. 246, n. 157, assumes that this is borrowed from the legend that Jacob's stones (Gen. 28:11) became one (cf. Ginzberg, *1*, 350; B. Ḥul 91b), and adds, "Perhaps there is such a legend in David's case as well." In Mrs. Ḥakham's version there are three stones, one for each patriarch (cf. n. 48, below), and all three competed to be the first to strike Goliath; God therefore turned them into one.

47. According to Rivlin, p. 246, n. 162, this is borrowed from the legend about Og who threw a mountain at Israel (Ginzberg, *3*, 345), but such heroic actions are common in Kurdish folktales as well. In Mrs. Ḥakham's version, Goliath tries three times to strike David with his lances but fails because of David's agility; probably influenced by 1 Sam. 18:11 (Saul's casting spears at David). David's quickness is hinted at also in 1 Sam. 17:48; 2 Sam. 22:30, 34.

48. It was customary in Kurdistan to swing the sling three times before releasing the stone, in order to assure a hit on the target. However, according to Rivlin, p. 247, n. 168, "it seems [that the number three] corresponds to the three patriarchs"; cf. n. 46, above.

Before Goliath was (able) to move,[49]
He (his head?) split into two pieces, and right there he collapsed.
Oh what a pity, etc.

27

When David saw (that) Goliath had collapsed,
He ran up and stood over him.[50]
Then he said to Uriah the Hittite,
"Give me a sword."
But Uriah replied, "I want my reward from you."
David asked, "What is your reward?"
Uriah replied, "I want a Jewish woman."
David said, "Very well, I shall fulfill your wish."[51]
But God answered David, saying,
"I shall give him thy first luck (wife).[52]
Oh what a pity, etc.

28

(Thereupon) David held Goliath's sword in his right hand
And took Goliath's head in his left hand.
(As) he was dancing (with them) in the camp of Israel,
Saul asked, saying,
"Tell me, ye whose son is this youngster,
How did he prove to be so knowledgeable, smart, and intelligent?
Indeed, he might take over my (entire) kingship."[53]
Oh what a pity, etc.

29

Word spread in the community (of Israel),
"This youngster is a descendant of Ruth."
(People) said further,
"It is forbidden for him to join Israel,

49. Or "while he was tottering." His splitting in two seems to be a borrowed theme from local folktales; cf. 1 Sam. 17:49.

50. Cf. 1 Sam. 17:51.

51. Cf. Ginzberg, *3*, 88; *6*, 252, n. 44. According to the Urmia version (Rivlin, p. 299), David commanded Uriah to open for him the collar of Goliath's armor so that he might cut off his head, and promised him, on his own initiative, to give him a pretty Jewish girl. According to another version (Rivlin, p. 253), David was looking for the key to the armor's collar but could not find it until Uriah appeared and found it in Goliath's beard; cf. the reference in n. 52, below.

52. Cf. Ginzberg, *4*, 103: "From the first, Bath-sheba [Uriah's wife] had been destined by God for David."

53. Cf. 1 Sam. 17:54–58, 18:8–9, with some modifications influenced by local folktales. Cf. v. 30, below.

Because he is an Ammonite."[54]
However, when Amasa the son of Jether[55] heard this,
He became very angry and said,
"Whosoever says that David should be excommunicated,
Right now I shall spill his blood with a sword.
Because I have learned from the prophet Samuel, my master,
Who said that it is permissible (for David to join Israel).
Moreover, he shall be the master of you ⟨them⟩ all.
Have you not seen with your own eyes
(That) this great deed and this honorable task
Which he has accomplished
Has (come to pass) because God (Himself) has made him great?"[56]
Oh what a pity, etc.

30

After David slew Goliath the Philistine
And cut off his head,
He held it in his hands and danced.
Then he stood up in the midst of Israel's camp
And gave the head to Saul.
He carried it (to him) as a gift.
Thereupon all Israel rejoiced.
Saul, too, was delighted.
Saul then said (in his heart),
"Now that David has accomplished this honorable task,
He might take over the (entire) kingship (as well)."[57]
Oh what a pity, etc.

31

After this the Israelites pursued the Philistines,
And slew them, and despoiled them.
When the Philistines were (completely) defeated ⟨broken⟩,
The Israelites seized their property and brought it (to their homes).[58]
They and the entire world wondered
How this Goliath the Philistine was slain.
All the nations said,

54. Error for "Moabite." Cf. Ginzberg, *4*, 88–89; *6*, 252–53.

55. Ginzberg, *4*, 89, has "Ithra, the father of Amasa," but in the quoted sources (e.g., B. Yeḇ 77a) this reading seems to be in doubt.

56. Amasa's praise of David seems to be a local addition.

57. Cf. v. 28, above.

58. Cf. 1 Sam. 17:52–53.

"O father, how much their God loves them!
This God is very great.[59]
Indeed, He is the one who brought them out of Egypt,
Who wrought miracles and wonders for them,
Defeated thirty-six (enemy) kings[60] for them,
Brought them to Jerusalem,[61]
And made them sovereign over it ⟨Jerusalem⟩.
Because He had sworn to their forefathers,
He now fulfilled His oath for them."

59. Cf. David's words to Goliath in 1 Sam. 17:46.

60. Apparently referring to the thirty-one kings mentioned in Josh. 12, plus the five Midianite kings mentioned in Num. 31:8.

61. "Jerusalem" in both lines probably refers to the Land of Israel in general, as is common in Jewish Neo-Aramaic. However, Jerusalem itself was conquered by David about ten years later (ca. 1000 B.C.E); see 2 Sam. 5:7. The anachronism may also be explained as a historical retrospect on the part of the redactor-singer of the epic. Such endings, which enumerate the miracles that God has wrought for Israel throughout the ages, are typical. In the Urmia version (Rivlin, pp. 299–300), however, the epic ends with a prayer for the salvation of Israel and the advent of the Messiah.

VII

King Solomon and the Queen of Sheba

SYNOPSIS AND GENERAL CHARACTER

The exotic meeting of King Solomon and the legendary Queen of Sheba, described in the Bible with only a few verses, has become the subject of numerous Jewish, Islamic, and Christian legends, as well as of early and modern artistic and literary works.[1] The Queen of Sheba and Solomon are credited in the Ethiopic tradition with being the ancestors of the royal house of Ethiopia.[2] In various Christian traditions the Queen of Sheba has become the symbol of the pagan world seeking the Christian Savior,[3] and in Islamic lore she is the prototype of the heathen convert to Islam.[4] The similarity of many details of this legend in the Jewish and Islamic sources is striking. Solomon, in contrast to David, is a prominent figure in Islamic literature but much less so in the Jewish aggadic sources. It is probable therefore that the Jewish sources which idealize Solomon and elaborate on his wisdom and grandeur are generally late, that is, from the Islamic period.[5]

The Neo-Aramaic epic seems to be based on the Targum Sheni (enlarged Aramaic version) to the Book of Esther, as well as on other Jewish and popular oral Islamic sources. Yet it differs from them in several details.[6] It begins with Solomon's dream in which God grants him wisdom and wealth and makes him the ruler of the entire world (v. 1). Among the birds that Solomon used to send out all over the world, apparently for intelligence purposes, was one named Ziz Śaḏay.[7] It told Solomon about the Queen of Sheba[8] and

1. A good summary of all these traditions and other aspects of this legend, such as its historicity, is found in Pritchard, *Solomon and Sheba* (see Bibliography, below).

2. See ibid., chap. 5, by E. Ullendorff, pp. 104–14; and nn. 14, 38, below.

3. See ibid., chap. 6, by P. F. Watson, pp. 115–45; Bamberger, pp. 245–46.

4. See ibid., chap. 4, by W. M. Watt, pp. 85–103; Bamberger, p. 245.

5. See ibid., chap. 3, by L. H. Silberman, pp. 65–84; Bamberger, p. 246: "This may well apply, if not to the entire Targum Sheni, at least to the section about the Queen of Sheba, which appears to be an awkward insertion in its place." Cf. Ginzberg, 6, 287 ff., nn. 34, 38, 41, 85; Schwarzbaum, pp. 199–203; below, nn. 12, 13, 15–19, 27, 38.

6. See, e.g., nn. 13–20, 22–24, 29, 32–33, 37, below.

7. See n. 13, below.

8. See n. 14, below.

advised him to conquer her land if he wished to be a truly great king. Solomon sent messengers to demand that she submit to his rule (vv. 2–4). The queen thereupon assembled her councilmen and informed them of her plan to visit Solomon, bring him gifts, and ask him riddles.[9] She brought with her to Jerusalem loads of gold and silver and hundreds of lads and maidens. On her way to Solomon's palace she was met by Benaiah the son of Jehoiada, Solomon's captain of the guard, whose imposing appearance led her at first to assume that he was the king (vv. 5–10). When she arrived at the palace she saw Solomon waiting for her in his glass pavilion, and thinking that he was sitting in water, she raised the hem of her dress, which brought forth a dubious compliment from the king (vv. 11–12). She then asked Solomon some unspecified riddles, all of which he solved. He thereupon gave all her servants gifts of fruit. The queen, very pleased, accepted Solomon's rule for her land and married him. With the tribute and the gold that Solomon's army brought from the queen's realm he built the Temple in Jerusalem (vv. 13–18).

Bibliography

Neo-Aramaic text: Rivlin, pp. 261–67.

1 Kings 10:1–13; 2 Chron. 9:1–12.

Targum Sheni to Esther, 1:2 (Moritz David, *Das Targum Scheni,* Berlin, 1898).

Ginzberg, *4,* 142–49 (synopsis); *6,* 288–91 (notes).

Koran 27:15–44 (translation by A. J. Arberry, New York, 1955).

Pritchard, J. B., ed. *Solomon and Sheba.* London, 1974; reviewed by B. J. Bamberger, *JQR* 66 (1976): 245–46.

1

(After) Solomon became king
He dreamt a dream,
(In which) God bestowed upon him
Wisdom, intelligence, and wealth,[10]
(By which) he ruled the entire world.[11]

9. See n. 20, below.
10. Cf. 1 Kings 3:5–15.
11. Cf. v. 18, below; Ginzberg, *6,* 289, n. 40.

2

(When) King Solomon asked all the animals[12] (to bring him news about faraway lands)
(Only) the bird Ziz[13] Śaḏay reported to him,
(For) it had flown and gone (all the way) to the land of Havilah,[14]
(When) King Solomon sent it away (together with all the other birds);
(Only) this bird brought all the news
And reported to the king.[15]

3

It said, "O King, you are a king
(Who) rules over the entire earth.
(Yet) if you see the Queen of Sheba,
(And) if you possess (and) conquer her land,
You will become a great king (indeed)."[16]

4

Thereupon King Solomon sent out messengers,[17]
Saying, "I am Solomon.
I rule the entire world.
I wish to conquer your land.
I shall collect tribute from you.
I shall establish my rule in your (land)."

12. On Solomon's knowledge of animal languages see 1 Kings 5:13; Ginzberg, *4*, 142, and especially *6*, 289, n. 38; Koran 27:16.

13. In the printed Neo-Aramaic text, *Ziw.* This may be a typographical (or copyist's) error, influenced perhaps by *Ziw,* the Hebrew name of the month of Iyyar, in which Solomon began the building of the Temple; see 1 Kings 6:1, 37. The Biblical *ziz śaḏay* is translated as *the wild beasts of the fiield* (Ps. 50:11) or *that which moveth in the field* (Ps. 80:14). However, in the aggadic literature *Ziz* is the proper name of a giant bird or the king of birds; cf. Ps. 50:11, where *ʿof harim* (the fowls of the mountains) is paralleled with *ziz śaḏay.* In the Targum Sheni the name of the bird is *tarnĕḡol bĕraʾ,* "wilk cock"; Ginzberg and Koran 27:20 have "hoopoe." For details on the identity of these birds, their various aggadic roles, and their Iranian and Arabic origins, see Ginzberg, *1,* 28–29; *4,* 142; *5,* 46 ff., nn. 129–39; *6,* 289, n. 39; 299, n. 85.

14. For this and other names given as the queen's realm, see vv. 16–18 and nn. 39, 42, below. Targum Sheni has "the city of Ḳiṭor," alluding to the smoke (*ḳiṭor*) of the famous frankincense (cf. Pritchard, p. 66). However, in Gen. 10:7, 29, and 1 Kings 10:11 the names Sheba, Havilah, and Ophir are closely related.

15. This seems to differ somewhat from the other sources, according to which the hoopoe was missing at first and reported to Solomon only after it was chastised; see Ginzberg, *4,* 142–43; Targum Sheni; Koran 27:20–22; Pritchard, pp. 96–97.

16. Compare this brief account with the detailed versions in Ginzberg, *4,* 143; Targum Sheni; Koran 27:22–26; Pritchard, pp. 70, 96–97.

17. According to the sources cited above (n. 16), he sent the message with the hoopoe itself.

5

When the Queen of Sheba heard (this message),
She gathered all her councilmen together
(And) gave counsel and advice.
She herself attended the session.[18]

6

The Queen of Sheba said, "I shall go (to Solomon).
I shall bring (him) a great present.[19]
I shall state my conditions[20] to Solomon.
I shall either win or lose."[21]

7

When the Queen of Sheba set out (for Jerusalem),
She brought forty loads of silver (and) gold of Ophir.[22]
She (also) brought four hundred circumcised youths and four hundred uncircumcised.
She dressed uniformly four hundred youths (and) maidens of the same age.[23]
(With all these) she rode away (and) came to Jerusalem.

8

(Before) she entered Jerusalem,
She placed (all) those youths before her.[24]
(When) she arrived in Jerusalem,
She saw Benaiah the son of Jehoiada[25] (coming) toward her.

18. Cf. the detailed versions in the sources cited in n. 16. According to these sources, her councilmen advised her to ignore Solomon's threats, but she intuitively decided to appease him by sending him presents and visiting him.

19. It seems that she herself accompanied her presents to Jerusalem; cf. vv. 7–8. However, according to the sources mentioned above (n. 16), she first sent her gifts to Solomon and only years later visited him, although she had been quite impatient to do so. According to 1 Kings 10:1–2, she did accompany her gifts, but she came on her own initiative, after hearing of Solomon's fame.

20. The Neo-Aramaic *šarṭe* (Arabic *šarṭ*), "conditions, terms," appears throughout the epic; cf. vv. 13–15. However, the other sources speak of *ḥido̱t* (*hard questions,* 1 Kings 10:1), *mĕṯalin,* "parables, conundrums, riddles" (Targum Sheni); see Pritchard, p. 9; and n. 34, below.

21. Cf. the rivalry between Solomon and Hiram in solving riddles, in Ginzberg, *4,* 141–42; *6,* 288, n. 36.

22. Cf. 1 Kings 10:2, 10–11; Ginzberg, *4,* 144; Targum Sheni, with modifications. The number "forty" seems to be a local addition, and is also given as the number of maidens in the retinue of Pharaoh's daughter; see chap. IV, n. 12, above. Cf. n. 23, below.

23. The number in Ginzberg, *4,* 144 (Targum Sheni), is "six thousand youths and maidens," without any distinction between circumcised and uncircumcised. However, this distinction plays a significant part in one of the riddles propounded by the queen; see Ginzberg, *4,* 146, riddle 4; Pritchard, p. 97. Cf. n. 37, below.

24. This seems to reconcile the various versions mentioned in nn. 16 and 19, above.

9

She bowed and prostrated herself before Benaiah,
(But) Benaiah said, "I am not King Solomon.
I am (just) one of his servants.
I stand at his gate (as a guard).
I am (merely) a slave and a servant of Solomon."

10

The Queen of Sheba said, "Is he (just) a servant?
(Yet) he is so beautiful, (so) good-looking.
His appearance is (like) that of kings.
He is very graceful, (very) fine."[26]

11

Benaiah escorted the Queen of Sheba
(And) brought her (to Solomon's palace).
King Solomon was (waiting) in a glass pavilion.
(Since) the glass was glittering at that moment,
She thought ⟨said⟩ that Solomon was (sitting) in water.

12

She (therefore) raised the hem of her (dress).
(When) Solomon saw (her) from afar,[27]
He said to her, "Your flesh is the flesh of women,
But your hair is the hair of men."[28]
Then Benaiah said,
"This is Solomon.
He is a wise king."[29]

13

The Queen of Sheba said, "So you are Solomon![30]
(Now) if you fulfill my conditions,

25. According to 1 Kings 4:4, he was Solomon's captain *over the host*; cf. v. 9, below; Ginzberg, *4*, 172.

26. Cf. Ginzberg, *4*, 145 (Targum Sheni); *6*, 290, n. 42; but there Benaiah's beauty is described by the author rather than treated as a direct statement by the queen.

27. The revelation of her hairy legs, specifically mentioned in Targum Sheni and Koran 27:44, is omitted here, perhaps for delicacy's sake. For the Arabic origin of the legend that her excessive bodily hair was due to her being a female jinni, or queen of demons, see Ginzberg, *6*, 289, n. 41; Pritchard, pp. 78 ff., 99; for a Yemenite Jewish version see Pritchard, pp. 70–71, 81–82.

28. Cf. Ginzberg, *4*, 145 (Targum Sheni); Pritchard, p. 71: "Thy beauty is the beauty of women, and thy hair is the hair of men; hair is becoming to men, but to a woman it is a shame."

29. These words of Benaiah are not given elsewhere. They are added here perhaps to counter the negative impact of Solomon's indelicate remark to the queen, which was evidently ignored by her altogether.

30. Cf. vv. 4, 18. See chap. 1, n. 5, above.

(Namely, if) you solve ⟨say⟩ whatever (riddle) I ask ⟨say⟩,[31]
I will know (that) you are a great king,
(And) you shall receive my gifts.
In the end you shall (also) rule my land."[32]

14

King Solomon said,
"O Queen of Sheba, tell me then, so that I may hear (your words).
If I (can) answer ⟨say⟩ your riddles ⟨conditions⟩,
I will take your land.
Then I will take you (for my wife),
So that you may (truly) know that I am King Solomon."[33]

15

She stated her conditions.
Solomon fulfilled all of them.[34]
(Then) he called (all her) youths and maidens[35]
(And) served them fruits.
The boys held (them) in their breast pocket,[36]
(While) the girls held (them) in their lap.[37]

16

The Queen of Sheba bowed before Solomon.
She accepted Solomon's rule.

31. See n. 20, above.

32. The last two lines seem to be a local addition; cf. v. 14, below. All she says in Targum Sheni is, "Then I shall know that you are a wise man, but if you do not [solve them] you will be a man like all the rest."

33. See v. 16, below. Contrast this boastful reply with the humble quotation of Prov. 2:6 (missing altogether in Targum Sheni) in Ginzberg, *4,* 145; Pritchard, p. 74.

34. The specific riddles (see n. 20, above) are omitted here, probably so as not to interrupt the flow of the originally oral epic. Targum Sheni has three riddles, but Ginzberg, *4,* 145 ff., has twenty-two; for their sources see Ginzberg, *6,* 290, n. 46; Pritchard, pp. 74 ff.

35. See v. 7 and n. 23, above.

36. The Neo-Aramaic text has *ʿeba,* translated by Rivlin as Hebrew *ʿerwah,* "genitals," and derived from Arabic *ʿayb,* "blemish, shame." However, this does not make much sense, and the word should be vocalized *ʿubba* or *ʿibba* (Arabic *ʿubb, ʿibb*), "breast pocket." See n. 37, below.

37. It is a typical Kurdistani custom for males to use their breast pocket as a receptacle and females their lap. According to this version, the fruits served as gifts (cf. Pritchard, p. 11), whereas according to Ginzberg, *4,* 146, riddle 3, the fruits played a part in Solomon's solution of a riddle: "She placed a number of males and females of the same stature and garb before him and said, 'Distinguish between them.' . . . The males, who were not bashful, seized them [nuts and corn] with bare hands; the females took them, putting forth gloved hands from beneath their garments." Cf. v. 7 and n. 23, above; Pritchard, p. 97.

She turned over the land of Havilah to Solomon.
She herself became the wife of Solomon.[38]

17

Solomon sent his own army to the land of Havilah.
He brought all the gold of Ophir to Jerusalem.
He conquered ⟨took⟩ the land of Abyssinia.
He collected large tribute from them.[39]

18

Solomon said, "I am Solomon.[40]
I (now) rule the entire world.[41]
I have conquered the land of Abyssinia and Havilah.[42]
I have carried away its gold.
I have brought (it) to Jerusalem.
I have built the Temple (with it)."[43]

38. Cf. vv. 2, 13–14 and nn. 14, 32, above. While this happy ending and her marriage to Solomon are at least alluded to in the sources, nowhere is it implied that she remained permanently in Jerusalem as Solomon's wife, as suggested in this version. Cf. 1 Kings 10:13, *And King Solomon gave to the queen of Sheba all her desire . . . so she turned and went to her own land.* Pritchard (p. 9) sees sexual relations subtly implied also in 1 Kings 10:2, *When she was come to Solomon.* Targum Sheni has only, "And he brought her into the royal palace." According to Koran 27:44, she submitted with Solomon to Allah. In 2 Alphabet of Ben Sira, 21b, it is stated that Solomon had intercourse with her after using a depilatory to remove her bodily hair; see nn. 27–28, above; Pritchard, pp. 71, 77–78. Cf. the Arabic sources on this union in Pritchard, p. 99; Ginzberg, *6*, 289, n. 41. According to the Ethiopic sources, this union between Solomon and the Queen of Sheba resulted in the birth of a son, the ancestor of the Abyssinian royal house, but the queen afterward left Jerusalem and returned to her land; see Pritchard, p. 109. In the Neo-Aramaic epic "Solomon and the Cushites," below, chap. VIII, Solomon followed his wife, "the daughter of the king of the Abyssinians," to Abyssinia, where he was captured, but he later escaped with her and returned to Jerusalem.

39. The whole verse seems to be based on 1 Kings 10:11. Cf. v. 2 and n. 14, above; Pritchard, p. 107.

40. See n. 30, above.

41. See v. 1, and n. 11, above.

42. Josephus designates her as the "queen of Egypt and Ethiopia"; see Ginzberg, *4*, 291; Pritchard, p. 11; cf. n. 14, above.

43. Probably based on 1 Kings 10:12. Cf. chap. VIII, vv. 18–19, below.

VIII

Solomon and the Cushites

Synopsis and General Character

What makes this legendary epic unique is that much of its subject matter is unknown in the Jewish classical as well as late aggadic sources. The only Hebrew source that seems to have a vaguely similar story is a Yemenite manuscript copied in 1702 by a certain Saadiah ben Joseph.[1] However, it seems that both these accounts have independently borrowed some elements from popular oral Islamic sources and have reshaped them into a Jewish version.[2] Wandering Muslim beggars who recited or chanted Islamic legends in exchange for alms were common in Kurdistan in Jewish neighborhoods as well as Muslim. They took their literary material from popular written Arabic sources, such as the Tales of the Arabian Nights and Life Stories of Prophets, thus serving as intermediaries between these sources and Jewish storytellers. It is quite possible that these late Jewish tales, as well as the Arabic ones, borrowed much of their material from old Jewish sources that were later lost or are still unpublished.[3]

The image of Solomon in this epic differs from the one in "King Solomon and the Queen of Sheba."[4] There the Queen of Sheba is overwhelmed by Solomon's power, wisdom, grace, and grandeur, and their marriage is blessed with happiness and harmony. In this epic, however, Solomon is a pitiful character, submissive to his Abyssinian wife,[5] whom he follows into exile, risking his throne as well as his life, to be finally rescued only by a miracle. Their marriage is marked by personal discord and religious conflict, and ends tragically when Solomon kills his wife by fire. Yet even in this

1. Published by J. Avidaʿ (see Bibliography, below); an English summary is in Pritchard, pp. 70–71, 81–82 (the author's name there is erroneously given as Yeshayahu Aviad instead of Judah Avidaʿ). See nn. 3, 7, 10, below.

2. Cf. nn. 8, 15, below.

3. Cf. Pritchard, pp. 85–87; Avidaʿ, p. 1; Rivlin, p. 108. However, 1 Kings 11:1–13 seems to be the basis of all these legends; cf. nn. 7, 10, below.

4. See chap. VII, above.

5. See n. 7, below.

generally tragic legend there is no escape from the traditional happy ending, according to which Solomon is eventually restored to his throne and imposes his rule on Abyssinia.

Bibliography

Neo-Aramaic text: Rivlin, pp. 268–72 (general comments, pp. 106–08).
1 Kings 11:1–13.
Avidaʿ, J. "The Tale of the Queen of Sheba" (in Hebrew). In *Sefer Assaf*, pp. 1–17. Jerusalem, 1953.[6]
al-Kisāʾī. *Qiṣaṣ al-anbiyāʾ, Vita Prophetarum*, pp. 293–95. Edited by I. Eisenberg. Leiden, 1922.
al-Thaʿlabī. *Qiṣaṣ al-anbiyāʾ*, pp. 178–80. Cairo, no date.
Mujīr ad-Dīn al-Ḥanbalī. *al-Uns al-jalīl*, pp. 139–44. Amman, 1973.
Burton, R. F., trans. *Thousand Nights and a Night* (the Arabian Nights), 6, 97–101. New York, 1934.
Pritchard, J. B., ed. *Solomon and Sheba*. London, 1974.

1

Solomon brought the daughter of the king of the Abyssinians[7] (to Jerusalem).
She brought Cushite servants with her.
She did not follow the Jewish religion.[8]

2

She was very youthful.[9]
She imposed her rule on Solomon.
She worshiped the idols of her father's house.[10]

6. Mainly chap. 2, which is an independent story.

7. This version is the only one that connects this legend with Abyssinia; cf. vv. 4, 5, 8, etc. The other sources refer only to an unnamed sea island, but the Arabic sources give the name of the king as Ṣīdūn (on Solomon's love of Zidonian women see 1 Kings 11:1, 5), Ṣadūf, or Nūrīyah, and his daughter's name as Šujūbah ("misfortune") or Jarādah ("locust?"). Cf. n. 13, below.

8. This is unique to this version. The Arabic sources speak of her halfhearted conversion to Islam; cf. n. 15, below. In the Jewish source of Avidaʿ this religious conflict between Solomon and his wife is ignored, and the worshiping of idols is ascribed only to her father.

9. Her unusual beauty is mentioned in all other sources. Cf. Burton, p. 97: "She was the fairest woman of her day, accomplished in beauty and loveliness, elegance and grace."

10. The Arabic sources speak of her asking Solomon to provide her with a likeness of her father, in order to mitigate her loneliness and assuage her longing for her father's house. Solomon agreed to do so but was much disturbed when he later found out that she worshiped this likeness as an idol; cf. n. 8, above. See 1 Kings 11:1–13 on Solomon's love of foreign

3

One day a wise man ⟨ḥaḵam⟩ visited Solomon
(And) told him a story,
Saying, "I shall reveal to you
And tell you whatsoever I have seen."

4

"You are Solomon.
You rule the entire world,
Yet you cannot prevail over the land of the Abyssinians."[11]

5

(When) Solomon went to the land of the Abyssinians,[12]
All the Abyssinians gathered around him.
They said (mockingly), "So this is the king of Israel!
How can you (now) escape from the hands of the Abyssinians?"

6

They said (further), "If you are (indeed) Solomon,
How can you escape from our hands?
You shall never see Jerusalem again.
We want you to show us (proof of) your kingship."

7

He said, "I am (indeed) Solomon.
I will cry out in a loud voice —
Perhaps (then) I will have some good tiding
(To demonstrate that) I am Solomon, the king of Israel."

8

Solomon went to the land of the Abyssinians.
He went (there) after[13] his wife.

---

women, their negative influence on his piety, and his resulting punishment by God; cf. n. 13, below.

11. This motif is unique to this version and is obviously borrowed from the legend of King Solomon and the Queen of Sheba (see chap. VII, v. 2, above), with the wise man replacing the bird Ziz Śaḏay. Cf. n. 12, below.

12. See n. 7, above. The rest of this version is quite different from all the other sources, and its immediate source, if any, remains unknown. The other sources include only some vague allusions, as indicated in the following notes. According to the Arabic sources, Solomon first slew the king of the island, after hearing of his great power, and then took his daughter to wife. It seems, then, that vv. 1–2 of this version either are out of place or serve merely as an introduction. Still another motivation for Solomon's journey is given further on in v. 8; cf. n. 22, below.

13. In the Neo-Aramaic text the preposition "after" is repeated twice, suggesting persistence on his part to follow her. It seems that she had run away and returned to her father's house; cf. nn. 12, 22. The Arabic sources entitle this legend *Fitnat Sulaymān,* "The Erring of Solomon," on account of his marriage to a woman who worshiped idols in his own house, as a

(Thus) he fell into the hands of the Abyssinians
(And) was captured by the king of the Abyssinians.

9

Solomon had appointed Benaiah (to rule) in his place in Jerusalem,[14]
(When) he went away to the land of the Abyssinians.
Solomon (now) pronounced the Ineffable Name,[15]
(And) Benaiah heard It on the roof of the palace in Jerusalem.[16]
Benaiah sat down and wept;
He was distressed about Solomon.[17]

10

Solomon said (mockingly) to the king of the Abyssinians,
"If you (wish to) slay me,
You must assemble all your governors ⟨kings⟩
(And try me) before all your peoples.[18]
(Thus) you will make for yourself a great name."

11

The king of the Abyssinians assembled all his government
(And) placed each (of his peoples) in a separate camp.[19]
He (also) brought along great viziers and kings.
He presented Solomon to his entire nation.

12

The king of the Abyssinians said,
"Look ye, I am a king.
I have captured Solomon.
I want to slay Solomon,
So that I may rule the entire world (in his place)."[20]

---

result of which God punished him with temporary exile and loss of his royal identity; cf. Ginzberg, *4*, 169–72; Garbell, pp. 128–33; n. 14, below.

14. The Arabic sources mention Asaph the son of Berechiah (1 Chron. 15:17; Ginzberg, *4*, 162) as the intimate friend of Solomon who helped him to recapture his throne from the demon who assumed his royal identity while Solomon was in exile. On Benaiah as Solomon's confidant see chap. VII, n. 25, above.

15. This is obviously a Jewish motif; cf. vv. 1, 16, and n. 8, above.

16. This telepathic message is unique. The Ineffable Name is mentioned in Avida^c's source, but in an entirely different context; see n. 25, below, and cf. Ginzberg, *4*, 166. Cf. Abishai's rescue of David from the captivity of Ishbi, Goliath's brother — Abishai learned that David was in distress when he saw a bleeding dove; see Ginzberg, *4*, 107–09.

17. Cf. v. 13, and n. 21, below.

18. The Neo-Aramaic words *millityasa* or *ʾummityasa* (from the Arabic *millah* and *ummah*) mean "nations, ethnic-religious groups" (cf. vv. 11, 13, 18), a description which seems to fit Ethiopia quite well.

19. Literally, "he seated them camps, camps, groups, groups" (distributive).

20. According to Avida^c's source, Solomon sent a letter to the king demanding that he

13

When all his peoples heard (this),
They feared their king
(And) were unable to say anything.
They secretly wept for Solomon.[21]

14

Solomon said, "O king,
I wish to see my wife.[22]
I (also) have three things to say.[23]
(Then) whatever I can do, I shall do."

15

Thereupon Solomon called the guardian of fire (and) the guardian of wind.
Fire appeared from the east,
Wind appeared from the west.
The wind and the fire consumed all those peoples;
None of them was left.[24]

16

Thereupon Solomon flew upward —
He pronounced the Ineffable Name —
He carried with him (his) wife, the king, (and) the executioner.[25]
He brought along all three of them.
He landed with all three in Jerusalem.

17

(After) Solomon arrived in Jerusalem,

---

accept Judaism and give him his daughter to wife. The king refused and decided to wage a fierce war against Solomon.

21. According to the Arabic sources the Israelites regretted their treatment of Solomon as if he were a beggar (al-Ḥanbalī, p. 143), and the angels wept for him out of pity (al-Kisā'ī, p. 294); cf. v. 9, above.

22. From this it seems that either the king had taken his daughter away from Solomon or she had previously returned to her father's house; cf. v. 8, and nn. 12–13, above.

23. It is unclear what these things (or words) are. According to Rivlin (p. 107), they are spelled out in Avidaʿ (p. 8): (1) he will inflict tribulations on the king's land; (2) he will deliver the corpses of the king and his people to the fowls of the sky and the beasts of the field; (3) he will break his idol. Cf. v. 15, below.

24. Cf. Avidaʿ, pp. 8–9: the wind carried the king and his peoples to an island where all of them except the king were devoured by wild beasts. The motif of fire may have been borrowed from Dan. 3:22 (Rivlin), but cf. Burton, p. 100.

25. Avidaʿ's source has a demon as adviser to the king. Solomon slew the demon by hanging him on an iron gallows inscribed with the Ineffable Name; cf. Burton, p. 101, and n. 27, below.

He burned (his) wife in the fire.[26]
(Then) he rewarded the executioner (and) sent him away.[27]
The king of the Abyssinians became a slave to Solomon for the rest of his life.[28]

18

All the Abyssinian people said,
"You, Solomon, shall be our king.
You shall rule over our land.
You shall collect much tribute from us."

19

Solomon replied, "I shall rule over your land.
I shall collect much tribute from you.
I shall gather all your gold into Jerusalem.
I shall rule over your land,
(But) I shall treat you justly."[29]

26. The Arabic sources say simply that he punished her when he found out that she worshiped idols.

27. The executioner is not mentioned elsewhere; cf. n. 25, above. According to Rivlin (p. 108), Solomon spared his life because he was one of those who wept and felt pity for him (v. 13). However, nothing is said about him in that verse.

28. According to Avidaʿ (p. 9), Solomon hanged the father.

29. This happy ending is borrowed almost literally from chap. VII, vv. 17–18, above. Cf. al-Ḥanbalī, p. 144: "Then he returned to his kingship, and all the kings of the earth obeyed him and brought him their treasures."

IX

The Prophet Elijah

There are many Jewish folktales about Elijah as the ever-ready prophet, who appears to mystics and learned rabbis as well as to innocent laymen, to aid them in moments of distress and danger.[1] He is also popular in Islamic lore and mysticism, where he is elevated above all other prophets.[2] This short Neo-Aramaic hymn, however, does not allude to any particular tale about Elijah but merely enumerates some of his attributes, especially his global role as herald of good tidings, friend in need, mediator between God and men, and precursor of the Messiah. The hymn was part of the *habdalah* liturgy, recited at the expiration of the Sabbath day (on Saturday evening).[3]

BIBLIOGRAPHY

Neo-Aramaic text: Rivlin, pp. 272–74.

1

Elijah owns twelve abodes.[4]

1. See Ginzberg, *4*, 195–235; Nissim ben Jacob ibn Shāhīn, *An Elegant Composition concerning Relief after Adversity*, translated by W. M. Brinner (New Haven, 1977; *YJS*, vol. 20), pp. 4–6, 13–16, 99–102; below, chap. XV, legend 2; chap. XVII, tale 8.

2. See Koran 6:86; 37:123–30; al-Thaʿlabī, *Qiṣaṣ al-anbiyāʾ* (Cairo, no date), pp. 122–30; *EI*, *2*, 861–65; *EI*², *3*, 1156. The legend of the rescue of Rabbi Kahana by Elijah (Ginzberg, *4*, 204) was narrated and sung in Kurdish by Muslim dervishes throughout Kurdistan. See also Schwarzbaum, pp. 241–45.

3. Rivlin, pp. 81, 101.

4. In v. 7, below, they are described as "caves." The Midrashic and Biblical sources speak of one cave; see Ginzberg, *3*, 137; 1 Kings 19:9, 13. The various Kurdish and Syrian towns in which these twelve caves are located are named in a manuscript; see Benayahu, pp. 121–22; above, Introduction, IV/4; cf. also Avidani, *4*, 558 (a legend about such a cave). The number twelve may stand for the twelve tribes of Israel. These caves seem to serve as terrestrial stations used by Elijah when he descends from his permanent celestial dwelling (vv. 3–5) to heal the sick (v. 8), etc. Cf. Ginzberg, *6*, 322–23, n. 32, on his terrestrial vs. celestial appearance.

5. In the plural, suggesting saviors in general who will redeem the Jews from their various lands of dispersion; cf. v. 9, below. On Elijah's role as the forerunner of the Messiah see Ginzberg, *4*, 233–35; Mal. 3:23.

6. This informal and childlike description of Elijah may be derived from the tradition that

He travels by himself (to) all twelve.
May he send us saviors[5]
To free us from prisons and jails.

2

Elijah is sweet.[6]
May he grant our homes full sustenance.
May the blessing of Elijah be upon this home.

3

Elijah says, "I am Elijah.[7]
I stand behind the (divine) screen.
I bring you good tidings.
I am the messenger of God.
I am the guardian of Israel."[8]

4

Elijah (dwells) among the angels.
He soars (over) the entire world in four orbits.[9]
He brings us calm and good tidings.[10]

5

He is a helper to us.
He grants Israel blessings in abundance.
He is very merciful.
He says, "I dwell in high heaven (to intercede) in your behalf."[11]

6

Elijah says, "O Israel, (if) today you obey the word of your God,[12]
He will redeem you from among the seventy nations,[13]

---

he belonged to the tribe of Gad, whose name means "good fortune" or "manna" (which tasted like honey); cf. Ginzberg, *1*, 365; *5*, 297, n. 183; Exod. 16:31. This explanation seems to be supported by the rest of the verse, which speaks of his role as the bearer of sustenance and material blessings; cf. vv. 5, 7, and nn. 16, 19, below.

7. Cf. chap. I, n. 5, above.

8. Cf. Ginzberg, *4*, 201–02; Rivlin, p. 273, nn. 5, 6; v. 5, below.

9. Or "wheels." Cf. Ginzberg, *4*, 203: "With four strokes of his wings Elijah can traverse the world. Hence no spot on earth is too far removed for his help"; *6*, 326, n. 46; B. Ber 4b.

10. See n. 6, above.

11. Cf. v. 3, and nn. 4, 8, above.

12. Cf. Deut. 28:1. On repentance as the necessary condition for salvation see Ginzberg, *4*, 233: "His task will be to induce Israel to repent when the Messiah is about to come"; *6*, 339, n. 106. Cf. p. 3, above.

13. This is the conventional number in rabbinic literature for all the Gentile nations of the world; see Ginzberg, *5*, 194–95.

He will build for you your Temple.
He will gather you into Jerusalem,[14] your land."

7

Elijah owns twelve caves.[15]
He travels (to) the four corners of the world.
(When) we make a request of him,
He grants blessings to every house in Israel.[16]

8

Elijah works wonders.
Every night he travels to villages and towns.
He brings healing from all ailments.[17]

9

Elijah performs many miracles.
He will free (us from) prisons and jails.
He will bring saviors (for Israel).[18]
He will crush the haughty and proud.[19]

14. Meaning the entire Land of Israel; see p. 54, n. 61, above.

15. See n. 4, above.

16. That is to say, he helps the poor and the needy with sustenance; cf. n. 6, above; Ginzberg, *4*, 204 ff.

17. On Elijah's role as a healer and physician see Ginzberg, *4*, 208–09. A common Neo-Aramaic blessing for a sick child is "May Elijah guard you (against illness)."

18. Cf. n. 5, above.

19. His crushing of nations seems to be derived from another etymology of the name Gad (see n. 6, above), "the cutter," "for from Gad was descended the prophet Elijah, who brings good fortune to Israel, and he also cuts down the heathen world" (Ginzberg, *1*, 365). Cf. 1 Kings 18:40.

X

Lel Huza: Women's Lamentations for the Ninth of Ab

Lel Huza is the name of a popular cycle of lamentations and narratives chanted and recited, respectively, by the womenfolk on the eve of the Ninth of Ab, the Jewish national day of mourning over the destruction of the Temple and Jerusalem. During the evening service, in which only men participated, the womenfolk gathered on the roof, where everyone in Kurdistan spent the hot summer nights, and sat in a circle around a woman well versed in this cycle, who chanted and recited for them the very moving dirges. While listening, the women burst into tears, wept, and sighed bitterly, and were deeply moved by the tragedies that had overtaken Jewish men and women in ancient times, "when Jews were killed and exiled from their homeland into strange lands" (quoting my informant).

Only a few women knew how to chant the entire cycle, which, according to my informant, was passed on orally from mother to daughter from time immemorial. Since most women were illiterate, the chants were never committed to writing. The present text was recorded on the night of the Ninth of Ab, A.M. 5725 (1965), in Jerusalem, as it was chanted by Mrs. Ṣabriyah Zaḳen, who had learned it from her mother.

The contents of the chants and of the supporting narratives are a mixture of tale and history, local Jewish realia and ancient Jewish legends. The entire history of the destruction of the Temple and of the exile of the Jewish people is represented by, and condensed into, the events that befell a lad known as Malka Ṣihyon ("King Zion") and two lasses, Halale and Šoše.

The contents of the cycle may be summarized as follows: (1) The tragic tale of the lost son Malka Ṣihyon, whose eight brothers were slain by the enemy but who himself was spared, only to die many years later under much more tragic circumstances; (2) The tragedy of Halale, the pretty Jewish girl who was captured by seven "infidel" brothers who all wanted to marry her; she was by a miracle drowned in a ritual bath and was thus saved from disgrace; (3) The fatal end of Šoše, killed by her father-in-law in a sacrifice ordained by divine edict in order to stop a drought threatening starvation for the whole family.[1]

I(A): The Story of Malka Ṣihyon

(1) This is (the story of) Lel Huza.[2] The Jews, were they not slain on the night of the Ninth of Ab? Whatever happened to them is recited in the synagogue. The mother of Curly[3] Malka Ṣihyon had nine sons. After the Jews were slain, these (sons) wandered on the highways (looking for refuge). Out came the infidels[4] and slew them on the highways. Eight they slew but left one (alive), Curly Malka Ṣihyon. They hoisted him on the tips of their spears[5] but did not slay him.

(2) His father and mother, too, the infidels pursued. What do we know? Once again they were exposed to taunts, (and) each one fled in a different direction. But after some time they returned to their home. They came (home) and saw that their sons were lost or slain.

1. For other details of background, as well as the musical notations of the chants, see Sabar (1976b). In order to retain the flavor of the informant's narrative style, I have translated as literally as possible. Note especially the numerous emphatic clipped sentences, which are typical of this nonliterary oral style, e.g., "Now that Jewish man, his wife told him," etc. (the emphasized logical subject precedes the grammatical subject). On the other hand, the common shift from the past tense to the present tense, e.g., "he says, they see," has not been retained, having been changed to "he said, they saw."

2. These obsolete words mean "the night demon of Judea" but have also become a synonym for "the night of the Ninth of Ab"; cf. Sabar (1976b), p. 140, n. 1. By common tradition, swimming in the river, a favorite pastime for the Jews of Zakho, was strictly forbidden for fear that Lel Huza, who dwelt in the river during this period, would carry away the swimmers and drown them. The prohibition of bathing during mourning for all Jews is based on rabbinic law (B. Ta 30a). On the relationship of Lel Huza to water, see I(B), below. For further details on the customs of the Kurdistani Jews on the Ninth of Ab see Brauer, pp. 249–53.

3. "His name was just M. Ṣ., but his mother adorned him by curling his side locks and called him Curly M. Ṣ. His hair was the color of gold water" (informant). Curiously enough, the Aramaic word *malka,* "king," is otherwise unknown in Jewish Neo-Aramaic, and *ḥakoma* (Arabic root, Aramaic formation) or *šulṭana* (literary) is used instead. Also, the spelling *Ṣihyon,* "Zion," is peculiar: it originated in Syriac and was borrowed in Arabic but is otherwise unknown in Jewish Neo-Aramaic; the male name "Zion" is pronounced *Ṣiyyon* (as in Hebrew) or *Čuna*; see Sabar (1974b), p. 45. However, *malka* as well as *Ṣihyun* (!) are used in Christian Neo-Aramaic; see Maclean, *Dictionary,* pp. 179, 263.

4. The enemy is called a variety of names: *kapore* ("infidels"; cf. Hebrew *kofĕrim*), *soraye* ("[Assyrian] Christians"), and *pilištanaye* ("Philistines"); see I(A) 4, 7, 12, below.

5. That is to say, took him prisoner.

(3) Thereupon the mother saw every night in her dream (a nightmare). She would go and tell (her dream) to (the sages in) the synagogue: "I saw this, I saw that. For God's sake, what shall I do? In the dream my soap, (when) I was about to (use) it, behold, it became a stone, and (when) I was about to (use) the tin basin (to rinse the laundry), behold, it became a stone basin. My cauldron, too, has turned to stone. Everything (else) has turned upside down upon me." But the sages would reply to her, "(May your dream) be of peace, (may your dream) be of peace."

(4) Now her son (Malka Ṣihyon), after the Philistines had slain his brothers, they took him down off the tips of their spears and let him go free. He did not know which way to go. He wandered about (until) he came to a town of (Assyrian) Christians. He was young, about ten, twelve, years, or twelve, thirteen.

(5) Now (while he was still) on the spears (a prisoner), he wanted to send a letter to his mother. He said (to himself), "If I send a letter to my mother on Thursday, she will throw herself into the sea (in despair).[6] If I send it on Friday, she will in her grief cook no meal for the Sabbath. I shall therefore send it on the Sabbath day. But I have no pen or ink, I have nothing." So he turned his left eye into ink. There was on his head a kerchief of white cloth, and he made it, or (rather) cut out of it, (a piece to serve as) paper. And he wrote (on it) with his small finger, (using it as a pen). Then he gave the letter to a stork, saying to him, "Go, carry it away." And on the Sabbath day the stork dropped it into the synagogue, while the Jews were standing up for the *ʿĂmiḏah* (prayer).[7] Anything that had happened to him and his brothers he described (in the letter) to his mother.[8]

6. "In olden times, [Jewish] women [in Kurdistan] used to wash their laundry at the seashore, [rather] at the river's edge on Thursday, so as to have clean clothes for the Sabbath. On Friday they were busy cooking, bathing, and otherwise getting ready for the Sabbath. There were then no washing machines and gas stoves as there are now." (informant).

7. Naming the stork as the letter-carrier reflects the realia of Kurdistan. Storks were a common sight in Zakho during late summer and early fall, and used to nest on the roof of the synagogue. Cf. I(B) 3, below. The ʿĂmiḏah (or "Eighteen Benedictions") prayer is a major part of the daily service.

8. Note that since this is women's literature, the main characters in it are women. Even in the story of Malka Ṣihyon, the hero seems to be his bereft mother. The womenfolk in the audience are constantly reminded of her suffering as a mother who has lost nine sons, the youngest, M. Ṣ., being extremely dear to her and handsome. The father is hardly mentioned. The lost son's letter is all about his mother's emotions, and even when it is dropped into the synagogue by the stork it is his mother who is informed of its contents, although women usually did not attend synagogue. In the story of Halale, the seven brothers go to their *mother*

(6) Now his mother had two daughters left at home — (there were all together) nine sons and two daughters. All the time the mother would sing and weep, saying, "By the life of Curly Malka Ṣihyon, lost in alien lands!"[9] She did not mention the sons who were slain (but sang) only about him.[10]

(7) So Malka Ṣihyon remained among the Christians. He married a Christian woman, but he would not eat their food. He ate only milk products, eggs, and suchlike food.[11] Now when it came to the eve of Sabbath, he would say to his wife, "Wife, light the Sabbath candle and turn it to face the Sanctuary (the Temple in Jerusalem)."[12] Although she was a Christian, she would say nothing (against this, for) she loved him. However, after he went out, she would say (to herself), "I am a Christian — I shall turn the candle to face Christendom, I shall light the wax candle for Christianity."

(8) Some time later he heard a herald proclaiming, "Hear ye, all the people, (the inhabitants of) a certain city in Israel have been slain; all those (who survived) have fled."[13] The Jews were slain on the Sabbath day, on the night of the Ninth of Ab. Of all the city people none was left except two girls, (who) hid themselves under the bridge, near the cave (above) the river.[14] They were sisters.

(9) Now that Jewish man (Malka Ṣihyon), his wife said to him, "In the city of Jerusalem all of them have been slain, the Jews, all of them, have been slain. Go up there, bring us some loot, property, and (other) things, (as well as) much money." So he came there in order to bring back property and money.

(10) He looked around (and noticed that in every house) all the Sabbath cooking (vessels) were plastered (with ashes to hold the heat),[15] (and he realized that the former owners) had been Israelites.

---

for advice and do exactly as she says (II[A] 4–5). For further details on the reflection of local social attitudes and values in this cycle see Sabar (1980), pp. 293–94.

9. Cf. Sister's Lullaby, I(B) 4, below.

10. Cf. chap. XX, proverb 70, below.

11. According to Jewish dietary law, meat products processed by non-Jews are not ritually clean for consumption.

12. Using the Hebrew word *ḳodeš*. Cf. the Arabic name for Jerusalem, *al-Quds*.

13. The purpose of this announcement was to induce non-Jews to loot the deserted Jewish homes. See below.

14. This detailed description of the hiding place is taken from the actual landscape of Zakho.

15. It was the custom in Kurdistan to plaster the cooking vessel with moistened ashes to keep the food hot during the Sabbath.

His blood froze, because they were Jews. His hands did not move to take anything, as he said to himself, "By God, I shall go back. To hell-fire with the one (my wife) who told me (to seize some loot)! How can I seize the property of Jews?"

(11) As he was about to return, to go back, he said to himself, "However, my way is long. Let me take some food with me." He took some out of a Sabbath dish, put it inside something, (namely) some bread, and began walking back, going down that same road under the bridge. He looked up, and behold, two girls were (hiding) there. He said to them, "What are you doing here, girls, (all alone, since you are) so little?" They replied, "As God liveth, the Jews, all of us, have been slain. They pursued us also, in order to hand us over (to the killers). None was left (alive). We have been hiding. It has been two or three days (that) we are here, with nothing to eat or drink. Surely we will soon die." He said, "Come with me to my wife. Perform some service for her, something of this sort, and we will give you shelter, and you will eat and drink." So they went along with him and remained there with his family.

(12) One day these girls saw this man say to his wife, "Turn the Sabbath candle to face Israel," but (when) he left, she turned it to face Christendom. Now one of them said to his wife, "Wife of my brother — long live my brother —why do you not bear my brother's burdens (i.e., obey him)? My brother has said, 'Turn the candle to face the Holy Land,' yet you turned it to face Christendom." So this girl arose and turned the candle back to face the Holy Land.

(13) Now his wife became enraged and angry. As soon as her husband came in, she said to him, "This girl is giving me orders! Did you bring me a rival wife, or what? I will never accept (this kind of treatment). (Other) people have brought property and suchlike things, (whereas) you brought me a couple of worthless and useless (girls). You must kill this girl forthwith. She has falsely accused me, saying 'You turned the candle to face Christendom.'" She continued saying things of this sort until she convinced him, and he slew his sister forthwith. He did not know, of course, that she was his sister.

(14) After he slew his sister, he went out (and stood) in front of the door, observing and reflecting. He stood before the door, and as God liveth, his hands cooled until they froze — after all, she was his sister, by his (own) father and mother. He listened (and over-

heard) his wife saying to his other sister, "Get up, accursed one! Rock my son, lest once again I should accuse you falsely. Just as I caused your sister to die, so shall I cause you to die." Behold, she replied, "Let him slay me; after all, what am I (good) for? I wish he would slay me right now. After you have falsely accused my sister, (what am I good for)?"

(15) She arose and went to rock the cradle, grief-stricken — not so? She began rocking it and singing this song:

I shall put you to sleep, to sleep, woe is me!
By the life of Curly Malka Ṣihyon, poor me!
Who is lost in alien lands, woe is me!
Woe is me, what has befallen me, poor me![16]

(Upon hearing this), her brother came back, bursting with grief, and said, "May my life (be) ransom for you. This Malka Ṣihyon, how was he related to you?" She replied, "All I know is, (when) I was small my mother wept all the time because my brother was lost, she did not know where." He said, "Well, I am (the one), there is no one else. My name is Malka Ṣihyon, but my mother used to call me Curly Malka Ṣihyon. Am I then your brother? Did I (just) slay my sister with my own hands? If so, I shall kill myself (as well)."

(16) Now she begged him, "May my life (be) ransom for you, my brother. You have done it, it is (already) done, so do not kill yourself. Even now we remain brother and sister; this too is good, we will comfort each other." He said, "No, never! After all, I brought you here so that you may live, and (yet) I slew my (other) sister. I have also heard my wife saying, 'I falsely accused your sister, and I shall do the same to you.'" Then he arose, slew his wife, and killed himself.[17]

(17) People tell that this girl now prayed to God, saying, ("May I be) Thy sacrifice, O Lord, mayest Thou turn me into a raven to dwell in the mountains." God accepted her prayer. Now people say that the raven is she. They say so; as for me, what do I know?[18]

16. See the complete song below, I(B) 4. Announcing tidings innocently by a lullaby is typical. Cf. chap. III, §31, and n. 33, ad loc.

17. Cf. the story of the son and daughter of R. Ishmael, who many years after they had been enslaved met as bride and groom. Eventually they discovered their true relationship and committed suicide (B. Giṭ 58a).

18. The black raven is a symbol of tragedy and gloom. Among the many legends about it in the Midrashic literature, there is one associating it with cruelty; see Ginzberg, 5, 185: "Noah, by sending out the raven, wished to indicate that God appeared to be cruel to mankind, even as this bird is cruel to his children." Cf. also p. 36, above.

I(B): The Chants of the Malka Ṣihyon Story

1. *Mother's Song, Warning Her Lost Son about Demonic and Human Enemies*

The Spirit of Judea (is hovering) over the waters — alas for the Spirit of Judea![19]
The Spirit of Judea (is hovering) over the waters — woe is me, mother!
Do not go, (my son), into the fields — alas for the Spirit of Judea!
Lest the field men find you — woe is me, mother!
Merciless and cruel (infidels) — alas for the Spirit of Judea!
They show no mercy to the Jews — woe is me, mother!
Do not go, (my son), into the mountains — alas for the Spirit of Judea!
Lest the mountaineers find you — woe is me, mother!
Merciless and cruel (people) — alas for the Spirit of Judea!
They show no mercy to the Jews — woe is me, mother!

2. *Mother's Nightmare about the Fate of Her Sons*

I went to (use) the tin basin, it has become a stone basin — woe is me!
I went to (use) the soap, it has become a stone — wretched me!
I went to (use) the cauldron, it was turned upside down — woe is me!
I went to (use) the soap, it has become a stone — wretched me!
I went to the (sages in the) synagogue — woe is me!
I said, "What is this trouble?" — wretched me!
They said, "May it be for peace" — woe is me!
"Do not fear" — wretched me!
And I did not know what had happened to me — woe is me!
And what had befallen me — wretched me!
Eight of my sons have been slain — woe is me!
And the ninth is on (the tips of) spears, (a prisoner) — wretched me!

19. It seems that the mother is calling upon Lel Huza to help her son along the waterway, Lel Huza's domain (see n. 2, above), because all the other routes are dangerous. The refrain "alas," etc., as well as most of the other refrains in the cycle, is mainly a prosodic device, without much particular significance.

3. *The Lost Son's Letter to His Mother*

(If) I send the letter to my mother — woe is me!
On Thursday — wretched me!
My mother at the sea(shore) — woe is me!
Washing laundry — wretched me!
When she hears (of our fate) — woe is me!
She will throw herself into the sea — wretched me!

(If) I send the letter to my mother — woe is me!
On Friday — wretched me!
When my mother (is) about to cook (for the Sabbath) — woe is me!
She will not cook for the Sabbath — wretched me!
I shall send the letter to my mother — woe is me!
On the Sabbath — wretched me!
(But) I have no pen and ink — wretched me!

My left eye, I shall turn it (into) ink — woe is me!
My small finger (into) a pen — wretched me!
My head-kerchief of *garawa*[20] (into) paper — woe is me!
I shall send the letter with the stork — wretched me!

4. *The Sister's Lullaby*

I shall put you to sleep, woe, to sleep,
By the life of Curly Malka Ṣihyon, wretched mother![21]

I shall put you to sleep — woe is me!
By the life of Curly Malka Ṣihyon — wretched me!

Who is in alien lands — woe, go to sleep;
Who is lost — wretched mother!

I said, "May my brother live" — woe is me!
"And you are my brother" — wretched me!

He said (to his wife), "Turn the (Sabbath) candle to face the Holy Land" — woe is me!
But she turned it to face Christendom — wretched me!
Woe is me! What has befallen me? — woe is me!
Woe is me! What shall I do? — wretched me!

20. A cheap whitish cloth used only by the very poor, hence indicative of his being a captive.

21. The first six lines are probably from a lullaby originally sung by the mother to her baby daughter after her brothers had been slain or lost. The rest is the daughter's addition, based on what she observed in her brother's house.

II(A): HALALE'S STORY

(1) Those Jews, the infidels were slaying them (again). The infidels were slaying the Jews, they slew them. Now any girl who was pretty, they would pursue her. Halale[22] too was pursued by seven infidels. She (fled and) entered the Sanctuary;[23] she (miraculously) cleft a column and entered inside it. She put her trust in God, (and) God, (may I be) His sacrifice, helped her (to hide there). However, part of her braid remained (outside).[24]

(2) These seven infidels came after her in order to take her out (of the Sanctuary). They looked, there was no Halale — she had disappeared. They said, "She is gone." They came out. But one (of them), aged one hundred years, suddenly said, "What? Has Halale disappeared?" They replied, "Behold, she has indeed disappeared." He said, "(Look) over there, her braid shows."

(3) They thereupon broke the column and took her out. (As) they took her out, they said, "Well, we will marry you, all seven of us." She said, "But for us, according to our religious law, (that of) Israel, this is impossible. (To only) one (husband) may one be married."

(4) Thereupon they took her away, saying, "We shall go to our mother (for advice)." They took her to their mother. They bound her (first) and carried her away. They came (to their mother). She told their mother, "We, among us, the Jews, we may marry one husband, we may not marry seven. I have been told (that our law is) like this. Also, I remember that my mother used to go to the ritual bath. Well, if she could not go to the ritual bath, she would not do that thing (have sexual intercourse)."[25] They said, "Very well."

22. "Meaning a pretty girl" (informant). The name may be derived from the Arabic *hilāl*, "crescent moon" (cf. the Hebrew *helel ben šaḥar* [Isa. 14:12], "the Morning Star, Venus"). But it may also be that the name was originally pronounced "Ḥalale," "Pure One," which suits her character and is connected with the Arabic root *ḥll*, "to be pure," in the Neo-Aramaic text of the song below.

23. Hebrew *hek̲al*, the innermost hall in the Temple; here meaning the part of the synagogue where the scrolls of Torah are kept.

24. Cf. the legend about Isaiah, who was swallowed by a tree but his hiding place was betrayed by his ritual fringe (*ṣiṣit̲*). See P. Sanh 10, 28c; Ginzberg, 6, 374.

25. The Jewish law of cleanness (see n. 29, below) was strictly observed by the Jewish women of Kurdistan. They used to take a ritual bath (*ṭabila*) in the river even on the coldest days of winter, when the river was almost frozen. If they saw a Gentile man on their way back, they would repeat the whole ritual; cf. Brauer, pp. 154–55, where it is related that the wife of a sage in Amidya repeated her bath 14 times until her skin began peeling from the frost. On the dangers facing Jewish women while having a ritual bath, see also Benjamin II, p. 104: "In the middle of the fields, about half an hour's journey from the town, stands a Synagogue,

(5) They then said to their mother, "This (girl) wants (only) one of us. Which one of us is she to marry?" The mother replied, "May the life of your mother be (ransom) for you; let the oldest brother, the one whose age is one hundred years, be the one to marry, let her be (married) to the oldest brother." The girl said, "I will not agree unless you take me to the river, to swim in it as (in) a ritual bath; will you?"

(6) They went (and) looked (at the river, but) there was no water in it. People say this was so because Zechariah the prophet had been slain (there), and many were slain on top of him, and their blood was seething in the river, but there was no water (left) in it.[26] They kept looking, they found an animal's hoof, that of a mule, there was a drop of water in it. They said to her, "Immerse yourself in this — swim!" They tied seven ropes to her waist and held the ends in their hands.

(7) Now this (girl), when she put her foot (in it), what happened? Only her toes got wet. But then, (may I be) His sacrifice, God performed a miracle so that she (could) swim. The water swelled; (first) it came up to her knee, then to her thigh, and

---

remarkable for its great age; nearby is a small reservoir, which serves as a bath for the women. Formerly the women there were exposed to frequent attacks from the Kurds; several facts were narrated to me, of which I will here mention a few. One day a woman was surprised while in the bath by four Kurds — she had, however, the courage to seize a large piece of wood, and to throw it at the head of one of the men, and thereby killed him on the spot. For this her own life was the penalty; for the three other Kurds murdered her. How sublime is this heroic and noble-minded courage of this daughter of our race who was willing to die for her religion! Another woman was seized by a Kurd; she defended herself and snatched from him a dagger which she buried in his side. A friend of the wounded man accidentally passing by, saw him weltering in his blood, immediately seized upon the woman, and stabbed her." Cf. ibid., p. 117: "A short time before my arrival a Jewish girl emptying some dirty water into the street, accidentally besprinkled with it a Mussulman who chanced to be passing by. Immediately a crowd assembled before the house, broke open the door, seized the girl, and heaped upon her all kinds of threatening abuse; asking her, how she, the daughter of an accursed race, dare offer to insult a true believer. The girl defended herself to the best of her ability, but the leader of the tumult cried out to her: 'There is only one way for thy escape, embrace our faith, and thou shalt marry one of our people, who is young, handsome, rich, and of a good family.' But the girl refused and answered: 'I am a Jewess, born so, and as such I will die; never will I deny my God, my people, and my faith. If you kill me, God will require of you my blood, and the Lord will avenge me.' — After that they seized her, killed her before the eyes of her parents by stabbing her with their knives, and then tore her in pieces."

26. Cf. B. Giṭ 57b; Ginzberg, *4*, 304; *6*, 396. The memory of this massacre is preserved by the Kurdistani Jews in their public ceremonies as well. On the Ninth of Ab, in the afternoon, they used to slaughter sheep at the riverside and sprinkle the blood with their fingers to the four corners of the world. Then they marked their necks, faces, and foreheads with the same blood; see Brauer, pp. 252–53.

(finally) to her waist. She immersed herself once, twice, thrice. She put her trust in God, saying, "This woman, mayest Thou rescue her from the hands of these infidels." Then, (may I be) His sacrifice, God drew her down, (and) she disappeared in that water.[27] She was carried away to paradise, or some such place. Now we say, "Halale, have a ritual bath," in song. Our mother (and) grandmother used to sing it, and we learned it from them.

II(B): Halale's Ritual Bath Song

Halale ("Pretty One"), purify yourself.[28]
Dalale ("Pampered One"), take a ritual bath.
Let the water reach to my ankle.

Halale, (lest) I not be purified,
Dalale, (lest) I not have a (proper) ritual bath,
Let the water reach to my navel.

Halale, purify yourself.
Dalale, take a ritual bath.
Let the water reach to my neck.

Halale, (lest) I not be purified,
Dalale, (lest) I not have a (proper) ritual bath,
Let the water reach over my head.[29]

III(A): Šoše's Story

(1) Šoše[30] too lived in that Jews' town. Once more the infidels began slaying them and robbing them. They were left with no crop, no wheat, and no anything at all. Now there were (some) people

27. For the theme of suicide by drowning, cf. B. Giṭ 57b: Four hundred Jewish boys and girls were captured for an immoral purpose, and when they realized what was awaiting them, they all jumped into the sea and drowned. H. N. Bialik's poem *Scroll of Fire* echoes this legend.

28. See n. 22, above. It is not clear whether the song is a dialogue between her and her captors, or, more likely, a monologue in which she addresses herself alternately in the first and second person.

29. She, of course, used the ritual bath as a pretext to avoid marriage with her heathen captors, since nothing is said or implied about menstruation, in which case ritual bathing is obligatory for Jewish women. Yet her story and chant reflect the rabbinic rules governing such a bath: the water must be from a natural source, such as a spring, and the woman's body must be totally immersed at least once. See *EJ*, *2*, 81–86, s.v. "Ablution"; *11*, 1534–44, s.v. "Mikveh".

30. "I do not know what her name means" (informant). Probably a hypocoristic form of *Šošannah*, "Susan, Lily."

who fled and went off to another place. Now they had nothing to plant, nothing to harvest, and nothing to eat. They were left in the wilderness with nothing at all.

(2) Their elder said, "(May I be) Thy sacrifice, O God. Now that we have fled into this wilderness, now then, what are we going to eat? God, (may I be) His sacrifice, (or) the Divine Voice,[31] announced and revealed, saying, "You must slay one (person) from your house; you may get rid of whomsoever you wish, and then you will eat and live; for one person from your house has not (yet) been slain" — it was a divine edict at that time (that from each house at least one person was to be slain)[32] — "now you must slay that person, whichever one you wish, from among either your daughters-in-law, (your) grandchildren, or your sons."[33]

(3) Now this man began thinking, "Whom shall I slay?" He had a daughter-in-law — she did not have too many relatives, only a sister, and she had (only) one son born (to her). Now her husband realized this, so he said to his father, "I know that you will slay my wife. If you do slay my wife, it will be a great sin. She is a stranger, she has no one but a sister in the (whole) world. You must not slay her — slay me instead of her." But his father, his hands could not move to slay his own son; and (yet) he had to slay someone.

(4) Nevertheless, one day his father arose and slew her, he slaughtered her on the roof.[34] Now, whenever her husband returned from plowing, she used to run toward him (to welcome him home). On that day she did not come running. Now her husband, his heart suspected the worst. He ran, came into the house, and said, "Father, have you slain Šoše?" The father replied, "No, I did not slay her."[35] He said, "You did kill her!" Now he gave way to his grief and began weeping and singing this song about his wife:

III(B): The Husband's Song on Šoše's Death

O Šoše the benevolent,[36] O Šoše the benevolent!

31. Hebrew *bat-kol,* literally "Daughter (echo) of the (Divine) voice."

32. Perhaps an echo of Exod. 12:30, *for there was not a house where there was not one dead.*

33. It is worthwhile to note the relative value placed on members of the family: most valuable — sons; less valuable — grandchildren; least valuable — daughters-in-law.

34. So that nobody would see him in the act, or perhaps echoing the ancient custom of offering sacrifices on house roofs; cf. 2 Kings 23:12; Jer. 19:13.

35. The denial perhaps indicates that he did it much against his will, and only in obedience to the Lord's decree.

36. This appellation probably indicates that through her death benevolence came to the family. Cf. also n. 37, below.

Šoše, alien among aliens,[37] O Šoše the benevolent!

Šoše was slain on the upper story, O Šoše the benevolent!
Her blood flowed down to the lower story, O Šoše the benevolent!

It was scooped with tiny spoons, O Šoše the benevolent!
To be used (as) kohl for the eyes of grooms and brides,[38] O Šoše the benevolent!

O father, you did not slay a lord's daughter, O Šoše the benevolent!
O father, you slew an alien among aliens, O Šoše the benevolent!

37. Hinting at her tragic status: not only was she an alien in her family, but now her entire family-in-law was in an alien land. However, the song contains some other allusions that are not clarified in the narrative; see the next note.

38. Apparently an indication of the magic use of blood — her blood was also probably considered beneficial. Brauer (pp. 99–100), in his long chapter on wedding customs, does not mention the use of kohl as a magical salve or as a cosmetic; henna is commonly used for both purposes.

XI

The Conversion of Onḳelos to Judaism

Synopsis and General Character

This legend is taken from a Neo-Aramaic Midrash to Exod. 13:21, *And the Lord went before them by day in a pillar of cloud, to lead them the way; and by night in a pillar of fire, to give them light; that they might go by day and by night.* The legend aims to show in a vivid way how fortunate the Jews are that the Lord God Himself pays court to them, His servants, leads them always on the right path, fights for them, and protects them by day and by night. This is in contrast to the custom of Gentile lords and kings, whose servants guard them, fight for them, and even get killed for their sake.

The old Midrashic sources include only brief versions of this legend. Our version, while omitting some of the details of Titus' sexual acts performed in the Temple, adds many embellishments and elaborations.

Onḳelos, a Roman Christian related to Titus, decides to be converted to Judaism, following the "commercial" advice of his uncle Titus' spirit (which he has) raised by means of necromancy. Caesar, upon hearing of Onḳelos' deviation, sends successive contingents of soldiers to arrest him, but Onḳelos succeeds in converting them all to Judaism. Divinely inspired, he translated the Hebrew Bible into Aramaic.

Bibliography

Neo-Aramaic text: Sabar (1976a), pp. 4–8 (Hebrew transliteration), 44–50 (phonetic transcription), 90–94 (English translation).

---

(1) Our masters, of blessed memory, say that Onḳelos the proselyte — a righteous proselyte,[1] may he rest in peace — was the son

1. Hebrew *ger ṣedeḳ*, meaning "sincere proselyte, who out of conviction has voluntarily adopted Judaism," in contrast to those who adopt Judaism for selfish and unworthy reasons; see *EJ*, s.v. "Appreciation of the Proselyte," *13*, 1185–90.

of the wicked Titus' sister, and Titus himself was the vizier of Caesar. And this is the (same) wicked Titus who because of our sins entered the Temple and committed foul abominations in the Sanctuary of the Lord.[2]

(2) But in the end the Holy One, blessed be He, exacted vengeance upon him by means of a gnat. It entered into his nose, proceeded to his brain, and kept eating it until he begged for death; but he could not die. He kept striking his head against rocks and walls but could not find rest. He continued for many years in this suffering until his head was split open with axes, and behold, a gnat the size of a young dove flew out of his brain, and (thus) he died in (great) pain.[3]

(3) After this event the thought occurred to Onḳelos, the son of Titus' sister, to forsake the faith of Christianity.[4] Onḳelos never did anything at all without asking Titus, his maternal uncle, for advice. He thereupon went to Titus' grave, and there, from his knowledge of various kinds of magic, performed magical rites, brought Titus out of the grave,[5] and said to him, "O my maternal uncle, I have a question for you — tell me honestly what I ought to do." (Titus) replied, "Tell me." (Onḳelos) said, "O my maternal uncle, I am about to go off to trade and to travel. Tell me, what merchandise ought I to buy?" (Titus) replied, "O my kinsman, go and see what merchandise is in little demand and (whose value) has gone down, so that no one looks for it — that one you ought to buy. For its value will certainly go up and increase; that merchandise will surely rise in value."[6]

(4) Onḳelos rose therefrom, reflected (over the matter), and said to himself, "At present there is no merchandise that is less in demand than Israel, nor any nation more humiliated. God will surely elevate it above all other nations."

(5) He took the road to Jerusalem, came before the sages, and

2. These abominations are omitted here probably for euphemistic reasons; see B. Giṭ 56b: "The wicked Titus blasphemed and reviled [Him who is] on high. What did he do? He seized a harlot with his hand and entered (with her) in the Holy of Holies, spread a Scroll of the Torah (on the floor), and committed over it a (sexual) transgression."

3. Cf. ibid. (with different details).

4. He lived in the second century C.E., but nowhere else is it stated that he was a Christian; see *EJ, 12,* 1405–06.

5. For Onḳelos' knowledge of necromancy and his consultations, prior to his conversion to Judaism, with Titus, Balaam, and a heretic (or Jesus), see B. Giṭ 56b–57a; *EJ,* loc. cit.

6. For somewhat different dramatis personae (Aquila for Onḳelos and Hadrian for Titus) see Tanḥuma (ed. Buber), Exod., pp. 81–82, and the editor's notes ad loc.; cf. *EJ,* loc. cit.

said to them, "Convert me. I am So-and-so. I have come to (adopt) the religion of Israel." Whereupon all those demands which, as we have said, Naomi had made of Ruth when she was converted were (now) set forth by the sages to him, and he agreed (to them).[7] He also accepted all the requirements of the commandments and of the toil in Torah (while one is) in this world, (knowing that) the reward for them is great in the next world.[8] Then they said to him, "O righteous one, it is impossible for a man who is still uncircumcised to come in under the shelter of the Divine Presence."[9] He replied, "Very well, (I will be circumcised) gladly." Thereupon he fasted for three days, the while he studied in a house of study. On the third day he went to a ritual bath, then came to the sages, who circumcised him forthwith.

(6) After this the Holy One, blessed be He, bestowed upon him some of His holy spirit and conferred upon him the illumination of the great prophecy,[10] so that he finally became the crown of all the sages of Israel. And all of the Torah, from *In the beginning God created* (Gen. 1:1) to *The Lord his God be with him, let him go up* (2 Chron. 36:23), he put into an (Aramaic) translation. Every difficult and obscure word that was in the Torah he illuminated and explained to the sages. (Thus) he established peace among them, for (heretofore) they used to disagree about every meaning. May God grant the same to all Israel.[11]

(7) Finally, when the wicked Caesar heard about what had happened, he sent men to Jerusalem after Onḳelos, (saying), "Go at once and bring him to me in chains." When Caesar's armed soldiers came to Jerusalem and saw Onḳelos among the sages — divine light surrounding him, as he shed light upon the sages — they were amazed at him. He summoned them, had them seated near him, and told them some of the meanings of the Torah and of the

7. See Ruth Rabbah, 2:16, 22; Ginzberg, *6*, 190, n. 44.

8. Meaning the world to come; a parallel Arabic expression has the same sense.

9. Cf. Tanḥuma, loc. cit.: "One may not study [Torah] unless he is circumcised." For the general rules regarding conversion see B. Yeḇ 46a–48a; *EJ*, s.v. "Laws of Conversion," *13*, 1183–85.

10. According to Professor G. Scholem (pers. comm.), "the great prophecy is that of Moses, in contrast to the other prophets, whose prophecy was from a mirror which does not illuminate."

11. Cf. B. Meḡ 3a. Onḳelos' Aramaic translation of the Bible (*Targum*) became sanctified almost as much as the original Hebrew text. The Jews of Kurdistan have a tradition that their Aramaic dialects, often called *lišan targum* ("language of the Targum"), are descendants of Onḳelos' Aramaic language.

commandments, and the reward for (keeping) them. (Thereupon) they, too, proclaimed the truth of the religion of Israel and acknowledged their belief in it, and through him they too were converted to Judaism.

(8) (When) Ceasar heard about this he sent other men, more numerous and more violent (than the preceding ones), to look for him. They also came to him, and he converted them as well as (he had) the others, by the sweetness of his teaching.

(9) (Of this), too, Caesar was told. This time, (however), he sent dire threats to Israel through very strong men whom he instructed, "You must not speak with him, neither for good nor for evil. Merely seize him as he is and bring him to me." When these strong men arrived, they did just that — they seized Onḳelos by force and took hold of him to carry him off. When they arrived with him at the gates of Jerusalem and were about to take him out, he stretched out his hand to the mezuzah of Jerusalem, saying "O you stupid men of Caesar's, do you have any idea of the benefit (to be derived from) the mezuzah?" They replied, "No." He said: "O you fools, this is the mighty name of the God of Israel. We write it down and put it upon our gates, and it protects us from all the harmful powers; no destroyer or demon dares to come into the house of Israel.[12] On the contrary, they (live) in tranquillity and comfort in their houses, and God protects them from all misfortunes. We are not like you, for you have to protect your master, Caesar. Night and day you maintain watches for his benefit, and still he is not at peace. On the contrary, he goes to sleep in fear and rises in fear."

(10) "Moreover, when your Caesar takes you into the army, you fight for him and you get killed, while he looks on from afar. As for us, Israel, this is not the way of our God. Instead, he makes war on the enemies of Israel, while Israel remains at ease, as it is said, *The Lord will fight for you, and ye shall hold your peace* (Exod. 14:14). Not only that, but you wear yourselves out day and night for the benefit of Caesar. In the daytime you (have to) provide him with shade, and at night you (have to) light lamps for him; he is at ease while you are put to pain. As for us, Israel, our God provides us with shade in the daytime, and at night, by means of His illumination, He furnishes us with light, as it is said, *The Lord went before them,* etc. (Exod. 13:21)."

12. Cf. Meḵilta (ed. Lauterbach), *1*, 88, and editor's note ad loc.

(11) "And do not say, 'This happened only on that (particular) day,' for each and every day, until the Messiah (arrives), God will do the same for Israel. All the other nations He leads in darkness and gloom, but Israel He illuminates with His light, as it is said, *For behold, darkness shall cover the earth, and gross darkness the peoples; but upon thee the Lord will arise, and His glory shall be seen upon thee* (Isa. 60:2)."[13]

(12) When these strong men heard this, they (too) expressed their belief in the faith of Israel and were converted by Onkelos. Thereupon Onkelos sent back an answer to Caesar, (saying), "O Caesar, all that I have done was done only on the advice of my maternal uncle, Titus. Now then, you know — and so does Titus — that I took a lowly hand and went to a nation of low estate. In the end God will raise us higher than all the (other) nations." When Caesar heard this, he held his peace and left him alone.[14]

13. Cf. Sifre Num. (ed. Horovitz), §83, p. 80; Yalkuṭ Shimʿoni, 2, §500.
14. Cf. B. AZ 11a.

XII

The Mission of Bar Ḳappara to Annul a Decree against the Jews

Synopsis and General Character

This *maʿăśeh* (folktale) is taken from a Neo-Aramaic Midrash to Exod. 18:12. The Midrash states that God allowed Jethro to eat bread before Him as a reward for his kindness to Moses, when he told his daughters, *Call him, that he may eat bread* (Exod. 2:21). Thus the famous verse Eccles. 11:1, *Cast thy bread upon the waters, for thou shalt find it after many days,* traditionally interpreted as an assurance that practice of charity is eventually rewarded, came true in this case.[1] The tale of Bar Ḳappara is then cited as a classic example of the truth of this traditional interpretation.[2]

The old Midrashic source includes two versions of this tale, a shorter one, the protagonist of which is Rabbi Eleazar bar Ḳappara,[3] and a longer one, whose protagonist is Rabbi Eleazar ben Shammuʿa.[4] Our version, while retaining the name of Bar Ḳappara, is similar in many details to the longer version. However, it includes or elaborates on some details while omitting others.[5]

Standing by the seashore, Bar Ḳappara saw a ship sinking, with only one out of many passengers surviving the shipwreck. Assuming that the man must have been righteous to survive the calamity, Bar Ḳappara was surprised to learn from him that he was actually a pagan on his way to buy some cattle to sacrifice to his idol. Nevertheless, Bar Ḳappara concluded that some good would come from him in the future (§§1–2). He therefore treated him kindly,

1. For a modern interpretation of this verse see R. Gordis, *Koheleth, the Man and His World: A Study of Ecclesiastes* (New York, 1968), p. 330.

2. See Bibliography, below. For other folktales (including Arabic) in support of this traditional interpretation of the verse, see Eccles. Rabbah, 11:1–3; Gaster (1924), nos. 99, 298 (with bibliography on pp. 204, 234); Gordis, pp. 329–30; Bin Gorion, *3,* 1280–82.

3. Lived at the beginning of the third century C.E.; see *EJ*, s.v. "Bar Kappara," *4,* 227–28.

4. Lived in the second century C.E.; ibid., s.v. "Eleazar ben Shammua," *6,* 598.

5. See notes below. Similarly, in the Yiddish version (Gaster [1934], *2,* 606–21) there is a great deal of local embellishment.

provided him with money, compensated him for all he had lost, and even more. Some years later this shipwreck survivor became king of his country, and like his predecessors in office began persecuting the Jews. To try to annul the decrees against them, the Jews chose Bar Ḳappara to intercede on their behalf and sent him to the new king with much gold (§§3–4). The king immediately recognized him, while Bar Ḳappara did not remember the king at all. Finally the king reminded him of their first meeting, rewarded him for his former kindness, and annulled the decrees against the Jews (§§5–7).

Bibliography

Neo-Aramaic text: Sabar, *Midrašim* (forthcoming).
Eccles. Rabbah, 11:1–2.
Gaster (1924), tale no. 300.
Gaster (1934), 2, 606–21.
Farḥi, Y. S. *'Ośeh Pele'*, pp. 312–13. Jerusalem, 5719 (1959).[6]

---

(1) Our sages of blessed memory told (this tale): One day Bar Ḳappara, peace be upon him, was standing[7] on the seashore. Suddenly he saw a ship approaching on the sea. It was not long before a tremendous flood of water swept the ship and plunged it into great distress, until it (was about to) sink into the sea and disappear. This righteous man (Bar Ḳappara) then swore an oath that he would not go away from there until he saw if anyone from that entire ship had survived. After an hour or two, lo and behold, the entire ship had sunk, together with a great many people who were in it. But then he saw that one person was (floating) upon a plank, having remained alive and well. Bar Ḳappara felt very happy, saying, "Blessed be the Lord! This one must be a righteous man, and that is why God has saved him."[8]

(2) He went toward him and asked him about the ship and the people (who were) in it, and the man told him a great many things

6. For additional bibliography see Gaster (1924), pp. 234–35.

7. The other sources have "strolling, walking."

8. This vivid description of the sinking ship is missing altogether in the other sources, which simply state the fact that the ship sank; cf., however, Gaster (1934), 2, 606. On the other hand, these sources mention that the survivor first pleaded with a group of Jewish pilgrims to give him some garments to cover his nakedness, but they repulsed him and even cursed him and his nation. Only then did he beg Rabbi Eleazar to clothe him. The latter immediately took off one of his own garments and gave it to him.

about them. Then Bar Ḳappara asked him, "You, now, what (kind of) person are you, and why were you traveling in this ship?" He replied, "I was traveling to such-and-such a place to buy fat and goodly cattle to sacrifice to my idol." (Now) this righteous man (Bar Ḳappara) became puzzled by the actions of the Holy One, blessed be He — (how was it possible that) all these people, the good as well as the bad, should have drowned, while this pagan survived? Upon reflecting (further), however, he said to himself, "Surely the actions of the Holy One, blessed be He, are just. Some good must yet come from this (person), and that is why God has saved him."[9]

(3) Thereupon Bar Ḳappara led him to his house, treated him respectfully, offered him food and drink, clothed him in garments of fine cloth, and gave him twice as many goods as he had had with him before the ship sank. Then this man, well satisfied, went back to (his) own town, (which was) under Christian[10] rule. It was not long before the town's ruler died, and the people brought forth this man and made him their king.

(4) Now, whenever a new king was enthroned, he proceeded to persecute the Jews, and this wicked (new king), too, severely persecuted them. He dispatched to Jerusalem (decrees) forbidding the Jews to observe the Sabbath, perform circumcision, and read the Torah.[11] When word (of the decrees) reached the Jews they became distressed and grieved, and said, "This wicked government has been accustomed to persecuting us; that is why this (king, too), has issued these decrees against us." Thereupon they collected much gold[12] in order to send it through a spokesman, virtuous and willing to go and try to have those decrees annulled, and then return. All the Jews said (unanimously), "Now there is none more righteous, wise, and virtuous than Bar Ḳappara," whereupon they sent him (on this mission).

(5) When the righteous Bar Ḳappara appeared before the king,

9. This section is missing altogether in the other sources and seems to be borrowed from another tale.

10. This seems to be a local addition that is contradictory to his previous description as a pagan (§2). In the other sources he is described as *ʾantipaṭa* "(Roman) proconsul" or "prince" (Gaster, loc. cit.).

11. These specific decrees are not mentioned in the other sources. According to them, he decreed that all Jewish men be slain and all their women be enslaved; cf., however, Gaster (1934), 2, 611.

12. See the end of §5, below. Cf. the other sources: "This government does nothing without bribe."

the latter recognized him immediately while Bar Ḳappara did not recognize the king. The king said to this righteous man, "(Do you remember) any incidents or happenings that occurred to you involving (other) people?" He replied, "No." The king said, "Take him out and let him come back after an hour." When Bar Ḳappara came back, the king asked him the same question, and he replied again, "Nothing at all (like this) has (ever) happened to me." Ten times he was taken out and brought back in, in order to help him recognize the king, but he did not.[13] (Then) the king asked him, "What is your wish, and why have you come here?" He replied, "May the king be well! The Jews are your servants and your subjects ⟨flock⟩, and they (constantly) pray for your well-being ⟨life⟩. They desire you to cancel the decrees that you have issued against them." The king said, "My good man, you will have to pay a lot of money to get me to annul them."[14] He replied, "Surely, I shall pay it." Thereupon he paid him as much as he demanded.

(6) Then the king asked, "You, O Jew, do you not know me at all?" Bar Ḳappara replied, "No, I swear ⟨by the life of your head⟩." The king said, "I am the one who found himself destitute after (my ship) sank into the sea. You then led me to your house, treated me very respectfully, and gave me as many goods as you could afford. Indeed, were you not the one who came to me today, (I mean), were it not for your generosity, I would not have annulled these decrees of persecution even if you had given me all the wealth in the world."

(7) Then the king brought Bar Ḳappara in, treated him as hospitably as he could desire, gave him back his gold and his property, adding a great deal more to it, and canceled the persecution decrees against the Jews. Thereupon Bar Ḳappara, peace be upon him, returned to the Jews satisfied and happy. Thus by the grace of this righteous man, who had performed an act of charity and favor for this pagan, the Jews were comforted ⟨their worries went away⟩, and

13. Cf. also §6, below. The other sources remain completely silent as to whether Bar Ḳappara recognized the king as the person who was shipwrecked; cf., however, Gaster (1924), in his English summary (but nothing indicating this in the original text!), p. 112: "He was not recognized by Bar Ḳappara, but he remembered the man's kindness." In Gaster (1934), 2, 613, the Roman prince is the one who did not recognize Bar Ḳappara, "for the incident had happened a long time ago." This complete forgetfulness of Bar Ḳappara perhaps indicates how very little he thought of his acts of kindness, since he performed them so frequently. It is also possible that he pretended not to recognize the king in order not to embarrass him by making him annul his decrees solely out of a sense of obligation for a former act of kindness.

14. See n. 12, above.

they had a great celebration.[15] For God did not lose sight of this (act of charity), as it is said, *Cast thy bread upon the waters, for thou shalt find it after many days* (Eccles. 11:1). Observe now, if when one does a favor for a pagan it is not lost (before God), and in the end one is repaid ⟨it comes back to him⟩, how much more so when one does it for a person possessed of righteousness, charity, and Torah. The Holy One, blessed be He, will surely reward him with many favors and sevenfold goodness.[16]

15. Nothing is said about a celebration in the other sources; cf., however, Gaster (1934), *2*, 618: "The Jews greatly rejoiced . . . as on a second Purim."
16. Cf. Farḥi, pp. 313–14.

XIII

David Alroy, the Messiah from Kurdistan

General Character

The revolt organized by David Alroy against the Persian king, Alroy's messianic movement, and his tragic death are first mentioned by Benjamin of Tudela, who visited Kurdistan about ten years after these events, ca. 1160.[1] His account, with various embellishments, was repeated by later Jewish chroniclers and even became the subject of a romantic historical novel by Benjamin Disraeli.[2] Alroy's revolt was preceded by three messianic movements in Iraq during the twelfth century, including one, ca. 1120,[3] led by Ibn Dugi, who promised the Jews of Baghdad that they would be miraculously flown to the Land of Israel on the first night of Passover.

These messianic movements indicate that the Jewish population in Kurdistan and its environs was quite substantial. Benjamin of Tudela mentions "more than one hundred Jewish communities" and estimates the number of Jews in the Kurdish town of Amidya, the hometown of Alroy, as twenty-five thousand.[4] The reports of these messianic movements, vague as they are, offer the first documentation of the presence of Jews in Kurdistan.[5] These old reports, as well as some living traditions (see n. 8, below), suggest strong ties among the Jews of Persia, southern Mesopotamia, and Kurdistan. It seems that many Persian Jews fled because of religious persecution to the rugged and inaccessible area of Kurdistan, which has served throughout the ages as a natural refuge for many rebels and persecuted individuals.

The story of Alroy's messianic movement as found in ḥaḵam

1. See Ben-Jacob, pp. 72–73; p. 43.

2. See Bibliography, below.

3. See Goitein, pp. 77–80; cf. idem, *PAAJR* 23 (1954): 37.

4. See Benjamin of Tudela, p. 51. This seems to be quite an exaggeration, and most probably refers to the entire Jewish population of Kurdistan; see n. 17, below. The Jews in Amidya in recent times (1945) numbered no more than 400 persons, and in all Kurdistan about 25,000; see Ben-Jacob, pp. 11, 81; Brauer, p. 18.

5. Not counting some vague Biblical and Talmudic references; see Introduction, II/1–2, and nn. 4–5 ad loc.

Avidani's book differs little from the accounts in other Jewish sources;[6] the main difference is that Avidani combines the story of Ibn Dugi with the one about Alroy.[7] It seems that Alroy's story has not been preserved as a living tradition among the Kurdistani Jews,[8] and all they know about him comes from Jewish sources written outside Kurdistan. Yet the messianic aspirations kindled by him eight hundred years ago have lasted among them until our own time, when almost all the Jews of Kurdistan emigrated en masse to Israel. One of their first rural settlements in the Land of Israel (near Haifa) was called Moshav Alroy, "Alroy's Settlement," after this messianic leader.[9]

Bibliography

Hebrew text: Avidani, *1*, 671–73.
Benjamin of Tudela, pp. 51–53 (Hebrew text), 54–56 (English translation).

6. Primarily the version of Ibn Verga, pp. 49–52; see n. 8, below.

7. The identification of Ibn Dugi with Alroy by Mann (pp. 257–58) and some other scholars was refuted by Goitein; see n. 3, above.

8. Cf. Brauer, p. 43, n. 12. Avidani's statement at the beginning of the story, that he had heard it from his teachers and forefathers, is dubious. In addition to the very similar content and wording, the common misspelling of proper names indicates that Avidani's version mostly follows that of Ibn Verga; cf. nn. 13, 16, 17, 19, 21, 24, 26. Avidani has changed the name from David al-Davidi, as used by Ibn Verga, to David Alroy, but he adds in parentheses about the foundation of Amidya allude vaguely to David Alroy. According to these traditions, Amidya was founded by two brothers, Joseph and David, who came from Persia and asked the governor's permission to settle 25,000 Jewish families in Amidya and in the surrounding area; see n. 17, below. According to one tradition, the date of the founding was 795, but according to another it was 1284. The brothers' shrine, called after their religious title *Be-Ḥazzane*, "the House of the Cantors," is one of the oldest and most venerated structures in Amidya. Cf. also the following legend, told to Brauer by an informant, probably Avidani:

"The brothers Joseph and David came to Amidya [disguised] as dervishes. When they saw how beautiful the place was, they asked the governor's permission to settle there. When the governor asked them which tribe they belonged to, they replied, 'We are from the tribe of the Children of Israel.' Since the governor was hostile to the Jews, he replied, 'I have no place for you here.' The two brothers therefore continued on their way to [a place called] Bebāde. While on their way, they used magic to make the governor ill by their witchcraft. In his despair he sent two horsemen after the brothers to ask them to return to the town and to tell them that he would fulfill their request. They returned, greeted the governor, and asked him [to grant them only] a plot of land that could be surrounded by the hide of a large ox. The governor agreed, and the brothers took the hide of a large ox and softened it in water for a few days, to make it pliable. They then cut it into a long thin strip, [spiral] like a snail. With that strip of hide they encircled a large plot of land on which they built the (old) synagogue and other structures." See Brauer, pp. 45–47; Ben-Jacob, pp. 73–74. This motif is common in legends of many nations, e.g., Egyptian, Turkish, Greek, Estonian, French, Icelandic, and North American Indian; see Thompson (below, Bibliography to chap. XVII), motif K 185.1: "Deceptive land purchase: Ox-hide measure. As much land bought as can be surrounded by an ox-hide. The hide is cut into very small strips." See also pp. xxviii, 187.

9. Cf. Ben-Jacob, p. 26.

Beaconsfield, Benjamin Disraeli, Earl of. *The Wondrous Tale of Alroy.* Philadelphia, 1833; London, 1833, 1853.

Goitein, S. D. "ʿObadyah, A Norman Proselyte." *Journal of Jewish Studies* 4 (1953): 74–84.

Joseph ben Joshua hak-Kohen. *ʿEmeḵ hab-Baḵaʾ.* Cracow, 1895. English translation, *The Vale of Tears,* by H. S. May. The Hague, 1971.

Ibn Verga, Solomon. *Šeḇeṭ Yĕhuḏah.* Edited by M. Wiener. Hanover, 1924.

Mann, J. "Obadya, prosélyte Normand converti au Judaisme, et sa *Meguilla.*" *Revue des Etudes Juives* 89 (1930): 245–59.

Samawʾal al-Maghribī. *Ifḥām al-Yahūd, Silencing the Jews.* Edited by M. Perlmann. *PAAJR* 32 (1964).

---

(1) There was (once) a man whose name was David Alroy, from the town of Amidya, which is more than four days' walking distance from Nineveh, and is my hometown. I, the humble ʿAlwan Avidani . . . have heard this story from my teachers and forefathers. David Alroy went down[10] from the town of Amidya to Baghdad, where he studied the Babylonian Talmud with the exilarch Raḇ Ḥasdai and the head of the academy, who was (also) a great man in that city. He also studied all the secular sciences,[11] (the pronunciation of) the Ineffable Name, and all the books of the Egyptian and Chaldean magicians, as well as astrology. He thus became greatly proficient in all kinds of wisdom, and no secret was too difficult for him. He became renowned in all the land as a miracle worker, and was therefore followed by all the Jews living in the Ḥaftun mountains, as far as the area of the Sambatyon River — a great multitude that included thousands of extremely rich, honorable, and successful people. This (area), which is the beginning of the land of Media and (extends) as far as the province of Golan and the mountains of Ḳardu (Ararat)[12] in Kurdistan, a walking distance of fifty days,[13] included more than one hundred (Jewish) communities. They were under the rule of the king of Persia many years after (King) Cyrus, and paid

10. Any traveling from the mountains of Kurdistan in the north to the lowland area in the south is referred to in the local dialect as "going down, descending"; cf. Sabar (1978b), p. 414, n. 57.

11. Hebrew *ḥoḵmaṯ ḥiṣonim,* literally "wisdom of aliens (Gentiles)," meaning profane (non-Judaic) learning.

12. See Introduction, I/1.

13. Cf. Ibn Verga, p. 50; but Benjamin (p. 51) has "25 days."

him a head tax of a gold piece for each man fifteen years old and older. Now this David Alroy, also called David al-Davidi, spoke seventy languages,[14] whereas all the Jews (in that area) spoke (only the language of the) Targum (Neo-Aramaic).

(2) Alroy took courage and wanted to rebel against the king (of Persia) all by himself.[15] (However), he incited the Jews to come out and fight all the Gentiles. He displayed to them omens and miracles, but they could not tell whether his great power was from God or was due to tricks and magic. At that time the town of Amidya[16] alone contained twenty-five thousand families,[17] as is also stated in the *Itinerary* of Rabbi Benjamin ben Rabbi Jonah of Tudela. (This event occurred in) the year A.M. 4920 (1160 C.E.).[18] This (number) included also (those who lived in the area) surrounding the town, beyond its high wall. When the king of Persia heard about this mighty man, his heart failed him altogether. Yet he invited him to come to him in order to see his power, (saying to himself), "If he is indeed the Messiah (sent) from God, blessed be He, we shall recognize him (as such) and believe in him,[19] for that would be God's will." Behold, David Alroy came to the king and stood before him without any fear. The king asked him, "Is it true that you are the Messiah?" He replied, "Yes, I am the Messiah. God has sent me to redeem the people of Israel from all the lands (of exile)." The king said, "I shall know whether this is true by casting you into prison. If you set yourself free therefrom, I shall know that this is true. Otherwise, you shall remain in prison all your life, but we shall not slay you, for you will be (shown to be) a fool."

(3) After David Alroy was cast into prison, the king sent for all

14. In no other source is it mentioned that he spoke seventy languages; on this phrase in Jewish literature see Ginzberg, 5, 194; Sabar (1976a), p. 86, n. 10.

15. Hebrew *lĕbaddo*; one would expect *ʿaṣmo*, "against the king himself." This adverb does not occur in any other source.

16. In the original text, *ʿAmādiya* (with *alef* after the *mem*). This spelling is that of the Hebrew and Arabic sources. The name is pronounced *ʿAmídya* by the local Jews. The spelling ʿAmariya in Benjamin of Tudela (p. 51) and Joseph hak-Kohen (p. 47) is an error due to the similarity of the letters *dalet* and *reš*; cf. Benjamin of Tudela, p. 54 (English), n. 2.

17. This highly exaggerated figure is repeated in another legend told by Avidani to Ben-Jacob (p. 73). It seems to be the result of combining Benjamin's estimate of "25 thousand *Jews*" (p. 51) with Ibn Verga's (p. 50) and Joseph hak-Kohen's (p. 47) "about a thousand *households*." Cf. nn. 4, 8, above.

18. Joseph hak-Kohen (p. 47) gives the date as 1163; cf. Ben-Jacob, p. 73, n. 3.

19. Hebrew *nodeh lo wĕ-naʾămin lo*; cf. Ibn Verga, *yodeh bo wĕ-yikkanaʿ lă-ʿăbodato*, "(the king) will acknowledge him and submit to serving him." Cf. below, §4.

his viziers and counselors, (saying), "Let us seek a solution against the wicked Jews who are rebelling against the kingdom." However, while they were still holding this evil consultation they heard that David had escaped by setting himself free, but they did not know how and by what means he had accomplished this feat. When the king heard (of this), he immediately sent a large army, including horsemen, after him to capture him. (When they arrived where he was), they could not see him but heard his voice saying, "I am here." They then came (back) to the king and told him what had happened. The king was amazed and said, "I thought that he had escaped by paying a bribe, but (now I see that) it was not so."

(4) The king immediately mounted his horse and galloped (all the way), until he came very near the river where his army had been unable to see David. Now (the king and his servants) called for him loudly, but he replied, "You fools! I am going on my way (before you), but you are confused and unable to catch me." Then he spread his shawl on the Gozan River and crossed it in front of them, while the king looked on. Then the king said, "This one, surely God's power is with him, and we must recognize him (as the Messiah)." But his servants changed his mind by telling him that David had done all this by magic and make-believe. The king then commanded them to bring boats, and he crossed the river with a great army to pursue him. Yet this (too) did not help, for David, by (using the pronunciation of) the (Ineffable) Name, which he knew, created a miraculous shortcut for a distance that (normally) takes ten days to walk.[20]

(5) When the king saw that this too had failed, he sent (word) to the exilarchs in Baghdad (ordering them) to capture David and deliver him into his hands, else he would slay all of them, young and old together, and would chastise the community leaders with terrible afflictions and set them on fire one by one, because David was their disciple. He also sent a letter to the commander of the faithful[21] (the caliph), who resided in Baghdad, asking him too to warn the exilarchs that they must deliver David (to the king). Then all the exilarchs, (including those) of Nehardea, Pumbeditha, Sura,[22] and all other places, sent (a message) to David Alroy (asking

20. Cf. Benjamin of Tudela (p. 52), "On that day he covered a walking distance of ten days to the town of ʿAmariya [Amidya] by [pronouncing] the Ineffable Name."

21. In Arabic *ʾamīr al-muʾminīn*; cf. Benjamin of Tudela (p. 52); Joseph hak-Kohen (p. 48). Avidani, following Ibn Verga (p. 51), has *ʾamir al-muʿdin* (!). Cf. nn. 24, 26, below.

22. These names are not mentioned in any of the other sources. Their inclusion here is

him) to give up his foolishness, so that he, as well as the Jewish community and its leaders, might be well, because they were now in great trouble and very grave danger.

(6) David,[23] however, replied that he had been informed by heaven that during the following Passover, which was to come very soon, they would be redeemed. They should therefore make ready on the night of the fifteenth of Nisan (the first night of Passover), (and wait) upon their roofs: at midnight, angels from heaven would carry them off on top of the clouds and bring them to Jerusalem. They all believed this and prepared themselves upon their roofs with their children and wives. They waited all night, watching the moon and the clear sky, until they gave up hope ⟨their eyes were finished⟩, for there was nothing to it. Thus it became known that the false Messiah did not have power to do anything.

(7) They then sent him a strong letter, as follows: "Know that if you do not change your mind regarding this matter, you will be excommunicated by all the rabbis in this world and in the next." They also sent a similar letter to the head of the Jewish community in Mosul, Rabbi Zakkay, and to Rabbi Joseph Burhān al-Falak,[24] the astrologer. They in turn also sent him (a letter), saying, "*It is a time of trouble unto Jacob* (Jer. 30:7), and we need the mercy of heaven, for the Holy One, blessed be He, has said in the Song of Solomon (2:7), *I adjure you . . . that ye awaken not, nor stir up love, until it please.*"[25] Yet David did not change his mind and did not fear them, although they were his masters and great scholars.

(8) When the situation became quite hopeless, the Holy One, blessed be He, wrought a miracle through the king of Turkey, whose name was Zayn[26] al-Dīn and who was a vassal of the king of Persia and a very good friend of the Jews. Since he was acquainted with David Alroy's father-in-law, he invited him to his house and said to him, "You must redeem all your people, who are in very

---

somewhat anachronistic, as these towns were no longer the prominent centers of Jewish learning that they had been in earlier centuries.

23. The event described in this section belongs to the messianic movement of Ibn Dugi, for which see Samaw'al al-Maghribī, pp. 72–74 (English); Mann, pp. 253–54; Brauer, pp. 42–43; Ben-Jacob, p. 14. See n. 7, above.

24. Meaning "proof of the celestial sphere" (Arabic); cf. Benjamin of Tudela, p. 53. Avidani, following Ibn Verga (p. 51), has *Burakan al-Fallaḥ*(!) Cf. n. 21, above.

25. According to the traditional allegorical interpretation, this verse prohibits forcing the advent of the Messiah before its proper time.

26. Avidani, following Ibn Verga (p. 51), has "Azyd," but cf. Benjamin of Tudela, pp. 34, 53.

great trouble with the king of Persia. Go, therefore, and redeem your people. I promise (to collect) from the Jews ten thousand gold coins and give them to you if you slay this man David, your son-in-law. By doing this you will redeem many people and be rewarded twofold from heaven."

(9) That night the father-in-law invited David to a banquet which he had prepared for him. David drank wine and became as drunk as Lot.[27] His father-in-law then leaped at him, cut off his head, and sent it to the king of Persia through Zayn al-Dīn and other trustworthy witnesses who testified that it belonged to David Alroy the false Messiah. (Only) then was the king appeased.[28]

27. See Gen. 19:32–35.

28. According to Ibn Verga (p. 51), the king still wanted to punish the followers of David and was appeased only after they paid him a hundred talents of gold; cf. Benjamin of Tudela, p. 53; Joseph hak-Kohen, p. 48.

Yona Gabbay, a well-known storyteller from Zakho. As a merchant who traveled throughout Kurdistan, he heard and told many folktales. He died in Jerusalem in 1972, when he was more than one hundred years old.

The author reading a Neo-Aramaic manuscript with ḥaḵam ʿAlwān Avidani

Sandor, a Jewish village in Iraqi Kurdistan, ca. 1934

Girl wearing case amulet with pendants

The Sandor village schoolchildren, ca. 1934

Man watching teapot

Woman at a nomadic-style loom

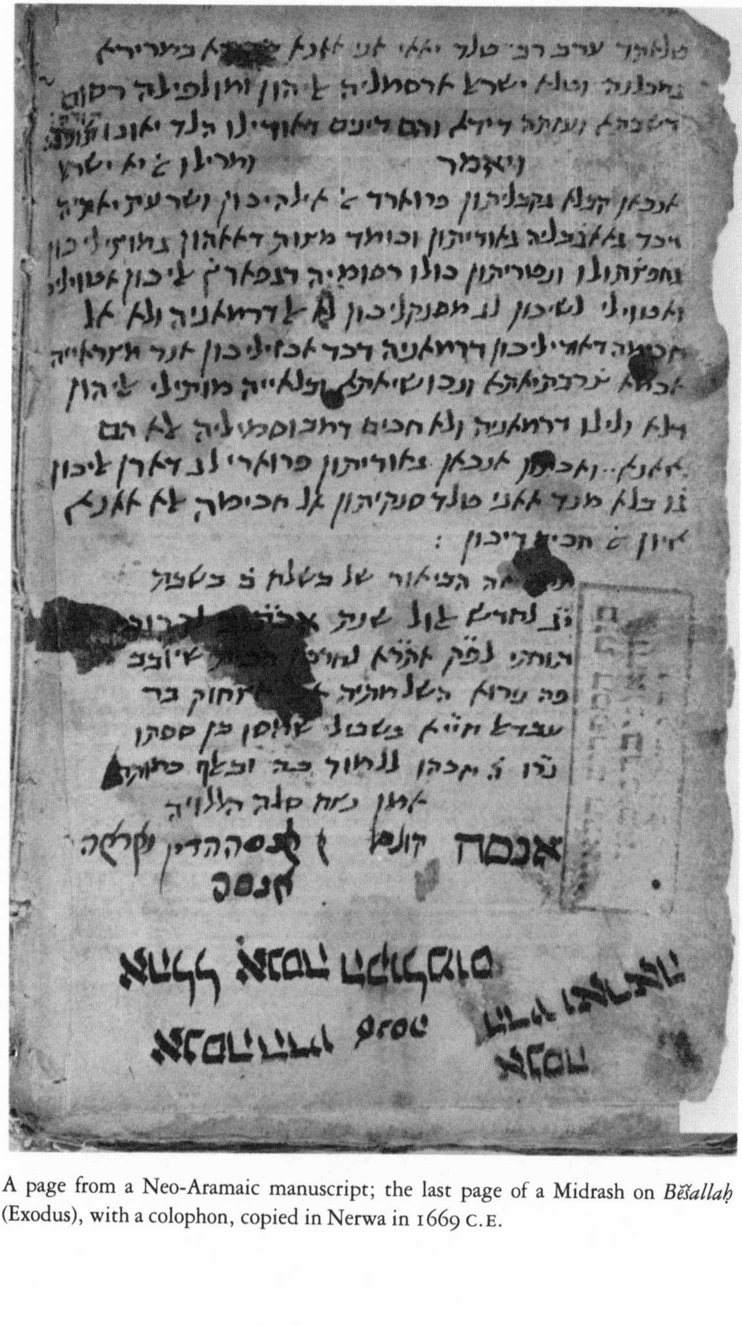

A page from a Neo-Aramaic manuscript; the last page of a Midrash on *Bĕšallaḥ* (Exodus), with a colophon, copied in Nerwa in 1669 C.E.

XIV

Apology of a Preacher

This apology, found in a manuscript of Midrashim (homilies) copied ca. 1650[1] by ʿAbd Allāh ben Sibar, offers some glimpses of the position of the *daršan* (preacher) in the community. We learn from it that there were wandering *daršanim* who traveled from one town to another, often because of persecution or adverse economic conditions[2] rather than by invitation. Thus the visiting daršan had to apologize, with much humor, self-deprecation, and flowery expressions, in order to gain the sympathy of the congregation and especially of the local ḥakamim. All this was done by way of homiletical interpretation of a Biblical verse.

Bibliography

Hebrew text: Sabar (1966), p. 412.

Go forth, O ye daughters of Zion, and gaze upon King Solomon, even upon the crown wherewith his mother hath crowned him in the day of his espousals, and in the day of the gladness of his heart (Song of Sol. 3:11).

An Investiture[3]

O ye of this congregation, go forth and gaze upon the ḥakam, upon the crown wherewith his Torah hath crowned him in the day of his teaching, and in the day of the gladness of his (heart) in his Torah.

Let us ask some questions about this verse. It says, *Go forth and gaze,* that is, you of this congregation, go forth and gaze upon the ḥakam. A question: Whereto should you go forth, outside (of your homes) or to the marketplace? No. Rather, step out of your eminence (do not be so proud) and listen to this new ḥakam who has

1. See Sabar (1976a), p. xliii.
2. See Benayahu, p. 43.
3. The Hebrew *halbašah,* usually meaning dressing or clothing, seems to mean here dressing or adorning a Biblical verse with homiletical comments. I did not, however, find this particular meaning in the Hebrew dictionaries.

joined you, even though you are not in need (of him). Blessed be the Lord, you are all ḥakamim (learned men), and many among you are (even great) ḥakamim. Indeed, were you not meritorious, the Holy One, blessed be He, would not have gathered together all these ḥakamim within you (your congregation).

Nevertheless, hearken and lend an ear to my words. Although I am not worthy of addressing a sermon to you, yet being the last to come to you, I hope to find favor in your eyes. This may be compared to fish in water. While in the water they do not drink it, but as soon as it rains they raise their heads out (of the water) and drink of the rain, for they find it more tasty than their (own) water. Now you too were compared to fish in the blessing with which Jacob, your father, had blessed you, (saying), *And let them grow into a multitude (multiply like fish)*[4] *in the midst of the earth* (Gen. 48:16). You too are like these fish. Just as they do not drink of their (own) water but wait for a drop of rain from the sky, so do you. Although there are many ḥakamim among you, and you certainly do not need any more, yet you are desirous of new words. (As for me), I am doing this neither for my own honor nor for my family's honor, but rather for the honor of my teachers.[5]

(How do we know that) *daughters of Zion* means the ḥakamim? From what is said, *The Lord loveth the gates of Zion* (Ps. 87:2), (that is to say), those who are distinguished[6] in halakah (religious law). (The words) *upon King Solomon* (indicate that) he too was a ḥakam, as he is called *King Solomon,* (for it is said), *By me* (wisdom) *kings reign* (Prov. 8:15), meaning, by My Torah kings reign. Furthermore, all Israel are sons of kings (hence they are all ḥakamim as well).

(How do we know that) *the crown wherewith his mother hath crowned him* refers to his Torah? As it is said, *Call understanding thy mother*[7] (Prov. 7:4), and it is also said, *Forsake not the teaching*[8] *of thy mother* (Prov. 1:8). (Furthermore), *in the day of his espousals* means the day of his teaching. For just as when one marries off his son, he, the (son's)

4. A play on words, as the word *yidgu* ("multiply") in this verse has the same root as *dag̃*, "fish."

5. An Aramaic quotation in the original Hebrew text; cf. Zohar, III, 144a (Aramaic variant); B. Meg̃ 3a (Hebrew).

6. A play on words: Hebrew *mĕṣuyyanim* ("distinguished") echoes the consonants of *Ṣiyyon,* "Zion."

7. Hebrew *'em,* so in the manuscript, although the Masoretic text has *moda'* "kinswoman." The first part of the verse reads, *Say unto wisdom, "Thou art my sister."*

8. Literally "Torah."

mother, and his family rejoice, so should the congregation rejoice when a ḥaḵam visits them. (Likewise), *in the day of the gladness of his heart* means the gladness one derives from study.[9]

Now, I have not been fortunate enough to study (much) Torah. What am I? What is my life?[10] *Surely I am brutish, unlike a man, and have not the understanding of a man* (Prov. 30:2). Yet I have been fortunate enough to see your faces, for whosoever sees the faces of the righteous, it is as if he has seen the face of the Shekinah, as it is said, *To eat bread with Moses' father-in-law before God* (Exod. 18:12). Is it possible that they ate before God? No. Rather, this teaches us that eating before Moses is considered by Scripture the same as eating before God.[11] Another piece of evidence is the case of Elijah, of blessed memory, who said, *As the Lord liveth, before whom I stand* (2 Kings 5:16). Did he really stand before the Lord? No. Rather, he stood before Ahijah the Shilonite, who was teaching (him) Midrash.[12] Yet Scripture considers it as if he had stood before the Lord himself.

9. Cf. Song Rabbah, end of sec. 3.

10. Expressions of humility adapted from 1 Sam. 18:18 and the prayer of the Day of Atonement; cf. B. Yoma 87b ("What are we," etc.).

11. Cf. B. Ber 64a, "Whosoever enjoys a meal with a disciple of the wise [*talmiḏ ḥaḵam*], it is the same as if he had enjoyed the splendor of the Shekinah."

12. According to the Midrash, he was Elijah's teacher; see Ginzberg, 6, 317.

XV

Legends about Rabbi Samuel ben Nathanael hal-Levi Barzānī Adoni and Other Rabbis of Kurdistan

Introduction

Like other Jewish communities, the Kurdistani Jews have, in addition to the corpus of traditional classical Jewish literature, a host of legends about their own rabbis and sages. The most prominent of these rabbis was Samuel Barzānī (died ca. 1630),[1] whose descendants and disciples served as rabbis throughout Kurdistan until our time. An imposing man and an illustrious rabbi, he became the subject of many legends, of which only a few were put down in writing. Many details in these legends are not supported by what we know of Rabbi Samuel from documented sources. Moreover, some legends, in all or in some of their details, contradict these sources or each other. Some contradictions may be explained as the result of a literary device, such as typological treatment of a legend in order to make it conform to well-known Biblical or Midrashic stories (see, e.g., legend 1). It is also possible that some legends which were originally told about other rabbis, especially if they too were named Samuel, were later assumed to be about Rabbi Samuel Barzānī.

Thus, according to one legend (4, below), he escaped from Barazān to Amidya as a young man and died there a few days later; but according to another legend (2, below), he was told by the prophet Elijah to leave Barazān and go to Mosul to become chief rabbi there. However, a burial prayer found in an old manuscript indicates that his burial place was in Amidya and describes in detail its exact location. It is also quite clear from his prolific literary and halaḵic works, as well as from documented sources, that he lived a

1. He usually signed his name "Rabbi Samuel ben Rabbi Nathanael hal-Levi"; cf. Benayahu, pp. 71, 82, 84, etc. The nickname Barzānī is derived from the town of Barazān, where he probably grew up and headed his first academy; cf. ibid., p. 26; below, legends 2, 4. Adoni, meaning "my master," is an honorific title given to him probably by his disciples; cf. ibid., pp. 28, 37; Ben-Jacob, p. 34. For his other titles as a spiritual leader see Benayahu, p. 36.

long life (contradicting legend 4) and that even at his death, like Moses, "his natural force was not abated."[2] His tomb in Amidya was revered as a shrine by Jews and non-Jews alike until our own time. Nevertheless, the Jewish communities of Mosul and of the neighboring town of Be-Tannure both have a tradition that Rabbi Samuel Barzānī is buried in their town.[3] It is possible that he lived at least for a while in Mosul, just as he did in a few other places. This tradition, however, may also be derived from the fact that the son of Asenath, Rabbi Samuel's daughter, was also named Samuel and served as rabbi in Mosul before being called to the rabbinate of Baghdad, where he and his descendants served in that office until 1743. In Mosul, too, descendants of the Barzānī-Adoni family served as rabbis down to our own time.[4]

From the documents written by Rabbi Samuel himself and by his disciples, relatives, and contemporary scholars,[5] he emerges as the most distinguished rabbi of Kurdistani Jewry, a charismatic spiritual leader, dedicated reformer, mystic, and poet. He was a scion of rabbis,[6] and his father, Rabbi Nathanael, is described as a prominent *dayyan* (rabbinic judge) who owned a large library of rare books and manuscripts.[7] In addition to Samuel, his oldest son, he had two

2. Benayahu, pp. 27–28; cf. Deut. 34:7.

3. Ben-Jacob, pp. 33–34, nn. 35, 38.

4. Ibid., p. 38; Benayahu, p. 28, n. 37. There are other contradictory details concerning his family. In legends 1 and 4 Samuel is described as an only child, but the documents tell us that he had at least two brothers and two sisters (Benayahu, p. 25). In legends 2 and 3 he is said to have had a son, Rabbi Isaac, and in a list of twenty rabbis of the Barzāni family in Mosul (Ben-Jacob, p. 38, n. 53), Rabbi Samuel's name is immediately followed by the name of Rabbi Isaac. However, in a letter written by his daughter Asenath she states that her father "had no sons but [only] daughters" (Mann, p. 511). Ben-Jacob (p. 37, n. 48) assumes that the son might have died young, while his father was still living. It seems, however, that the son, Rabbi Isaac of the legend, should be identified with Rabbi Samuel's younger brother, whose name was also Rabbi Isaac; see n. 5, below. For a study of these and other contradictions see Sabar, "Legend vs. Reality" (forthcoming).

5. Mainly his brother Rabbi Isaac, his daughter Asenath, and his son-in-law Rabbi Jacob. Most of the documents are religious regulations (*taḳḳanoṯ*) and epistles to various communities, pleading for financial support of the rabbinic academies.

6. Benayahu, p. 25.

7. How precious these books were to his descendants is apparent from a letter of his son Rabbi Isaac (Benayahu, p. 112): "My brother's [Samuel's] bequest did not include any money, vineyards, or fields but only these books, of which twenty-nine were lost by plunder and fire. The rest are not a cow or a goat that I could milk them, nor a mule, a horse, or a donkey that I could hire them out, nor homesteads, a field, or a vineyard that I could eat their yield. My father bought all these books and forbade anyone to sell [even] one of them. [Even] in that year of starvation, [when] a few people died and we incurred some debts, we did not sell any of them. They are rather to remain forever [in the family]. However, whosoever

more sons, Rabbi Isaac and Rabbi Reuben, and two daughters.[8] Samuel was probably born and raised in Barazān. All that is known about his childhood comes from the tradition preserved in legends (1, below), according to which he was a very slow-witted child. According to another version (2, below), as a young man he was "simple, honest, and God-fearing . . . He was, however, completely illiterate, as he had never studied Torah." However, it is not uncommon in legends for prominent learned men to be described as illiterate in their youth, to emphasize the contrast and to increase the dramatic effect.[9] In yet another legend (4, below) he is described as a learned young man studying Talmud and mysticism with his father while still in Barazān. This tradition seems closer to the truth and is supported by Rabbi Isaac's statement in a letter that he himself served as an aide to his brother (Rabbi Samuel) when the latter was head of the academy in Barazān.[10]

Apparently in the course of a dispute among the local aghas (nobles), the town of Barazān was set on fire, and Rabbi Samuel's family, as well as many others, had to flee.[11] It seems that the divine green fire which appeared, according to legend 4, over Rabbi Samuel's festal booth (*sukkah*) and resulted in his flight from Barazān to Amidya reflects this real fire. From Barazān he wandered to several other places, where he founded academies or served as rabbi.[12] He seems finally to have settled in Amidya and to have died there. However, he exerted his influence far beyond the place where he actually lived and also long after his death. He is the author of many hymns,[13] religious regulations, and halaḵic books,[14] one of which was copied as far away as in Yemen.[15] Since there was no

---

wishes to read any of them, let him do so . . . For they are not my books [alone], but rather belong to the entire world." Cf. also Mann, p. 484.

8. Benayahu, p. 25.

9. E.g., Rabbi ʿAḵiba, who according to legend was an illiterate shepherd until he was forty years old.

10. Benayahu, pp. 26, 116: "My brother could not teach, for he was [at times] preoccupied with his studies and would tell me not to let the students recite too loudly, in order not to distract him."

11. Ibid. Cf. the similar fate of the Jews of Nerwa at the beginning of this century (see Introduction, II/10).

12. Benayahu, pp. 26–27.

13. Some published: Ben-Jacob, pp. 158–64; Benayahu, pp. 91–108. Others have been incorporated in the prayer books of the Kurdistani Jews, and some were chanted and transmitted orally down to the present day; cf. Benayahu, p. 46.

14. Benayahu, pp. 46–54.

15. Entitled *Sefer ʾAḇne Zikkaron,* "Book of Memorial Stones," but popularly known as

printing press in Kurdistan, only a few of his writings survived in manuscript. No doubt most of the manuscripts originating in Kurdistan come from his school.[16] He encouraged his disciples to establish academies throughout Kurdistan, in line with his saying that "any community which does not have a *midraš* {religious school} is as if it did not have God."[17] He even established contact with the rabbis of the Land of Israel.[18] His son-in-law Rabbi Jacob claims that in his academy were students "from the four corners of the world, including Egypt, Constantinople, the Land of Israel, etc."[19]

Rabbi Samuel must have been a man of awe-inspiring appearance. He is described as being like "an angel, his face radiant like Adam's."[20] With his death there "disappeared a man whose candle was never extinguished at night, the mighty man of the congregation, a candle {permanently} burning in the *midrašim*."[21] Even Gentiles mourned his death and said that "he was the great *muʿallim* {Arabic: teacher} of the Jews, and that after his death the Jews will be destroyed and scattered."[22] Yet this great man, who had no profitable skill with which to support his family other than the rabbinate, for which he was paid a pittance, at times lived in abject poverty. His brother, who served as his aide,[23] sent many letters begging for support of the academies. He states, typically, "God knows, I have no bread in my house, nor even a dress for my wife, who is naked and barefoot, unable to go outdoors out of shame."[24] "All the communities," he tells us, "showed mercy to my brother {Rabbi Samuel} for God's sake. However, his accursed {wife} would not let him eat {enough}, and he used to weep out of hunger, for she took everything for herself."[25]

Šeḥiṭaṯ Barzānī, "Slaughter(-Book of Samuel) Barzānī." It is a manual for ritual slaughterers; cf. Benayahu, p. 51.

16. Including probably the numerous Neo-Aramaic Midrashim copied in Nerwa and Amidya between 1647 and 1670, not long after his death (ca. 1630); see Sabar (1976a), pp. xliiii–xliv, and *Midrašim* (forthcoming); Introduction, VI/4.

17. Benayahu, pp. 34, 86.

18. Ibid., pp. 30–31.

19. Ibid., p. 36.

20. Ibid., pp. 33, 110. Cf. above, chap. I, v. 20; Ginzberg (5, 103) speaks of "the splendor of the light which shone over Adam before the fall."

21. Benayahu, pp. 36, 110.

22. Ibid., p. 37.

23. See n. 10, above.

24. Benayahu, pp. 115–16.

25. Ibid., pp. 113–14.

Rabbi Samuel apparently had only daughters,[26] of whom the most famous was Asenath. She was married to Rabbi Jacob, his nephew and best-known disciple, who became the head of the academy in Mosul.[27] They had one son named Samuel after his grandfather.[28] Since this Samuel was too young when his father died, his mother Asenath took her husband's place as head of the academy in Mosul.[29] A female rabbi was a rare phenomenon in any traditional Jewish community, even more so in Kurdistan, and Rabbi Asenath was therefore venerated by the Kurdistani Jews almost as much as her father, and was given the title *tannaʾiṯ,* "female Talmudic scholar."[30] An appeal for funds that she addressed to the community of Amidya shows her profound erudition in the Hebrew language and in rabbinic literature and offers a glimpse at her difficult role as a religious leader. Her activities included teaching Judaism, preaching, and instructing her congregation in the laws of ritual ablution, Sabbath, prayer, and the like.[31] She acted as her husband's substitute in the academy even before his death, "since he was preoccupied with his studies and had no time to teach the students. I therefore taught them in his stead and served as his helpmeet. Now, however, he has gone to his resting place and has left me and the children to [our] sighs."[32] Her father, Rabbi Samuel, had taught her only to study and teach Torah, and when he gave her in marriage to Rabbi Jacob he adjured him not to make her do any housework.[33] In the legend about Rabbi Asenath (5, below) she is described not only as a learned and pious woman but also as a Kabbalist who wrought

26. See n. 4, above.
27. See Mann, pp. 480 ff.; Benayahu, p. 27.
28. Cf. Mann, p. 515, n. 156.
29. Ibid., pp. 481, 483.
30. Ben-Jacob, p. 35; below, end of legend 1.
31. Mann, p. 483.
32. Ibid., p. 511 (a pun in the original: *halaḵ huʾ li-mĕnuḥoṯ wĕ-ʿazaḇ ʾoṯi . . . lĕ-ʾănaḥoṯ*). For a popular and faulty English summary of her biography, see S. Henry and E. Taitz, *Written Out of History: A Hidden Legacy of Jewish Women Revealed through Their Writings and Letters* (New York, 1978), pp. 108–13. Cf. also S. D. Goitein, *Jews and Arabs* (New York, 1964), p. 187. That she was quite prominent is also evident from a letter by Rabbi P. Ḥarīrī in which he addresses her as a venerated queen: "My lady, my mother, my *Rabbaniṯ* [female rabbi] . . . After bowing, prostrating myself, kneeling, and falling to the ground [in reverence to you]. . . . We are always ready to revere you and serve you truly and faithfully, but please do not forget [to mention] us in your prayers, for surely your prayer is more accepted [by God] and is equal to peace offerings, ascending to high heaven and binding the upper worlds (with the earthly one)" (Ben-Jacob, p. 205).
33. Mann, pp. 483, 511.

miracles, as well as an attractive woman coveted by a Gentile, who one midnight climbed up to the roof of her house with unchaste designs against her. The legend alludes perhaps to the fact mentioned in her epistle about her having been "seized and stupefied by some wicked Romans [Christian Assyrians]," who by the order of a judge took over her house and confiscated all her and her daughters' effects, including the books that she had in front of her.[34]

In addition to the legends about Rabbi Samuel and his descendants, there are of course legends about other, less illustrious, rabbis and sages. Two such legends, about Rabbi Simeon Doga of Amidya and Rabbi Mordecai of Nerwa, serve as good examples. In legend 4, which recounts the flight of Rabbi Samuel Barzānī to Amidya, Rabbi Simeon Doga is mentioned as an astrologer and local rabbi who invited Rabbi Samuel to share a meal in his sukkah and helped him to hide from his persecutors. In legend 6, which deals with his tragic death, Rabbi Simeon is again described as a mighty astrologer who predicted, or even caused, the rise and fall of governors. When a local governor discovered one such augury about his own fall, he ordered Rabbi Simeon to be cast off the city wall. The documents from this period clearly indicate that Kurdistani Jews practiced augury. A certain Judah ben Rabbi Simeon of Amidya, most probably the son of Rabbi Simeon Doga, writes in a letter to a personal friend: "I have cast lots, and it fell on Aḥmad Beg, to the effect that he will be king [the Turkish governor of the district]. However, the day was cloudy, [making the augury doubtful]. . . . His vizier, however, must be on guard [for his life is in danger]. This is the result of my divination, but I am not sure of it, since the day was cloudy."[35]

One letter addressed to Rabbi Simeon Doga describes the recipient with a series of laudatory epithets, for example, "one who is constantly preoccupied with learning . . . outstanding figure of his generation . . . the excellent *dayyan* [judge]."[36] Among the scholars of Amidya mentioned in this letter is "the scion of holy men, the venerated sage Samuel," undoubtedly meaning Rabbi Samuel Barzānī. That Rabbi Simeon was indeed a leading *dayyan* is clear from an appeal addressed to him by the dayyan of Nerwa, asking him to warn all the local rabbis not to marry off an eight-year-old

34. Ibid., pp. 483, 510.
35. Ibid. pp. 485, 520–21; cf. n. 86, below.
36. Ibid., pp. 522–23.

girl who had been abducted from that town by a certain scoundrel named Hanukkah.[37] In a letter written by Rabbi Simeon himself he assures a disciple that he would willingly teach him how to be a sage and a ritual slaughterer, and adds, "provided that you are God-fearing and love Torah and its precepts."[38]

The last legend (7, below) deals with the conversion of the emir of Nerwa to Judaism after Rabbi Mordecai demonstrates its superiority to him. The conversion of prominent Gentiles to Judaism is a common theme in Jewish and rabbinic folk literature in general.[39] According to ḥak̲am Avidani, Rabbi Mordecai was the rabbi of Nerwa and the teacher of his grandfather, Rabbi Benjamin, who witnessed the event related in the legend. As an additional "proof" of the authenticity of this legend, ḥak̲am Avidani tells us that Rabbi Mordecai gave a manuscript book he had written, entitled *Interpretation of Dreams,* as a gift to his grandfather, and that he, Avidani, had that manuscript in his possession before it was acquired by the Jewish National and University Library in Jerusalem.[40] The manuscript includes, among other things, a few original letters written ca. A.M. 5548 (1788) indicating that Rabbi Mordecai served as rabbi in Amidya but probably moved later to Nerwa. In one letter he is described as *marē᾿ dĕ-᾿at̲ra᾿,* "the master of the town [of Amidya]."[41] The letters indicate that Rabbi Mordecai had strong ties to Nerwa. In one letter a *šaddar* (an emissary sent to collect contributions for Jewish institutions of learning in the Land of Israel), after his arrival in Amidya, appoints Rabbi Mordecai as his deputy and authorizes him to go to Nerwa and take his (Mordecai's) wife with him.[42] In another letter that Rabbi Mordecai signed and addressed to the rabbis of Nerwa and other localities, he informs them of the arrival in Amidya of Rabbi Aaron Ashkenazi, an emissary from Tiberias, and urges them to send generous contributions with his deputy, ḥak̲am Sasson.[43]

37. Ibid., pp. 486, 525.
38. Ibid., p. 524.
39. See *EJ,* s.v. "Proselytes," *13,* 1182–93.
40. Avidani, *4,* 550; Assaf, p. 140; Brauer, p. 46.
41. Assaf, p. 142.
42. Ibid., p. 141.
43. Ibid., p. 142. The emissaries, fearing travel difficulties as well as robbery or even murder by Kurdish brigands, usually did not dare to penetrate the rugged area beyond Amidya, and would send local ḥak̲amim as their deputies to more distant localities; cf. ibid., p. 143: "I am the emissary of Hebron. I intended to come [from Amidya] to your community as well, but since the road to your town is very perilous, [passing] through mountains and hills, rivers and bridges, and my strength is too weak, I am unable to come to you, especially now, in the season of rain and severe cold."

According to the legend, Rabbi Benjamin, ḥak̲am Avidani's grandfather, was a disciple of Rabbi Mordecai while he was in Nerwa. However, it seems that Rabbi Benjamin, too, lived in both Nerwa and Amidya, as he is listed among the ḥak̲amim who are buried in Amidya. His son ḥak̲am Simeon, who for about fifty years served as rabbi, teacher, and cantor, also lived in Amidya. One of his Sabbath hymns was quite popular throughout Kurdistan. He died in 1912.[44] His son ḥak̲am ʿAlwān Avidani, who settled in Jerusalem, was the "last Mohican" of a long line of ḥak̲amim and teachers in Kurdistan, among whom, "in spite of the unfavorable cultural and economic conditions of the environment, there was still a residue of knowledge of Judaism. . . . [They] endeavored to raise disciples and preserve Judaism for the future generations. The success of their efforts is to be found in the preservation of this Jewry to the present day."[45] Ḥak̲am Avidani, who died at the age of ninety-two, served as the spiritual leader of the Kurdistani Jews in Jerusalem and as a resourceful informant for many studies dealing with Kurdistani Jews. He owned a number of old and rare manuscripts and wrote or edited several books.

BIBLIOGRAPHY

Assaf, S. "On the History of the Jews of Kurdistan and Its Neighborhood" (in Hebrew), in *Bĕ-ʾOhăle Yaʿăk̲ob̲,* pp. 116–44. Jerusalem, 1943.

Brauer, E. "Der heilsame Granatapfelbaum." *Almanach des Schocken Verlags,* 5698 (1937/38), pp. 164–73.

Penuel, J. (J. J. Rivlin). "A Folktale about the Ḥak̲am Rabbi Samuel ben Nathanael hal-Levi *Babo Sava*" (in Hebrew). *ham-Mizraḥ 1/1* (1943): 11.

Rivlin, J. J. "Rabbi Simeon Doga," and "Rabbi Mordecai of Nerwa and the True Proselyte" (in Hebrew). *Hed̲ ham-Mizraḥ 1/17* (1943): 15.

1. How Rabbi Samuel, a Hopeless Child, Became a Poet and a Scholar[46]

(1) (This) story, which I heard from my dear father, of blessed memory, is about a pious and God-fearing man whose name was Rabbi Nathanael hal-Levi Barzānī, nicknamed *Babo Sava,*

44. Ben-Jacob, pp. 80–81.
45. Mann, p. 491.
46. The Hebrew text is found in Avidani, *1,* 1–2. A shorter version of this legend by a different informant is found in Ben-Jacob, p. 34.

"Grandfather,"[47] of blessed memory. He had an only son[48] whose name was Samuel. He wanted to teach him Torah and piety, but unfortunately the child was very slow-witted. Whatever he learned one day he would forget the next, as if he had not learned anything, not even a trifle. His father hired a tutor for him who sat with him day and night, yet he benefited nothing. Then he chastised him with all kinds of chastisements, but (they too were) of no use. Thus the boy reached the age of fourteen (some say he was only five years old)[49] and was still illiterate. His father then turned to God and prayed, saying, "Lord of the universe, if my son is to remain illiterate, I would rather have a willow plant, for (then at least) I would enjoy sitting in its shade."

(2) What did the father do (then)? He locked his son up in a room all alone for three days and three nights, without food or drink. Some people came by, and no matter how strongly they entreated the father to take the child out of his prison room, or (at least) give him some food, he refused to do so and did not accede to their plea. His wife wept and shed bitter tears, saying to her husband, "My dear husband, we are surely (quite) old, and (if our son should die), we shall remain (forever) childless. What (then) will be the end of us? My lord, my husband, please have mercy upon our only child, (who is all) we have." Whereat her husband reproached her, saying, "Your arguments and entreaties are in vain. (I shall wait) until the Holy One, blessed be He, responds to our prayer from heaven and bestows His spirit upon the child from His Sanctuary, so that I will not see him die in prison. I have one request from God: (He will) either (make) the child learn Torah or let him die there in his room." The wife wept, (saying), "Are we indeed to perish (childless)?" The child, too, was weeping and sobbing inside (his room), while his mother was wailing and shedding bitter tears outside.

(3) Our sages of blessed memory have said, "(The heavenly) gates of tears remain unlocked."[50] (Thus) any person who sheds tears (in prayer), the Holy One, blessed be He, accepts (his prayer) and delivers him from his trouble. In this case, too, God heard the

47. Cf. Benayahu, p. 24.

48. See n. 4, above, and n. 52, below.

49. In the original text this parenthetical phrase appears before the quotation of the hymn, end of §3, below. Cf. Ben-Jacob, p. 34: "He was five years old."

50. In contrast to the gates of prayer, which were locked after the destruction of the Temple; see chap. 1, n. 25, above.

weeping of the child. On the third day, early in the morning, before dawn, the Holy One, blessed be He, sent an angel from heaven[51] who taught the child all of Torah, with its revealed as well as concealed meanings. The child then began singing in a pleasant and clear voice this hymn, in which his name, Samuel, is alluded to acrostically . . .[52]

(4) When the father heard the pleasant and cheerful voice of his only son singing,[53] he immediately opened the door and cried out to him, "Samuel, Samuel, is it you (singing), my son?" He then hugged him and kissed him warmly, examined him in Bible, Mishnah, Gemara, and Kabbalah, and (found that) nothing was unfamiliar to him. Now the father rejoiced greatly and raised his hands toward heaven, saying, "Lord of the universe, it is revealed and known before the throne of Thy glory that I would have delivered my son, my only son, to death for Thy great, mighty, and awesome Name. But now I am very thankful unto Thee." Later on the child became famous as one of the great men on earth. Indeed, he is Rabbi Samuel Barzānī, the ancestor of the Barzānī family in the town of Mosul — which is (the Biblical) Asshur, situated near the Tigris River — and his daughter Asenath was nicknamed "Asenath the *Tanna'iṯ*."

2. How Rabbi Samuel, an Illiterate Weaver, Became the Rabbi of Mosul[54]

(1) There was a man in the town of Barazān whose name was Samuel Adoni. This man was simple, honest, and God-fearing, and

51. In Ben-Jacob, p. 34, the prophet Elijah appears instead of the angel; cf. legend 2, §3, below. The style as well as the content bear obvious allusions to the Biblical story of the binding of Isaac; cf. this and the following section with Gen. 22. Motifs such as the only child (Gen. 22:2), the angel's appearance at the last moment of despair (v. 12), three days (v. 4), the repetition of the name (below, §4; Gen. 22:11), and the concern about dying childless if the only child is harmed appears in both stories.

52. The hymn, mostly verses from Psalms, is here omitted. Samuel's name is alluded to acrostically in many of his hymns. On this and his poetic skill in general see Benayahu, pp. 47–48; above, n. 13.

53. According to the version in Ben-Jacob (p. 34), the father, after a day or two, took pity on the child and was about to open the door of his prison. Nothing is said there about the weeping of the mother and of the child or about the father's prayer.

54. *Hebrew text*: Ben-Jacob, pp. 206–07. According to Ben-Jacob, p. 33, n. 36, this legend was originally set forth in the "Arabic-Kurdish" dialect in a rare manuscript entitled *Sefer Sĕgulloṯ u-Ḳĕme'oṯ*, "Book of Remedies and Amulets," by Rabbi Aaron Barzāni, an eighth-generation descendant of Rabbi Samuel Barzānī. Several motifs, e.g., his illiteracy and the revelation of Elijah (cf. n. 52, above) appear both in this legend and in legend 1, above.

(always) kept away from evil. He was, however, completely illiterate, as he had never studied Torah. He was a weaver, and by this simple skill he earned his living with difficulty and sorrow. This is what he used to do: each day he would get up (early) in the morning, take up the tools of his trade — thread and yarn — as well as a hunk of bread and a jug of water, and go out to the mountain, outside of the town. There he would diligently do his work until sunset. When he wanted to pray, he would whisper the alphabet, which was the only thing he knew. Then he would raise his eyes toward heaven, saying, "Master of the world, Thou searchest minds and consciences ⟨hearts and kidneys⟩,[55] and Thou knowest the intentions of my heart. Mayest Thou set my prayer in order and accept it willingly."

(2) One day, when Samuel Adoni was diligently doing his work on the top of the mountain, he felt thirsty, but discovered that he had forgotten to take with him the jug of water. Although he was overcome by thirst, he was afraid to return to the town, lest thieves should steal his tools. So he raised his eyes heavenward, and his lips whispered the alphabet in devoted supplication. While he was praying, behold, a venerable old man appeared before him, (holding) in his hand a jug of water, and said to him, "God has heard your prayer and sent me to give you water to drink. Now get up, pronounce the blessing, and then you may drink." Samuel replied, "I do not know the blessing, for your servant is (I am) illiterate." The old man replied, "You are not illiterate. (Just) finish the recitation of the alphabet, as is your custom, and then you may drink."

(3) When Samuel finished drinking, the old man said to him, "I am the prophet Elijah. Now tell me your wish; even if it be for wisdom or wealth, it shall be given to you." Samuel replied, "It is God whom I fear, and my soul abhors the vanities of this world. My request is that God may grant me knowledge and intelligence, and light my eyes with the light of Torah."[56] Before he finished speaking, the old man stretched out his hand and touched his lips, saying, "Behold, this (hand) has touched your lips, and you shall be a great sage in Torah.[57] Now come, carry off your tools and the

55. Ps. 7:10. For this motif see Bin Gorion, *2*, 871.

56. Cf. Jonah 1:9, and Solomon's dream in 1 Kings 3:5–15.

57. Cf. Isa. 6:7. For Torah likened to water see Song Rabbah 1; Ginzberg *1*, 229, *2*, 304, 346.

instruments of your trade, because you will not need them any longer. Tomorrow you shall go to the town of Asshur (Mosul), for three days from now the rabbi of that town will die and you shall replace him ⟨sit in his chair⟩, and teach the children of Israel Torah and (its) commandments. Eleven generations of your descendants shall stand to perform the holy service,[58] and they shall be proficient in (preparing) remedies and amulets, with which they will make their living in comfort and success."[59]

(4) Rabbi Samuel Adoni traveled to Mosul as the prophet Elijah, of blessed memory, had commanded him. And behold, everything came true, for after three days the rabbi of the town of Mosul departed (this world), and Rabbi Samuel sat in the chair of the rabbinate. From that day on the prophet Elijah would reveal himself to him day after day and would engage in (teaching him) Torah. To Rabbi Samuel were born a son named Isaac and a daughter named Asenath.[60]

3. How Rabbi Samuel Wrought a Miracle[61]

(1) Years had passed (since Samuel became the rabbi of Mosul). Once, on the night when the Passover holiday was celebrated ⟨sanctified⟩, Rabbi Samuel and the members of his family were reclining at the table in accordance with the custom of this holiday. Suddenly the old man (Rabbi Samuel) stamped his foot and closed his eyes as if he were praying.[62] After a short while a smile appeared on his lips, and he told the members of his family to go on with the ceremonies of the seder. All the participants were puzzled by what they saw, and ḥak̲am Isaac, his son, asked him the meaning of it; but he replied, saying, "Wait until the eve of the Festival of Weeks — may we celebrate it in prosperity — then you will receive your answer."

58. The printed text has *šemot̲*, "names," which may be an error for *šerut̲*, "service." Ben-Jacob (p. 38, n. 53) lists the names of twenty members of the Barzānī family who were rabbis of Mosul at various times.

59. See n. 54, above. This seems to be a kind of grant of divine sanction to the preoccupation of these rabbis with practical mysticism. The style remains that of Gen. 17:6, 35:11.

60. See n. 4, above.

61. This is a continuation of the preceding legend; see n. 54, above.

62. That Rabbi Samuel saw visions is mentioned in his own letter (Benayahu, p. 81): "While I was dozing, I saw in my dream that lo and behold, a tall figure in human shape woke me up, as one does when he is awakened from his sleep. Then he said to me, 'Son of man, arise! What meanest thou that thou art asleep?'"

(2) The son waited with great impatience. On the eve of the Festival of Weeks, behold, the son saw heavily laden camels standing at the gate of their house, led by Arab men who inquired if this was the house of Rabbi Samuel. When they received an affirmative answer, they began unloading their camels and offered their gifts to the rabbi,[63] whereupon, while they sat down to eat, they told what had happened to them:

(3) "We were going by boat on the Tigris River from the town of Basra to Baghdad. (Just) before we arrived at the port of our destination, a large crack appeared in the bottom of the boat, and water began entering and flooding (the boat so rapidly) that we could not reach the shore. It being springtime, the river was overflowing and the boat was about to sink. There was with us a Jewish traveler who sat calmly and quietly at the side of the boat. When we asked him why he was sitting so calmly while we were all in mortal danger,[64] he replied, saying, 'What will you give me if I save you now?' Although the man seemed to us to be a lunatic, we agreed on his reward and swore an oath that we would give it to him. Then the Jew said, 'I will pray, and you must say Amen after me,' and he recited loudly, his eyes raised heavenward, 'Samuel Adoni, stand up in prayer in our behalf before your Creator — perhaps God will have mercy upon us for your sake and will save us from this imminent death.' Behold, as soon as we responded with Amen after him, the crack in the bottom of the boat was filled in and the water that had (already) entered dried up completely.[65] After a few hours we arrived safely in the city of Baghdad, to our great joy. This is what happened to us. Now we have brought our tribute to the rabbi, our master, and we beg him to accept it kindly from our hands."

(4) All those who were listening were amazed at this wonderful tale. Isaac, the rabbi's son, asked the Arabs, "When did this happen to you?" They replied, saying, "This happened on the night of the fifteenth of the month of Nisan, on the night of the (Passover) holiday of the Jews." The son then turned to his father and asked

63. These generous gifts, probably of grain and fruit, seem to allude to the local custom of bringing new fruits to the synagogue on the Festival of Weeks (Brauer, p. 246), as well as to the Biblical offering of choice first fruits (Exod. 23:19). The caravan of loaded camels seems to allude to the story of Joseph, Gen. 37:25. Cf. also the end of §1.

64. Apparently an allusion to the Biblical story of Jonah (Jonah 1).

65. An apparent allusion to the splitting of the Red Sea, Exod. 14:15–22, which forms an essential part of the Passover night service (Haggadah).

him, "Father, why did you stamp your foot on the night of the seder?" Rabbi Samuel replied, "At that same moment I filled in the crack in the boat with my foot." Isaac asked further, "But why did you smile?" The father replied, "Because the calamity was averted ⟨the evil decree was torn up⟩."

4. The Flight of Rabbi Samuel from Barazān to Amidya and His Death There[66]

(1) This happened to Rabbi Nathanael and his son Rabbi Samuel Barzānī, may they rest in paradise. They hailed from the town of Barazān,[67] a place of (Jewish) sages and eminent scholars. . . . It lies far from the town of Amidya, a walking distance of two days. . . . Once, on a Friday that was one of the intermediate days of the Festival of Tabernacles, father and son were in the sukkah (festal booth) studying the second chapter of the tractate Ḥăgīgah of the (Babylonian) Talmud. They concentrated on the twenty-second verse of Ezekiel's prophecy, chapter 1, *And over the heads of the living creatures there was the likeness of a firmament, like the color of the terrible ice, stretched forth over their heads above.*[68]

(2) While they were pleasantly discussing the mystical and plain meanings of this verse, a green fire descended from heaven upon the booth and surrounded them. All the Gentiles, including the great sheikh of Barazān, saw this fire, and the sheikh commanded (his servants), "Go and see what is this green fire upon the booth of the Jews."[69] When they came near and found that son and father were sitting in the booth alone, busy with their study, they returned to the sheikh, saying, "We saw only (two of) your Jews, father and son, sitting and studying, and nothing more." He sent for them, and when they came to him he said to them, "You are not Jews but rather our *sayyids,* because we saw a green fire upon your booth.[70] I

66. *Hebrew text*: Avidani, 4, 553–56. Two other very similar versions were published by Penuel (in Hebrew) and Brauer (in German); see Bibliography, above. The informant's name is not given in either version, but Brauer (p. 165) mentions Amidya as the hometown of the informant, most probably ḥak̲am Avidani.

67. In the district of Arbil; see Ben-Jacob, pp. 96–97.

68. The verse is not quoted in the other two versions.

69. Cf. Penuel: "How is it possible that the green fire, the holy fire which rests only upon the residence of a *sayyid* [a descendant of the prophet Muḥammad], is now resting upon the roof of the Jews? It surely means that there is a *sayyid* inside that booth."

70. There seem to be two conflicting popular traditions about the appearance of the green fire. The local Jews, probably influenced by the nonconsuming fire revealed to Moses in the bush (Exod. 3:2; cf. Elijah in 1 Kings 19:22), connect the fire with great rabbis, as a sign of divine inspiration (cf. below, legend 6, §5, and n. 108), whereas the Muslims believe that it

decree that you be immediately converted to Islam.[71] We will honor you as (we honor) our sayyids. But if you are not converted, I shall put you to death." They replied, "God forbid! We cannot do this."[72]

(3) Thereupon the sheikh immediately imprisoned them in a cattle shed, and they were tormented by burning animal dung which filled the place with smoke. When the time came to welcome the Sabbath,[73] Rabbi Nathanael said to the sheikh, "You know that we are forbidden to leave our homes on the Sabbath (hence we cannot escape). Please, let us therefore go home. On Sunday we will give you our (final) answer, yes or no." The sheikh agreed and believed them, as it was well known among the Gentiles that a Jew would not leave his home (to travel) on the Sabbath.[74] He therefore freed them, and they returned to their home.

(4) After the advent of the Sabbath, when they had finished the afternoon and evening prayers, pronounced the sanctification blessing, and eaten the festive meal of Sabbath eve, the son asked his father whether one may profane the Sabbath to save a life.[75] The father replied, "Yes, one may do so. My dear son, arise and flee. I, however, am ready and willing to give up my life for the sanctification of His blessed Name. I am already grown old, but you are young and an only child to me,[76] which is why I feel pity for you. Arise and go whithersoever you can."

(5) Thereupon Rabbi Samuel took his linen shoes, which are called *raškiye,* repaired them, for they were torn, and put them on. Then he kissed his father's hand and his mother's hand and said to

---

indicates a descendant of the prophet Muḥammad. Cf. S. D. Goitein, in *Journal of Jewish Studies* 4 (1953): 80: "The Bagdad Jews were reported to have on green robes for their flight to Jerusalem in the time of Menahem ben Solomon ibn Dugi, green being the color of Paradise as well as of the Muslim prophet's family."

71. On forced conversions of rabbis and their resultant wanderings from town to town, see Benayahu, p. 43, and chap. XIV, above. Rabbi Samuel himself has written several appeals to redeem Jews threatened by forced conversion; ibid., pp. 87–91.

72. In Brauer's version, Rabbi Nathanael denies having seen any green fire.

73. Penuel's version is different: "A few hours later they were taken out and asked again to be converted." Cf. Brauer, p. 167: "Rabbi Nathanael reflected in his heart, 'I do not care if they kill me, but I am worried about my son, and I must rescue him.' Then he called the sheikh's servant and asked him to take him to his master."

74. Cf. below, chap. XX, proverb 55. That there were close relations between Jews and Kurds, including some discussions of religious matters, is evident from the documents as well; cf. Benayahu, p. 45; legend 7, below; Introduction, end of I/5 and n. 13 ad loc.

75. Cf. B. Yoma 85a.

76. See n. 4, above.

them, "My dear father and mother, may you have a Sabbath of peace!" They, however, kept weeping bitterly, so the son said to his father, "My dear father, it is forbidden to weep on the Sabbath." The father replied, "I am weeping out of delight in the Sabbath."[77] Then the son departed.

(6) The son walked all night until daylight, when he arrived at a river crossing with no bridge (over it), called Ruyešin,[78] where it is joined by another river, called Zabe; both rivers merge together at a town called Ṣoriya, where he wanted to cross. Early on the morning of the Sabbath, when two ordinary Jews went out to the river to relieve themselves (as was the local custom), they noticed a (pious) Jew with side-locks and beard standing on the other side of the river, motioning to them and pleading to the effect that he wished to cross the river. The two Jews summoned the Gentile (in charge of the river crossing), and he came out to transport the son (across the river) on a raft.[79] When these two Jews looked at him (closely) and recognized him as the famous Rabbi Samuel Barzānī, they were amazed. They said to him, "Rabbi, if you profane the Sabbath, we (too) will forthwith go to work." He upbraided them,[80] saying loudly, "Woe unto you, you wicked villains!" At that very moment they turned into two dry willow trees with only a few fresh branches at the top. Some old men told me that they have seen these trees.[81]

(7) Then Rabbi Samuel continued on his way, arriving at the town of Amidya that same Sabbath day, at the time of the afternoon prayer.[82] He entered the old synagogue, (the one) dedicated to the memory of Ezra the scribe,[83] peace be upon him. At that time there lived in Amidya a rabbi named Simeon Doga, who was famous; he

77. Cf. Brauer, p. 168: "Let me weep, for this too is Sabbath's delight, whereby my soul is relieved." This seems to be influenced by the legend about Rabbi 'Aḳiba, who used to weep on the Sabbath. When his disciples reminded him of the verse, *And call the Sabbath a delight* (Isa. 58:13), he replied, "This too is my delight." See H. N. Bialik and J. Ravnitzky, *Sefer ha-'Aggadah* (Tel-Aviv, 1956), p. 180.

78. The name appears as *Kuyšin* in Penuel's version and is absent in Brauer's.

79. So Brauer, but Penuel has: "They immediately recognized that he was Rabbi Samuel. . . . They [themselves] went to fetch a boat and ferried him over."

80. Brauer has, "He looked at them with sparkling eyes."

81. Cf. Penuel, "They are still there down to the present time." It seems that they were punished so severely because they showed lack of faith by thinking that Rabbi Samuel would carelessly profane the Sabbath.

82. Penuel adds, "at the ninth hour in the afternoon" (3 p.m.). Cf. Introduction, IV/5.

83. According to the tradition of the Iraqi Jews, his shrine is near Basra, in southern Iraq. However, there were many synagogues named after him; see Ben-Jacob, *Ḳĕḇarim ḳĕḏošim bĕ-Ḇaḇel* (Jerusalem, 1973), p. 179.

too was (later) slain on a false charge.[84] He was sitting (in the synagogue), delivering a sermon to which the congregation was listening attentively. When they saw the famous Rabbi Samuel Barzānī suddenly entering the synagogue, they began asking each other, "Was Rabbi Samuel your guest last night?" Each one answered "No," and everyone was puzzled about it, but they kept silent until the afternoon prayer was over. Then Rabbi Samuel proceeded to the pulpit and said, "Sirs, I confess my sin — I have desecrated the Sabbath; I am ready to accept the (deserved) judgment." Rabbi Simeon replied, "Our masters of blessed memory have already said that to save life one may profane the Sabbath. You are hereby invited, with all respect, to partake of the third Sabbath meal at my booth. I have (already) prepared for you a bottle of wine and a fattened hen, and you and I shall have this meal together. This is your judgment, nothing else."

(8) People say that on the preceding Friday Rabbi Simeon Doga himself went to the marketplace, bought two fat hens, and told his wife to prepare both of them for the Sabbath. His wife asked, "Why two? One would be enough." He replied, "Tomorrow we will have an honored guest. Leave one of the hens for the third meal." He already knew, by way of the science of astrology, what was going to happen. That honored guest was Rabbi Samuel.

(9) After the *Haḇdalah* prayer at the expiration of the Sabbath, Rabbi Samuel Barzānī told Rabbi Simeon Doga about all that had happened to him, and asked for his advice as to what he should do. Rabbi Simeon Doga replied, "It is a sore affliction that we Jews have no government of our own to save us (from persecution). And there is no trust to be placed in Gentiles. The hand of the sheikh of Barazān is (even) harsher than that of the Turkish governor of Amidya. I have no other advice except that you wait for a little while until this danger is past."[85] The people then hid Rabbi Samuel in the synagogue and supplied him with bread and (other) food, and he remained there (for a while).

(10) We shall (now) return to Rabbi Nathanael Barzānī, the aged father. On Sunday morning the sheikh sent for him and asked him where his son was. He replied, "My son has run away out of fear. However, I am in your hands — do with me as you wish. I

84. See legend 4, below.
85. This section is missing altogether in the other two versions.

will gladly endure all torments, but I will never abandon the religion of the Torah, which we received on Mount Sinai." When the sheikh heard his words, he was filled with anger and was about to slay him. One of his counselors, however, said to him, "If you will accept my advice, leave this old Jew alone. After all, he will soon die, and our religion will derive no benefit from him. If, however, you could bring back his young son who has escaped, our religion will benefit greatly from him." The sheikh agreed with the counselor and let Rabbi Nathanael go free to his home. He then sent (his servants) to look for Rabbi Samuel in all the Jewish communities, but he could not be found.

(11) Finally the sheikh learned[86] that the rabbi had escaped to the town of Amidya. He sent a letter to the governor of Amidya, (saying), "I have heard that a Jew of mine is with you. Look for him and send him (back) to me. It is quite clear to me that he is indeed with you. If you do not (send him back), I am prepared to come and wage war against you." When the governor heard his harsh threats, he became sorely frightened, and his heart failed him, for (he knew that) he was not strong enough to fight the sheikh.[87] He thereupon sent his servants to look very carefully for the rabbi in every possible place, so much so that he did not leave even one place unsearched, including pits, bushes, and caves. When the Jews saw what was happening, they put Rabbi Samuel into the *genizah* (storeroom) of worn-out books in the synagogue (named after) the prophet Ezekiel, who was called Sayyid Ezekiel.[88]

(12) They hid him there after closing and plastering over the entrance (of the *genizah*), and he remained there for three days and three nights. However, the sheikh's decree was enforced more and more strictly day after day.[89] When Rabbi Samuel realized this, he

86. According to the other versions, he found this out through geomancy (Brauer) and casting lots, a skill that he had learned from the Jews (Penuel).

87. Cf. Penuel: "Although the Emir Sayf al-Dīn, the Turkish governor, was kind to the Jews, he could not stand up against the Barzānī sheikh, for the latter was a violent man."

88. It is interesting to note that the title *sayyid,* literally "master" and usually designating a descendant of the prophet Muḥammad (see end of §2 and n. 69, above), is used here as the title of a Jewish prophet; cf. Sabar, "The Arabic Elements" (forthcoming), §8.3 and n. 67 ad loc. The synagogue, according to a tradition, is one of the oldest in Kurdistan, its original construction dating from the year 1248. It was built in accordance with the description of the Temple in Ezek. 40; see Ben-Jacob, p. 73.

89. Cf. Penuel: "On the third day, Sayf al-Dīn issued an order to demolish all the walls built by the Jews recently." According to Brauer (p. 172), Rabbi Samuel knew well that the sheikh would eventually discover his hiding place through geomancy.

grew weary of life in this world and asked to be taken out of his hiding place in the *genizah,* which contained more than three hundred scrolls of Torah and countless old books. (What a pity that all these books remained there and were eventually lost).[90] They complied with his wish and took him out. He then asked for a prayer shawl and a set of phylacteries, which he put on, and stood up in prayer, saying, "Master of the world, take my soul, and do not deliver me into the hands of mine enemies." Forthwith he was summoned to the Assembly on High (passed away), just like Rabbah bar Naḥmani, who is mentioned in the Talmud.[91] (My father, may he rest in paradise, showed me the wooden pillar in front of which Rabbi Samuel prayed, and told me, "Rabbi Samuel Barzānī passed away on this spot)."[92]

(13) After he had passed away, he was found still clad in prayer shawl and phylacteries. This was related to the governor of the town, who came by and saw him thus, whereupon the governor said, "Only Jews know how to be (true) martyrs." Then he himself, with his army, marched (solemnly) in Rabbi Samuel's funeral procession, and the latter was buried with great honor in the cemetery of Amidya.[93] Many fruit trees[94] were planted around his grave. Whosoever became ill would take a fruit from those trees and say, "I plead with this righteous man who is buried here to cure me," and his ailment would immediately be healed.[95]

(14) The location (of his shrine) is well known down to the present day. He is called in the Kurdish language *šēra-dīn,*

90. The parenthetic sentence is in the original text. Some of these books and manuscripts, however, were eventually rescued during a visit to Kurdistan by the late Walter J. Fischel and Rabbi Lippa Schwager, and were sold to various libraries in the United States and England; see Benayahu, p. 49, n. 175. A detailed description of the genizah is found in Brauer, p. 171: "It had three chambers, one for storing the synagogue wine for the Sanctification benediction, one for storing the Scrolls of the Torah in winter, and the third, innermost and darkest, held discarded books."

91. B. BM 86a. According to this legend, Rabbah (3rd–4th centuries), the Babylonian amora and head of the Pumbeditha academy, died like Rabbi Samuel, as a result of persecution, after making several attempts to hide. Cf. n. 71, above.

92. The parenthetic sentence is in the original text. The synagogue had twenty-five wooden pillars (Ben-Jacob, p. 73). According to Penuel, this pillar, which faced in the direction of Jerusalem, was five meters high and so wide that a person could not encircle it with both arms.

93. The governor's participation in the funeral and his remark are missing in the other two versions.

94. The other versions mention only the pomegranate tree.

95. According to the other versions, if anyone took the pomegranate without first asking Rabbi Samuel's permission, he would become ill with fever.

meaning "the lion of the faith."[96] The governor of Amidya sent (a message) to the sheikh of Barazān to inform him of all this, whereupon his anger subsided. People say that after thirty days the sheikh too died, and all the Gentiles realized that he was punished and perished for this very reason. Thus was God's name sanctified among all the Gentiles.[97] Rabbi Nathanael hal-Levi (Samuel's father), however, lived on to reach one hundred and twenty years,[98] and only then was he summoned to the Assembly on High. He is called in the language of Kurdistan (Neo-Aramaic) *Babo Sava,* meaning "Grandfather." He was buried right there in the town of Barazān.

5. The Power of Rabbi Asenath, the Daughter of Rabbi Samuel[99]

(1) Asenath, the daughter of Rabbi Samuel Adoni Barzānī, was a great sage and a woman learned in Torah. She (even) learned the wisdom of the Kabbalah (mysticism) and became greatly renowned for (performing) miracles and wonders. After she had borne one son and one daughter to her husband, she prayed to God to terminate her menses, so that she might devote herself to Torah in sanctity and purity, and God fulfilled her request.

(2) Asenath was also a pretty and attractive woman. It happened one day, when she went up to the roof to spread out her laundry (to dry), that she was seen by a Gentile who conceived a desire for her. At midnight the Gentile (tried to) sneak up to the roof, his heart filled with evil intentions against this learned woman. She immediately pronounced the names of (several) holy men, and (as a result) the Gentile remained hanging on the beams of the roof, unable to move. In the morning the matter became known to everyone. A large number of people gathered to see this unusual sight, but all their efforts to remove the Gentile from his place were in vain.

(3) When the *wālī,* the governor of the town, heard about this,

96. The Kurdish words are translated in Penuel's version as "the Light of Religion," and in Brauer's as "the Crazy Lion." All three translations are etymologically possible; the letters *šyrʾ* may be read also as *čirā,* Kurdish < Persian *čirāğ* < Aramaic *šĕrağaʾ,* Neo-Aramaic *šraʾa,* "lamp, light"; *dīn* (Kurdish), "crazy," < Persian *dēwān,* "demons, devils."

97. Nothing is said in the other versions about the death of the sheikh.

98. This detail is missing in the other versions and seems to be a typological addition, influenced by the number of years lived by Moses (Deut. 34:7), Rabbi ‹Aḳiba, etc.; cf. also Gen. 6:3.

99. *Hebrew text*: Ben-Jacob, p. 37. Translated from a Judeo-Arabic text found in a manuscript, for which see n. 54, above.

he himself entreated the sage Asenath to set the Gentile free, but she refused, saying, "Had this Gentile come to steal something from my house, I would have remained silent. Since, however, he came to me with the intention of corrupting my morals, he shall remain hanging in his place." The governor then swore to her that if she set the sinning Gentile free, he would punish him properly and hang him publicly, whereupon Asenath set him free, and he was hanged from a tree to the amazement of all the people in the town.

6. THE DEATH OF RABBI SIMEON DOGA, THE ASTROLOGER[100]

(1) There was once a (legal) dispute regarding the widow of a brother who had died without issue (*yĕḇamah*). Rabbi Simeon allowed the widow to remarry forthwith outside (of her late husband's family), while all the (other) ḥaḵamim and rabbis of Amidya said that she first had to perform the rite of *ḥaliṣah*.[101] They sent the problem to the (Jewish) court in Baghdad and received an answer that the rule was according to Rabbi Simeon. Still the (other) ḥaḵamim disagreed with him,[102] whereupon they sent the problem to the court in Jerusalem, which also replied that the rule was according to Rabbi Simeon. Still the ḥaḵamim and the rabbis of the town persisted in their disagreement, whereat Rabbi Simeon said to them, "I wish I could send this problem to the river Sambatyon,[103] so as to receive an answer from there; (unfortunately) I cannot do so."

(2) It is related that when the rabbis of the Land of Israel saw from his halaḵic decision how brilliant Rabbi Simeon was, an eminent rabbi from Jerusalem decided to come over and see him. He took with him as presents a book on geomancy and astrology, a whetstone, and a ritual slaughtering knife.[104] Then he set out from Jerusalem on his way to see Rabbi Simeon.[105]

100. *Hebrew text*: Avidani, *4*, 556–68. Another version, differing in several details, was published by Rivlin (see above, Bibliography). Its informant is not mentioned but was most probably Avidani.

101. The rite releasing the surviving brother-in-law from the obligation of marrying the widow; see Deut. 25:5–10, and *EJ*, s.v. "Levirate Marriage and Ḥaliẓah," *11*, 122–31.

102. According to Rivlin's version, the dispute was between Rabbi Simeon and an emissary (*šaddar*) from the Land of Israel.

103. The name of the legendary Sabbath River, across which, according to a tradition, the lost ten tribes of Israel were led into exile; see *EJ*, s.v. "Sambatyon," *14*, 762–64. Rabbi Simeon's remark is meant to be sarcastic.

104. None of these is mentioned in Rivlin's version.

105. Avidani adds here in parentheses: "(I had owned this book on astrology, in manu-

(3) While the rabbi from the Land of Israel was still on his way to Amidya, misfortune befell Rabbi Simeon. One day the Turkish governor of Amidya noticed under his chair a paper covered with square Hebrew script.[106] He called in an ordinary Jew and said to him, "Translate for me what is written on this paper," and the Jew innocently translated it, saying, "It is written on it, 'Topple over the governor and set up someone else in his place.'" The governor then asked him, "Do you perhaps know who wrote this paper?" He replied, "I do not know." After much investigation the governor eventually learned that Rabbi Simeon Doga had written it.

(4) It is said that that same day was the eve of the Festival of Weeks. The governor sent four men after Rabbi Simeon to slay him, commanding them, "Do not bring him to me, but rather take him straight to the high city wall and cast him down from it. For if he comes to me, he will surely win me over with his words."

(5) They did just that. They came right over to take Rabbi Simeon from the old synagogue named after Ezra the scribe, peace be upon him, where they saw him lying on his belly and studying Gemara. They told him that the Turkish governor wanted him, and he forthwith went along with them. When they reached the governor's barracks ⟨*qišla*⟩, they continued going further, so he asked them, "Where are you taking me? Is the governor not at the barracks?" They replied, "You (just) come along with us." When they took him inside the city wall, Rabbi Simeon became very disturbed. He immediately cast lots with his hands and quickly realized that they were taking him to be slain. When they arrived at the top of the wall, they suddenly cast him off that wall, which was more than thirty meters high, but immediately saw a green fire surrounding him.[107] He fell on the rocks at the foot of the wall, but no harm came to him. Thereupon he got up, walked a few steps from where he had fallen, and sat down. When the four men saw that he did not die, they came down and slew him on the spot.

---

script, until [A.M.] 5694 [1934], when I left the town of Amidya on my way to the Land of Israel, where I handed it to a man whose name was Samuel Miškafa, a descendant of [Rabbi Simeon] Doga's family)." Cf. §8, below.

106. According to Rivlin's version, he was told about this and was shown the inscription which predicted that he would be removed and that someone else would be installed in his place.

107. Hurling someone down from the top of a wall was a local method of capital punishment; cf. Introduction, n. 40. Rivlin has: "A green fire descended from heaven, surrounded him, and protected him." Cf. n. 108, below.

(6) They then came back to the governor and told him about the miracle they had seen. The governor replied, "I said that his sentence was to be (only) that he be cast off the wall. If he did not die as a result of this, why did you kill him?"[108] He then grew furious, and said, "I shall be innocent of his blood, but you shall be condemned (by heaven) for it."

(7) It is related that all four men who took part in slaying Rabbi Simeon did not live beyond that year, and all died. As for the (local) Jews, when they heard (of the rabbi's death), crowds of men and women assembled before the barracks yard, shouting and screaming so intensely that they (even) cursed the governor and held him up to contempt. He heard this but said to his servants, "Be quiet and do not answer anything to the Jews, whether good or evil, because they are right."[109]

(8) We shall now return to the rabbi from the Land of Israel who was mentioned above. He arrived at the town of Amidya on the same day of the eve of the Festival of Weeks. When he heard that Rabbi Simeon had been slain by being cast off (the wall), he fell to the ground, lamented, and wept, saying, "Woe unto me that I was not fortunate enough to see his face!"[110] He gave the presents (that he had brought with him) to Rabbi Simeon's family. This is all; there is more to tell,[111] but I did not want to make it long and tried to be brief in my account.

108. Cf. Rivlin: "I said to drop him, not to kill him. Behold, he was a *sayyid,* a holy and wonder-working man. You have seen this with your own eyes. Why then did you kill him?" Cf. nn. 69 and 70 above.

109. Rivlin's version of this section reads: "That same day on which Rabbi Simeon Doga was slain was the eve of the Festival of Weeks. It was the custom of women on that day to go to the Khābūr River to wash their clothes and to immerse themselves [for ritual purification], while the men were at the market place. Thus the death of Rabbi Simeon did not become known until the authorities informed the mukhtār [the official representative of the Jewish community] that So-and-so had been slain. [Only then] did men, women, and children gather before the governor's courtyard and lamented in Kurdish, saying, 'O governor, may God remove you from your office!' However, the governor, whose name was Sayf al-Dīn, did not harm the Jews, as he was afraid of them because of the miracle which was wrought for Rabbi Simeon when he was cast from the wall. [Even when] the Jews brought plates full of ashes and poured them upon the governor's house, no one dared to say anything [against them]."

110. Cf. Rivlin: "When the rabbi arrived at the town's gate, he found the Jews returning from the cemetery. He was riding his mule, but when he heard about the death of Rabbi Simeon Doga, he fell off the mule, tore at his hair, and slapped his knees, saying, 'Woe unto me!", etc.

111. Rivlin's version begins with an anecdote about how Rabbi Simeon revealed the secret place of a precious silk handkerchief that belonged to a poor widow's only son. It ends with a remark that Rabbi Simeon was buried next to Rabbi Samuel Barzānī, near other famous shrines in Amidya.

7. The Conversion of the Emir of Nerwa to Judaism by Rabbi Mordecai[112]

(1) My grandfather told this (story) about his teacher, ḥakam Rabbi Mordecai of the town of Nerwa, the birthplace of many rabbis and scribes.[113] He said that once the Turkish [114] emir of Nerwa sent for this Rabbi Mordecai and said to him, "I want you to tell me the truth about what you say, that all Gentiles will go to hell, while the Jews will go to paradise.[115] If you do not clarify this for me, I swear by my faith that I will do to the Jews one of these three things: slay all the Jews under my rule, expel them destitute and stark naked, or convert all of them (by force to Islam)." Rabbi Mordecai replied, "Give me eight days' time. Then I will bring you an answer." The emir agreed to this.

(2) Rabbi Mordecai went forth, gathered all the Jews, and proclaimed a fast of prayer and recitation of penitential hymns (*sĕliḥoṯ*) for three days and three nights. They also took a scroll of Torah to the Jewish cemetery.[116] Behold, on the third day the sheikh of the Muslims, that is to say, their grand sage,[117] suddenly died. On the

112. *Hebrew text*: Avidani, *4*, 549–50. A similar version was published by Rivlin (see Bibliography, above).

113. Cf. Introduction, II/10; Mann, p. 481.

114. Here, and elsewhere in the original text, *yišma'eli*, "Ishmaelite," which may designate a Turk, a Kurd, or a Muslim in general.

115. Rivlin's version begins differently: "This story happened in Nerwa, which is one day's walking distance from Amidya. A ḥakam lived there named Rabbi Mordecai. In his time a plague broke out which took many lives in the area surrounding Nerwa, but did not reach Nerwa [proper]. One night Rabbi Mordecai saw in a dream that the plague was to break out in Nerwa [as well]. His house was the first from the entrance into the town, so already in the first hour of that same night he lit a candle, stood up next to the window, and studied the holy [book of] *Zohar* until it was exactly midnight, when he saw through the window between thirty and forty horsemen riding by. Whenever one of them arrived at the window, he would stop right there [and wait] until the last of them arrived. [Then] they asked the first man, 'Why do you not enter into the town?' He replied, 'Behold, the town is surrounded by a fence. I am therefore unable to enter because of the fence.' When Rabbi Mordecai heard this, he intensified his study and raised his voice [even louder], and continued in this manner for about half an hour, while they were arguing, until they went off toward another town named Ašīṯa, inhabited only by Gentiles, north of Nerwa. They caused so much destruction in Ašīṯa that not even a rooster survived. When the report of this reached the emir, he sent for Rabbi Mordecai and said to him, 'I have heard that you said such-and-such." He replied, 'Yes.' The emir said, 'How dare you say that you know all this, when you [Jews] are the sons of Hell?' Rabbi Mordecai, greatly upset by this, replied, 'Very well, then. Let us have a test and see who are those who will inherit Hell.'"

116. To pray for intercession by their deceased forebears. The threats of the emir as well as the fasting proclaimed by Rabbi Mordecai are not mentioned in Rivlin's version.

117. Cf. Rivlin: "The Gentile had the rank of *dawāzdah 'ilm,* 'twelve kinds of knowl-

same day an ordinary Jew also died, a dyer by occupation,[118] who knew nothing more than praying out of his prayer book. At the end of the eight days set by the emir for Rabbi Mordecai, he sent for him, saying, "Tell me now your answer." He replied, "First of all, send all the other people out of here, then I shall tell you what I intend to do." Thereupon all the people were sent out of there, and they remained by themselves.

(3) Rabbi Mordecai then said to the emir, "Seven days ago (your) grand sheikh and our ordinary Jewish dyer died. Let us — you, me, and my disciple, who is trustworthy[119] — go and open the grave of the Jew at night, by moonlight. Then we shall go and open the grave of the sheikh, and see which one of the two is resting more comfortably in his grave. Now it is known that our masters, of blessed memory, have said that after seven[120] days the belly of the corpse splits and decays. In this way we shall find out the truth, and (everything) will become as clear as the sun." The emir agreed to Rabbi Mordecai's suggestion.

(4) On that night the moon was full, as (it always is) on the fourteenth day of the (lunar) month. All three went forth and opened (first) the grave of the Jew, and behold, he was lying as if (asleep) in bed, his face covered with sweat, (as though) nothing had happened to him.[121] No maggots had taken over his body. Rabbi Mordecai then said, "Let us go now and open the grave of your sheikh." They went on and opened that grave, and saw the sheikh buried with iron chains binding him from head to foot, his hands and head (bent) over his knees.[122]

(5) When the emir saw this miracle,[123] he ordered the grave

edge,' that is to say, he was knowledgeable in the twelve classes of wisdom of the Gentiles. Whosoever reaches this rank, no one can be higher than he."

118. Cf. Rivlin: "He used to dye the wool which was brought to him by the Gentiles." This was a common occupation among the Jews. My own family's surname was Ṣabagha, "Dyer," before it was changed to Sabar; cf. Introduction, III/1.

119. In Rivlin's version nothing is said about the disciple, i.e., Avidani's grandfather; it has instead "and the beadle of the congregation."

120. The sources (e.g., B. Shab 151b) mention only three days. Perhaps the letter *zayin* (7) in the original text is a misprint for *gimel* (3).

121. Rivlin: "They opened the shrouds and found him to be like a man who had drunk wine and brandy, his face covered with sweat.

122. Rivlin: "They found an iron nail driven into his brain and sticking out from the back of his head, and his hands and feet hollow."

123. Rivlin adds: "When the emir was lying in his bed, he saw the sheikh in the shape of a dog, nibbling at a bone in his mouth. The emir said to him in his dream, 'Behold, you held the highest rank [yet look at what has happened to you]!' He replied, 'True; but in this place,

covered and said to Rabbi Mordecai, "You are truthful, and your Torah is truth. I want to be converted and to become a Jew, but on condition that no Muslim learn of it. You need only advise me what to do." Rabbi Mordecai replied, "First go and appoint your son emir in your stead, and enjoin him to treat the Jews properly. Then come to me secretly every night until I teach you (the prayer) 'Hear, O Israel' (Deut. 6:4) and (other) precepts (of Judaism). Thereafter you will leave your native country and go to Baghdad, to be with the exilarch and remain there."[124] The emir did exactly as he was told by Rabbi Mordecai and was successful (in his escape), and the decrees (against the Jews) were repealed.[125]

(6) This was told to me by my father, Rabbi Simeon, who had heard it from my grandfather, Rabbi Benjamin, who was that trustworthy disciple of Rabbi Mordecai and who saw all this story (happening) with his own eyes.

---

the other world, there is no partiality, and the [true] religion is that of Israel. If you only can, go and adhere to [the religion of] Israel.'"

124. Rivlin: "Rabbi Mordecai said to him, 'I cannot convert you, for the hand of the Gentiles is strong in our places.' He replied, '[Just] teach me the first verse you say when you recite the *Shĕma'* prayer.'"

125. See end of §1, above. Rivlin: "Eventually the emir set up his son in his stead, went to a place where he would not be recognized, and became a true proselyte."

XVI

Selections from the Chronicle of Jonah ben Gabriel

The manuscripts originating in Kurdistan usually contain only traditional literature, such as Midrashim, tales, hymns, halaḵic rules, and the like. Jonah ben Gabriel's manuscript, however, contains, in addition to the traditional material, many notes on contemporary events — some of which do not concern Jews at all — as well as detailed descriptions of natural disasters that befell his hometown of Arbil[1] during his lifetime. Many brief notes on private events, such as births and marriages in his own family, as well as on communal matters, such as the building of a synagogue, are also included. The more traditional material in the manuscript comprises, among other things, halaḵic questions and answers, nostrums and cures, interpretations of dreams, the casting of lots and the use of the signs of the zodiac, as well as forms of promissory notes and commercial bills. The manuscript probably served as a thesaurus for this learned man and community leader, in which he jotted down all that was of interest to him and that he thought worthy of preserving for future generations.

As he records in his manuscript, Jonah ben Gabriel was born on the fourteenth of First Adar, A.M. 5532 (March 1772), and took a wife on the eighteenth of Tebet, A.M. 5552 (February 1792). Since his notes about public events cover the years A.M. 5553–5603 (1793–1843), he must have lived more than seventy years. His notes indicate that he was a public figure in his town. He was in charge of the building of a synagogue and of the symbolic purchase of the town area from the Turkish governor, in order to enable the Jews to move their belongings from place to place on the Sabbath.[2] He entertained a guest from the Land of Israel and lent him some

1. Pronounced *'Árwil* by the Kurdistani Jews. It was an important Assyrian center, situated east of Nineveh (Mosul). A Jewish community existed in Arbil (Arbel) continuously from the end of the Second Temple period, when it was the capital of the kingdom of Adiabene, whose royal house was converted to Judaism, until the 1950s, when its Jews emigrated to Israel; see *EJ*, s.v. "Irbil (also Erbil, formerly Arbil)," *8*, 1452–63; Ben-Jacob, pp. 88–94; Brauer, p. 38; Introduction, II/2.

2. See §§1–2, below.

books.[3] That he was a learned man is apparent also from his remarkably modern, clear, and succinct Hebrew style.[4] A pious Jew who regarded every catastrophe as decreed from heaven, he often ends his notes with a brief prayer for salvation,[5] and in his description of natural catastrophes he pays special attention to the suffering of the Jewish community. However, he limits himself to stating the facts, without adding any sentimental comments.

BIBLIOGRAPHY

Hebrew text: Ratzaby (Raṣahbi), J. "Lĕ-Tolēdot Yĕhude Kurdistan bam-Meʾah hak-kodemet" [On the history of Kurdish Jews in the preceding century]. *Sinai* 42 (1958): 371–77.[6]

---

1. *Building a Synagogue*

We built the first structure of the synagogue in the year 5553 (1793). A second structure was erected (added) in the year 5563 (1803). We began building it on the first day after the Passover holiday and finished it on the first day of the month of Tammuz (July). We had a ceremonial meal for the dedication of the synagogue on the first day of the blessed (month of) Tammuz. In charge of the construction were David Michael and I, the humble servant Jonah (ben) Gabriel. May the Lord guard us and keep us alive.

2. *Symbolic Purchase of the Town Area*

It should be recorded that on Passover of the year 5566 (1806), during the reign of Sultan Selīm,[7] may he be exalted, we purchased

3. See §7, below.

4. In only one instance does he resort to a mixture of Arabic and Hebrew; see Ratzaby, p. 377.

5. See end of §§3–6, below.

6. Ratzaby has published only selections from the original manuscript and has summarized other passages in his introductory remarks. The present translation includes only a few selected portions from this article. The passages concerning general political events that would be of little interest to the reader of this book are omitted here. In reply to my inquiry about the present whereabouts of the manuscript, Ratzaby said that he had borrowed it from its owner, a bookseller named L. Schwager, who has in the meantime passed away, and that he does not know where it is at present. Having had no access to the original manuscript, I owe most of my introduction and notes to the information contained in Ratzaby's article.

7. Selīm III, who reigned from 1789 to May 1807, when he was dethroned; cf. Ratzaby, p. 373, n. 1.

the town of Arbil from the high official[8] Ḥājjī Qāsim Āghā, in order to obtain the right of (symbolic) possession of the town, and thus to be able to move (our belongings) on the Sabbath day.[9] We did not[10] manage ⟨reach⟩ to purchase the town area during the reign of Sultan Muṣṭafā[11] because he reigned for (only) six months and then died. However, we purchased it once more during the reign of Sultan Maḥmūd,[12] may he be exalted, on Passover of the year 5569 (1809).

3. *The Plague of Hailstones*

The year 5573 (1813) was a leap year (in the Jewish calendar). On the twenty-fourth of Nisan, the Sabbath right after Passover, after midday, the skies became overcast and rain fell. Afterward it hailed for about half an hour. The hailstones were large and small, some as big as walnuts. However, a few people came forth afterward and claimed that they had seen hailstones as big as hens' eggs. Thereupon the floodwater surrounded the town wall and destroyed about three hundred houses — some say about four hundred — and killed some Gentiles. Some died indoors and others were carried away by the flood. The hailstones remained in the fields for about fifteen days. The Gentiles would bring them and sell them in the marketplace.[13] On that Sabbath, in the morning,[14] the governor's palace ⟨*sarāy*⟩ collapsed and about eight Gentiles died beneath it. Ten days later the Gentiles brought a hailstone (to town) and weighed it, and it weighed one *waqīyah* (about 1½ lbs.). Moreover, before the Passover a Jew (from another town) came forth and declared that in his town it had hailed (so heavily) that the hailstones killed several people, and that each hailstone that was

8. Hebrew *śar,* probably the local governor; cf. the source cited in the next note: *śar ha-ʿir,* "the town governor."

9. Such a symbolic purchase enabled the Jewish community to consider the entire town area as one domain for the purpose of moving their belongings from place to place on the Sabbath; see *Šulḥan ʿAruḵ, Oraḥ Ḥayyim,* Sabbath laws, 391. The purchase was renewed whenever a new ruler was installed.

10. Ratzaby reads *ʾgʾ*, "agha," followed by a question mark. This makes no sense and seems to be a misreading of *lʾ*, "not," which is required by the context.

11. Muṣṭafā IV, who succeeded Selīm III in 1807.

12. Maḥmud II, who came to the throne in 1808 and died in 1839.

13. Hailstones and snow were often stored by Kurdish villagers in cool pits in the mountains, to be sold to the townspeople in the summer for refrigeration.

14. The author has stated above that the rain began after midday (Hebrew *ḥăṣoṯ hay-yom*). The collapse of the palace would therefore seem to have been due to some other cause, perhaps an earthquake, rather than the flooding.

weighed came to one *ḥuqqah* (about 2¾ lbs.).[15] May it be (God's) will to have peace in the world. Amen, so be it.

4. *The Plague of Locusts*

In the year 5584 (1824) there was (so) much blessing and abundance in the world that one Arbil bushel[16] of wheat cost (only) one *akilej*[17] and a half. However, in the year 5585 (1825), (although) crops were good, locusts appeared but did not do much damage, except that one Arbil bushel now rose in price to eight akilej. In the year 5586 (1826) crops were also good, but (this time) locusts ate up half of the grain, and one Arbil bushel sold for twelve akilej. In the year 5587 (1827) there was little rain, crops were poor, and locusts ate up all the greenery in the fields. As a result, one Arbil bushel rose to sixty akilej, and the people in all the villages around Arbil fled (elsewhere). Some died of starvation, and some kept fleeing further on. The villages, with no people left in them, went to ruin. In the holy (Jewish) congregation of Arbil about two hundred Jews died — men, women, and children, having had nothing to eat. Horses and cattle died (as well). The Gentiles ate the flesh of (dead) donkeys, horses, dogs, and cats. People offered to sell their household belongings very cheaply but found no buyers. In the year 5588 (1828) the area surrounding Arbil was replanted, but one Arbil bushel (still) cost twenty-five akilej, for locusts remained active. However, they ate only some (of the crops) and left others (untouched), so that later on one Arbil bushel cost (only) eight akilej. May the Holy One, blessed be He, send us our righteous Messiah and resurrect our dead. Amen, so be it.

5. *The Plague of Pestilence*

In that year (1828) there was also a horrible pestilence (which spread) from the gates of Diyarbakir[18] to the gates of Qantara[19] and

15. Both *waqīyah* and *ḥuqqah* (or *uqqah*; Arabic-Turkish) are derived from the Latin *uncia,* "ounce."

16. The author uses the Arabic term *ʿulbah,* which means literally "vessel, case" but as a loanword in Neo-Aramaic it has the meaning "bushel"; cf. Maclean, *Dictionary,* p. 236. Since this measure of grain has several local varieties, the author carefully specifies each time "Arbil bushel," that is, the local measure, which was about 6½ dry liters; cf. Ratzaby, p. 375, nn. 31–32.

17. Probably a local coin; perhaps derived from the Turkish *akçe,* "coin, third of a *pārah,* money."

18. A town in southeastern Turkey, on the left bank of the Tigris River. On its Jewish community see Ben-Jacob, pp. 133–37.

19. The name of several localities in Syria.

carried away several thousand Gentiles, (so many) that they could not be counted. Also, from among the Jews (of Arbil) about a hundred and fifty died. The Jews fled to the villages, but even there some people died. In the year 5591 (1831) there was (another) pestilence in all the provinces as well as in Arbil. On the first day after Passover the (Jewish) community fled again to the villages and remained there for about three months, returning on the first day of the month of Tammuz. About seventy people from among the Jews died (this time). May the Holy One, blessed be He, deliver us from all kinds of misfortunes. Amen, so be it.

6. *The Pillar of Cloud*

In the year 5603 (1843), in the month of Second Adar, a white pillar shaped like a long cloud appeared (nightly in the sky), beginning with the first hour of the night. It would appear in the west and turn to the south, remain there for about two hours of the night, and then gradually diminish. The pillar appeared every night until the first night of Passover, but (afterward) did not appear again. Scripture says, *And be not dismayed at the signs of heaven* (Jer. 10:2). May the Holy One, blessed be He, send us our righteous Messiah and swiftly and soon resurrect our dead. Amen, so be it.

7. *On the Borrowing of Books*

An emissary from the Land of Israel, (named) Joseph Uzziel,[20] borrowed from me the book *Midrash Samuel,* the book *Beṯ Pereṣ,* and the book *The Joy of the Festival.*[21] He (promised that he) would send them back to me from (the town of) Kirkuk[22] or from Baghdad, but he never did.

20. He was an emissary from Jerusalem to the Arab countries, and was in Baghdad in March of 1859; see Ratzaby, p. 372, n. 4.

21. For details about these books see Ratzaby, p. 377, nn. 54–56.

22. A large town south of Arbil, with about 300 Jewish families in 1947; see Ben-Jacob, pp. 117–22.

XVII

Folktales

Abbreviations and References

Alfiyah, Meir. *Maśśa' Gey' Ḥizzayon.* Jerusalem, 5725 (1965).

AT — Thompson, Stith, and Aarne, Antti. *The Types of the Folktale: A Classification and Bibliography.* Helsinki, 1961. The classification numbers following the letters *AT* refer to the universal number of the tale type. Any classification letter added (by IFA) to the *AT* type index is indicated by an asterisk. *See also* Thompson.

Avitsuk, Jacob. *Ha-'Ilan šes-Safag̱ Dĕma'ot* [The tree that absorbed tears]. Haifa, 1965.

Baharav, Zalman. *Šiššim Sippure-'Am* [Sixty folktales]. Haifa, 1964.

IFA — Israel Folktale Archives

Marcus, Eliezer. *Min ham-Mabbu'a* [From the fountainhead]. Haifa, 1966.

Mizraḥi, Ḥaninah, *Bi-Yĕšišim Ḥoḵmah* [With elders is wisdom]. Haifa, 1967.

Motif. See Thompson.

Noy-Diaspora — Noy, Dov. *Golah wĕ-'Ereṣ Yiśra'el* [Diaspora and the Land of Israel]. Jerusalem, 1959.

Noy-Folktales — Noy, Dov. *Folktales of Israel.* Chicago, 1963.

Noy-Iraq — Noy, Dov. *Han-Na'ărah hay-Yĕfefiyyah u-Šĕlošeṯ Bĕne ham-Meleḵ* [The beautiful maiden and the three princes (120 Jewish-Iraqi folktales)]. Tel-Aviv, 1965.

Noy-JAT — Noy, Dov. *Sippure Ba'ăle Ḥayyim* [The Jewish animal tale in oral tradition]. Haifa, 1976.

Noy-Libya — Noy, Dov. *Šiḇ'im Sippurim wĕ-Sippur mip-Pi Yĕhuḏe Luḇ* [Seventy-one folktales of Libyan Jews]. Jerusalem, 1964, 1967.

Noy-Morocco — Noy, Dov. *Šiḇ'im Sippurim wĕ-Sippur mip-Pi Yĕhuḏe Maroko* [Seventy-one folktales of Moroccan Jews]. Jerusalem, 1964, 1967.

Noy-Schwili — Noy, Dov. *Jefet Schwili erzählt* (Yemenite-Jewish folktales). Berlin, 1963.

Noy-SMYK — Noy, Dov. *Sippurim mip-Pi Yĕhuḏe Kurdistan* [Folktales of the Jews of Kurdistan, in simple Hebrew]. Jerusalem, 5728 (1968).

Noy-Tunisia — Noy, Dov. *Šiḇ'im Sippurim wĕ-Sippur mip-pi Yĕhuḏe Tunisyah* [Seventy-one folktales of Tunisian Jews]. Jerusalem, 1966.

Stahl, Abraham. *'Eḏoṯ Mĕsappĕroṯ* (Folktales of various Jewish communities). Jerusalem, 1969.

TEM — *Ḥodeš Ḥodeš wĕ-Sippuro* [A tale for each month]:
TEM 1961. Edited by Dov Noy. Haifa, 1962.
TEM 1963. Edited by Z. Kagan. Haifa, 1964.
TEM 1964. Edited by Z. Kagan. Haifa, 1965.
TEM 1965. Edited by Dov Noy. Haifa, 1966.
TEM 1966. Edited by Dov Noy. Haifa, 1967.
TEM 1968–1969. Edited by E. Cheichel. Haifa, 1970.
TEM 1972. Edited by E. Cheichel. Haifa, 1973.
TEM 1974–1975. Edited by Dov Noy. Haifa, 1978.
Thompson, Stith. *Motif-Index of Folk-Literature*. 6 vols. Copenhagen and Bloomington, 1955–58.
Weinstein, E. *Sabta' 'Ester Mĕsapperet* [Grandma Esther's tales]. Haifa, 1964.

---

1. The Angel of Death and the Rabbi's Son

Hebrew text: *TEM 1965*, no. 3, pp. 25–26 (IFA 6441); notes, pp. 108 (Hebrew), 121 (English). Recorded by Rivka Ashkenazi from her father, Sasson Ashkenazi, born 1926 in Qaṣr-Shīrīn, Persian Kurdistan.
A combination of *AT* 934*F (IFA), "Charity saves from death," and *AT* 934*G (IFA), "Studying Torah changes fate of rabbi's son, who is to die on his wedding night." The influence of the Alcestis motif (*AT* 899) is evident. For IFA versions of these types see *Noy-Morocco*, nos. 12, 39, 69; Marcus, no. 35 (Persian Kurdistan); *Noy-SMYK*, no. 2. Cf. Gaster (1924), no. 139.

In a certain town there lived a rabbi who studied Torah day and night. He had only one son. One night the rabbi had a dream in which he saw the angel of death coming to his son in order to take away his soul. The rabbi woke up frightened but did not tell his dream to anyone.

One day an old man clad in rags appeared at the gate of the rabbi's house and announced to him, "I am the angel of death. I have come to take away the soul of your son, because he has reached the end of his life."

The rabbi was seized with fear and began thinking about how he could change this evil decree. Suddenly he thought of something and said to the angel of death, "My son is about to celebrate a festive occasion — the preparations for his wedding have already been made. Please do not blight his joy and the joy of my guests and of my family."

The angel of death replied, "Very well, I will take away your son's soul after the celebration"; and having said this, he departed.

The rabbi then hastened to make final arrangements for the wedding. He prepared delicious food and set the tables as in a royal palace. While he was busy with these preparations he met another old man who said to him, "I know that your son's soul is in danger and that the angel of death is about to return here. I would advise you, therefore, to gladden the angel's heart with wine and feed him delicious food. Perhaps he will then agree to let go of your son's soul."

The rabbi did as he was advised by this old man. He served delicious food to the angel of death and gave him choice wine to drink, and the angel of death truly enjoyed himself. At the end of the festive meal the angel approached the bridegroom and said to him, "Long ago I borrowed from a certain man some straw which I mixed with clay, and with it I built my house.[1] Now the man has come to me and demands that I return his straw. What shall I do?"

The bridegroom replied, "Buy some other straw and give it to the man instead of the straw you used." The angel of death said, "I too thought of doing that, but the man wants no other straw but his own." The bridegroom replied, "In that case you have no other choice but to demolish the house and return the original straw to its owner."

The angel of death then said, "The straw is nothing other than your soul. God demands it back and will not accept any substitute."[2] "If so," pleaded the bridegroom, "give me time to take leave of my bride and my family."

When the bridegroom's family heard of this evil decree, they began weeping and imploring God for mercy. Thereupon the bride came out to the angel of death and said to him, "According to the Torah, a bridegroom may not be sent to battle to face death before the end of one joyous year after his wedding."[3]

1. Mixing straw with clay in order to make better building material was the most common method of construction in Kurdistan. For this and other details about Jewish houses in Kurdistan see Brauer, pp. 56–63.

2. For the comparison of the human body to a house in Midrashic sources (e.g., Exod. Rabbah 4) see *TEM 1965*, p. 108. The tactic used by the angel of death is similar to the one used by the prophet Nathan against David (2 Sam. 12:1–6). For other Biblical as well as Islamic parallels see Schwarzbaum, p. 137.

3. Cf. Deut. 24:5.

Having heard her words, the angel of death decided to seek advice from God. He went up to heaven, and behold, two angels were standing before the divine throne and pleading for mercy for the rabbi's son.[4] When God saw that the young man was a righteous person who deserved joy and happiness after his wedding, He changed the decree against him and relieved the angel of death from his duty.

The rabbi's son and his wife lived on for many years thereafter in joy and happiness.

2. The Jewish Cobbler and the Kurdish Robber

Hebrew text: *TEM 1963*, no. 1, pp. 12–16 (IFA 4825); notes, pp. 82 (Hebrew), 100 (English). Recorded by Z. Baharav from Jacob Tshaprak, the son of a cobbler, born 1896 in Bashkala, Turkish Kurdistan. Thompson, *Motif-Index* N 705*, P 475.2. For a similar deed of courage see *Noy-Diaspora,* no. 1. Cf. Baharav, no. 50; *Noy-SMYK,* no. 3 (notes, p. 56).

In the town of Diyarbakir, on the border of Turkey and Iran,[5] there was a large Jewish community from time immemorial. Many of them were craftsmen — tailors, shoemakers, and tanners who tanned leather for coats. There were among them also merchants, who supplied clothing and shoes to the Kurdish farmers and tribes who lived in the remote mountains. The Jewish cobblers wandered from one village to another, repairing the villagers' shoes and receiving in exchange rice, lamb's wool, goat's hair, pine tree resin to be used for lighting at night, and similar necessary items.

One day, in the months of Tammuz-Ab (July–August), a group of cobblers working for the merchant Jacob ben Ḥawwah[6] were sent out to the villages, where they worked and slept as well. The members of the group kept working for about ten days, until their working materials were exhausted and they did not have any leather

4. This and other details in the story are reminiscent of the legends about the angel of death in Jewish and Islamic sources; cf. Schwarzbaum, pp. 53, 281–318.

5. An error for Syria; cf. the end of the story, where the Syrian border is mentioned. On Diyarbakir and its old Jewish community see Ben-Jacob, pp. 133–37.

6. Eve, his mother's name. People were usually known by their father's name (as a surname), but when the father died early the mother's name was used instead; cf. Sabar (1974b), p. 47.

left to sew. The merchant Jacob gave his workers a list of goods and sent them back to the town to fetch more untanned cowhides, which are good for soles, and other kinds of leather as well as a variety of haberdashery.

After the cobblers had bought what they needed, they soaked the hides in water, dried them, put them in bags, loaded the bags onto seven donkeys, and set out on their way back to the villages. The small caravan, which consisted of only five Jews, proceeded slowly along the mountain paths toward its destination. At sunset the five men encamped by a spring. Since in these mountains there were dark caves where wild beasts lived — wolves, bears, and foxes — the five Jews maintained a watch during the night, each man doing one shift in turn.

At midnight it was the turn of Jacob, the apprentice, to stand guard. He was the youngest in the group, but none was as courageous as he. As he walked around the camp, watching the sleeping men and the donkeys tied to the men's feet to ensure that the beasts would not be stolen or run away, he suddenly saw some glittering lights coming toward him and recognized them as the eyes of a wolf. Indeed, soon after he saw many such lights, all of them eyes of wolves searching for prey. What did Jacob do? With the help of his cigarette lighter and a wick he made a bonfire, and the wolves, frightened by the fire, disappeared in the direction from which they had come.

The next day, at noontime, when the sun was beating down on their heads, the five men decided to set up camp in the shade of some trees. As they sat eating, after having fed their animals a mixture of grass and grain, they suddenly saw a tall figure approaching them. It was a Kurd, wearing cartridge belts and holding a rifle in his hand. The Kurd greeted the men and then asked Jacob, who was smoking a cigarette, for some tobacco, so that he could roll a cigarette for himself. Jacob handed him his tobacco pouch and his cigarette lighter, but the Kurd, without saying a word, put them in the pocket of his coat.

When Jacob saw the Kurd behaving in this way, he immediately became wary of him and said to his friends in Arabic,[7] so that the

7. In an abridged version (*Noy-SMYK,* p. 21) the language is (Neo-)Aramaic. Perhaps *'arb̠iṯ,* "Arabic," is a misprint for *'ib̠riṯ,* "Hebrew," since Hebrew, rather than Arabic, was used by the Kurdistani Jews as their private language in dealing with Gentiles; cf. Sabar

Kurd would not understand, "Let us take the rifle of this Gentile away from him because his intentions are evil — he surely intends to kill us, because he has noticed that we are Jews whose blood is *hefḳer* (abandoned property). We must, therefore, act before he does, and right now!"

The other four men, whom Jacob was calling to action and who had wives and young children at home, remained standing in their places, fearful and trembling, and did not respond to his call. Nevertheless, Jacob the apprentice did not give up his idea. He watched the Kurd "with seven eyes" (i.e., very closely) in order to anticipate his evil intentions, and finally, all by himself, without any help from his friends who stood aside, he took advantage of the moment when the Kurd bent down to get a drink of water from the spring. He leaped up from his place, brought his foot down on the Kurd's right hand, and seized his rifle with his own strong hands.

Without giving the Kurd a chance to stand up, Jacob loaded the gun with cartridges and pressed lightly on the trigger. Then he ordered the Kurdish robber to return the tobacco pouch and the cigarette lighter and to surrender all the cartridge belts. The Kurd handed over all his belongings to Jacob, realizing that the young Jew was not merely trying to be clever and might pull the trigger at any moment.

Then Jacob motioned to his friends to tie the Kurd up with ropes. They tied him securely to one of the donkeys, so that he would be unable to free himself. Then all five loaded their goods onto the donkeys and went on to climb the mountain path, while the Kurd followed the donkey and Jacob guarded him with the rifle in his hand.

Near the first village on their way they met an old woman, and when she saw the Kurdish robber, she shouted, "Behold the notorious murderer, who has already shed much innocent blood of villagers and tribesmen and has stolen the best of our property!"

When the caravan reached the top of the mountain, Jacob fired three shots into the air, whereupon twenty-five horsemen emerged from a tribal tent camp in the area. They were greatly astonished to see the prisoner of the Jews. They immediately called the tribal chief ʿAbd al-Qādir, who invited the entire group into his stone house.

(1974a), p. 216. However, Arabic was commonly spoken by the Jews of Diyarbakir, as well as Neo-Aramaic, Kurdish, and Turkish; see Ben-Jacob, p. 136.

Sheikh Sulaymān, a tribal elder and brother of ʿAbd al-Qādir, blessed God for turning the Kurdish robber over to the Jews and said to Jacob, "You and your friends were saved from great trouble."

The Kurdish robber kissed the hands of ʿAbd al-Qādir and his brother Sulaymān, but this self-humiliation proved of no avail to him. The tribesmen knew that this was the robber who had stolen their horses several days before. They flogged him with a whip until he admitted the theft and revealed to them where he had hidden the horses.

In the evening, bonfires were lit on the mountains to inform all the villagers in the region that the famous marauder had been captured. The next day the family members and the tribal chiefs of the Kurdish robber arrived at the tent camp to redeem him. The tribesmen flatly refused to free him before he had a trial according to the tribal rules of Kurdistan. When the negotiations to redeem the prisoner brought no results, the chiefs of the robber's tribe declared war against the tribe of ʿAbd al-Qādir. The battle went on for three whole days without a decisive victory by either side.

On the fourth day Ẓafrullāh Shāh, the grand sheikh of Kurdistan, who considered himself a descendant of the prophet Muḥammad, arrived at the place, holding in his hand a white flag as a sign that it was time to end the conflict and make peace between the two fighting camps. Both sides stopped the battle, during which the robber had been kept the whole time under heavy guard, with his hands and feet tied.

By the order of the grand sheikh all the tribal chiefs and sheikhs in that great mountainous area gathered in the tent camp of ʿAbd al-Qādir. Then the grand sheikh spoke in a loud voice, saying, "First, let us thank the Jew who overpowered the robber and turned him over to us." Then he ordered the marauder to be brought before him and asked him, "Why do you lurk in ambush, seize travelers, and shed innocent blood?" The marauder replied, "That is the way I make a living." The sheikh went on, "Do you call stealing things like a cigarette lighter and tobacco making a living? This is the despicable doing of common thieves and not of mountain brigands."

The sheikh then ruled that the marauder should be hanged and his tribe expelled beyond the Syrian border, and this was done after the rifles and the horses that he had stolen from the tribe of ʿAbd al-Qādir were returned.

As the grand sheikh Ẓafrullāh Khān was about to leave, he

blessed Jacob the apprentice, gave him many gifts, and said to him, "The prophet Moses forbade the Jews to kill.[8] You did well therefore that you did not kill the robber with your own hands but brought him to the tent camp, where he was sentenced by tribal law."

3. By Virtue of a Single Good Deed

Hebrew text: *TEM 1964,* no. 4, pp. 33–34 (IFA 5804); notes, pp. 92 (Hebrew), 104 (English). Recorded by Raḥamim Ḥakīmzādeh from his father, Sulaymān, born in Kermanshah, Persian Kurdistan. *AT* 809*–*A, "The single good deed — The companion in Paradise." Cf. Marcus, no. 20; *Noy-SMYK,* no. 7 (notes, pp. 58–59); Weinstein, no. 14 (several old Jewish sources are mentioned in the notes, p. 79); Gaster (1924), nos. 323, 413a, 413b.

There was once a wicked man who caused trouble to many people. Eventually he died and his soul ascended to heaven for trial before God. There, at the heavenly court, he was questioned about his deeds, and when it was ascertained that he had committed many sins, crimes, and iniquities, he was condemned to hell-fire.

When the wicked man heard the verdict, he pleaded, "No one has ever taught me the good way. If you will give me back my soul and return me to life, I will not be wicked or sin anymore." God accepted the plea of the wicked man and gave him back his soul, but the man did not change his ways, and his deeds were even more evil than before.

Once more his time came to die, once again he was brought before the heavenly court, and once more he was condemned to hell-fire. This time, too, the wicked man begged and entreated, "Please let me live a few years more. I promise that I will behave like a righteous man."

For a second time his soul was returned to him, but when he came back to life he persevered in his wickedness and committed even more crimes. Once, however, in his two lives, he did do a good deed. When it was again his time to die, on that same day a very righteous man also died. Both men, the righteous and the wicked, ascended to heaven to be judged before the heavenly court.

8. Probably referring to the Biblical commandment *Thou shalt not murder* (Exod. 20:13).

The wicked man was found to have committed many iniquities but also one good deed, while the righteous man was found to have performed only good deeds except for one small sin. It was decided to send the wicked man to paradise for only one hour, and then to transfer him to his permanent place in hell. As for the righteous man, it was decided to send him to hell for only one hour, and then to transfer him to paradise.

The righteous man was very grieved about this one hour in hell, and when the wicked man saw how the righteous man was grieving and weeping, he appealed to the heavenly court, saying, "I am willing to give up my one hour in paradise and grant it to this righteous man, so that he might go there directly."

When God saw this good act on the part of the wicked man and his readiness to give up his one hour in paradise, He forgave him all his sins. Thus both men, the righteous and the wicked, inherited the bliss of paradise.

4. The Old Man's Treasure

Hebrew text: *TEM 1968–1969*, no. 17, pp. 119–20 (IFA 8244); notes, pp. 162 (Hebrew), 286–87 (English). Recorded by Ziona Cohen from her father, Abraham M. Mizraḥi, born in Jazīrah, Turkish Kurdistan. Motif D 1812.3.3, "The prophetic dream," is the main motif in many Jewish legends, wherein the hero is supernaturally advised to "ascend" with his family to the Land of Israel. The end of this tale is derived from Motif N 521, "The treasure in the stick."

There lived once in Syria an old, wealthy Jewish man who had many sons and daughters, grandchildren, and great-grandchildren. One day he arose and appealed to his children, saying, "Let us arise and go up to Zion, to the holy city of Jerusalem."

His children looked at him in great amazement and asked him, "Father dear, why should we go up to Zion, when the Jews, wheresoever they live, still have no real home,[9] whereas we, thank God, live a very good life here? So far we have not lacked for anything. You worked all your life — do you want now

9. Probably meaning political independence; cf. below, the end of this paragraph. The time of the story seems to be the 1940s, before the establishment of the state of Israel. For similar IFA stories see *TEM 1968–1969*, pp. 162, 286–87.

to lose everything that you have here? Surely you know that we cannot take our money and property out of this country, for all the roads to Zion are swarming with robbers and marauders. No, we cannot get out of this country without spending all our possessions as ransom in the various places which we will have to pass. And what will happen when we arrive in Zion? We have nothing there, not even a state."

The wealthy father, however, remained quite stubborn and said, "Rabbi Meir the miracle worker appeared to me in a dream, saying, 'Go up to Zion, for there is your right place.'" When the family members heard these words from the old man, who was already one hundred and six years old, they all, with their babes and wives, arose and packed their belongings, secreting in them as much money and precious objects as they could, and set out on their way to Zion.

The roads on which they traveled swarmed with brigands, and they had no choice but to pay ransom, since they were primarily concerned with arriving safely. Indeed, when they (finally) arrived in Zion, nothing was left of their wealth. They immediately went to Tiberias to visit the shrine of Rabbi Meir the miracle worker. As they looked for a place, an inn or a house, in which to spend the night, the old man announced, "My place is next to the shrine, under the canopy of heaven. Here I shall sleep, and nowhere else."

His children, not wanting their old father to sleep outdoors, begged him not to do so, but to no avail. He remained stubborn and stayed there to sleep next to the shrine, and Rabbi Meir the miracle worker appeared to him in a dream, saying to him, "You are a good man, and you have fulfilled my commands. Tell me now what you are in need of, and I shall help you."

The old man replied, "O Rabbi Meir the miracle worker, I gave away all my wealth as ransom on my way here, and now I am destitute." Rabbi Meir replied, "Buy some garlic and plant it, and you shall make a living out of it."

The old man again did just as Rabbi Meir advised him. He bought some garlic and planted it on the parcel of land next to his house. As the garlic grew, it was blessed with abundance and flourished unendingly. The more it was plucked and sold the more it increased. The old man sold the garlic and became very wealthy once more.[10]

10. Garlic as the source of wealth (by turning into gold) appears also in tale 27, below.

He was very happy with his lot, and gave away much to charity. He kept his wealth in his walking cane, so that no one knew what happened to his wealth and where it was hidden. When in due time he returned his soul to his Creator, at the age of one hundred and thirty-five, the cane split apart, for it could not bear its sorrow at its master's death. Only then did his family members find out where their father's treasure was hidden, and they rejoiced greatly.

5. The Poor Man's Trust in God

Hebrew text: *TEM 1966*, no. 8, pp. 57–60 (IFA 7315); notes, pp. 106–07 (Hebrew), 133–34 (English). Recorded by Ziona Cohen from her maternal uncle Mordecai Mizraḥi, a native of Turkish Kurdistan. Combination of two types: *AT* 1645 *B, "God takes care of all (Donkey of lazy man who trusts in God brings treasure)," and *AT* 763, "Those who find the treasure kill each other." IFA has 12 versions of *AT* 1645 *B; cf. *Noy-Schwili*, no. 146 (Yemen); *TEM 1964*, no. 7 (Iraqi Kurdistan); Baharav, no. 9 (Iraq); Marcus, no. 44 (Persia); and 8 versions of *AT* 763; cf. *TEM 1961*, no. 3 (Yemen); Marcus, no. 6 (Persian Kurdistan); Mizraḥi, no. 3 (Persia). For this motif in old Jewish, Christian, and Islamic sources see Bin Gorion, *3*, 1317, "The inheritance of the wicked" (references on p. 1528): Schwarzbaum, pp. 249 ff.

There was once a poor man who had twelve sons and daughters. He also had a donkey. Every day he went with his donkey to work, laboring from morning to evening. Still, he earned hardly enough money to sustain his family.

In the evening, as he returned from work with his donkey, he used to see a shepherd taking his sheep out to pasture. The poor man would stop and look at the herd and then go on home.

One day the poor man looked at the herd longer than usual. And what did he see? All of a sudden, one of the sheep left the herd and disappeared over the horizon. He decided to pay special attention to this matter the next day as well, and once again the same thing happened: while the shepherd was not watching, one of the sheep left the herd and disappeared.

At this the poor man said, "I shall follow this sheep and see whither it disappears." The next day, as another sheep left the herd, the poor man followed it. And what did he see? The sheep entered a cave and disappeared there. What did the poor man do now? He came close to the cave and peeked inside. And what did his eyes see? A big crippled bear, which had only its hind legs, standing on them and eating the sheep.[11]

The poor man grew very angry and called out to heaven, "Lord of the universe, how is it that Thou takest care of this bear and providest for it so that it receives its meals without making any effort? And how is it that I have to work from morning till evening, and yet I can hardly support my family? I do not receive *my* meals. No more! From now on I shall not go out to work."

The poor man returned home and told his wife all that he had seen, adding, "Wife, from this day on I shall not go out to work." His wife waxed very angry and began shouting at him, "Have you gone out of your mind? How can you stay home when we have nothing to eat?" The poor man replied, "The crippled bear gets all its necessities for free. I too want everything for myself to be free, ready and prepared."

The next morning, two friends of the poor man went out to their regular job, uprooting trees and clearing away rocks in the field. They approached the nearest tree and pulled at it until it was uprooted, although not at the ground level like other trees but at the lower part of the trunk. And what did they see? A great treasure of silver and gold. What were they to do now? They consulted each other at length and finally decided to hire a donkey or a horse to transport the treasure, and also to buy some food to eat in the meantime.

It was difficult to find a donkey or a horse for hire at that time of the day, since all were at work. But they remembered that the poor man's donkey was free and ready for hiring, since its owner had not gone out to work that day. So one of the two friends came to the poor man's house and knocked on the door. The poor man agreed to hire out his donkey, but he asked no less than one hundred dinars for it.

The friend agreed, and the poor man was so happy that he danced with joy, saying to his wife, "Do you see? I regret now that I have

11. That God provides for all creatures, not forgetting even the smallest of all, is a common theme in old Jewish (including Falasha) and Islamic literature. Cf. Ps. 145:9, *The Lord is good to all, and His tender mercies are over all His works;* B. Shab 107b: "The Holy One, blessed be He, feeds all the [creatures in the] world, from the horns of the wild ox to the eggs of lice." In Islamic and Falasha legends about the death of Moses he is worried that after his death his children will have no one to provide for them. God shows him a rock at the bottom of the sea inside of which there is a tiny red worm holding a green leaf in its mouth and saying, "Praise and glory be to Him who does not forget me, who am sunk in such a desolate and lonely place." See Schwarzbaum, pp. 47–48, 304–18, for this and other references; cf. Leslau, p. 111.

worked so hard all these years." He ran to the marketplace and bought many delicious foods that he had never eaten before, and having spent all his money he returned home.

And what did the friends do? The one who had hired the donkey went with it until he reached a restaurant, where he bought *pita*-bread filled with lots of meat, one portion for himself and another for his friend. But suddenly he thought in his heart, "Why should I divide the treasure with my friend? It is better to get rid of him and keep all the money for myself." What did he do? He bought some poison, sprinkled it on his friend's food, and set out on his way.

At the same time the other friend, who had stayed to watch the treasure, thought, "Why should I divide the treasure with my friend? It is better that I keep all of it." What did he do? He dug a pit in the ground, stuck a sharp pole in it, and covered the pit with straw and tree branches. Then he sat down in his place and waited as if nothing had happened.

The friend with the donkey arrived at the place and gave his friend his portion of the food, but while doing this he fell into the pit, was impaled on the sharp pole, and died. The other friend, now alone, felt happy and thought to himself, "Behold, I now have all the money. First I shall sit and eat, and then I shall continue on my way." What did he do? He took the first portion of the food, which belonged to his dead friend, and ate all of it. Then he loaded the treasure onto the donkey.

Having finished loading, he ate the portion that was intended for himself, that is to say, the poisoned one, and forthwith fell to his knees and died. As for the donkey, it stood there, loaded and ready to go, and waited for a long time. In the evening it was still waiting there, hungry and shivering from the cold.

Meanwhile at the house of the poor man, husband and wife were arguing, the wife shouting, "Look what you've done! Even the donkey has now gone and disappeared. What will we do now?" In reply the husband tried to explain to his wife, "Wait patiently. What does the proverb say? *The ass knoweth his master's crib*"[12] (Isa. 1:3).

Suddenly they heard a noise outside. It was the donkey, which had found its way home and was now knocking at the door. The poor man opened the door and wondered how the donkey had come

12. Which is filled with fodder.

home by itself. As the donkey entered, it bumped against a wall and the bag on its back split open. What did they see? Gold and silver coins, a precious and great treasure.

The poor man turned to his wife, saying, "Wife, do you see? Just as God sent the sheep to the bear, so did He send sustenance for me. And all this is because of my trust in God."[13]

6. The Unfortunate Shoemaker

Hebrew text: Baharav, no. 46, pp. 209–11 (IFA 4566); notes, pp. 262 (Hebrew),[14] 278 (English). Recorded by Z. Baharav from Jacob Tshaprak, a native of Turkish Kurdistan. *AT* 947 *A: "Unfortunate person remains unfortunate forever." Ten other versions have been recorded by IFA from Turkey, Palestine (3), Yemen (*Noy-Schwili,* no. 105), Iraq (3), and eastern Europe (2).

A poor shoemaker worked day and night yet could not support his wife and his many children. Since he was a very proud and self-respecting man, it mattered not to him what people said about him. Whenever someone asked him "What do you and your family eat?" he would reply boastfully, "My economic condition is strong, my income is secure, and I have no worries."

The shoemaker and his family lived in a dark basement, his children were clad in rags, and in his house there was not even one penny to buy the food his children needed.

One night the sultan, poorly dressed and disguised as a beggar, passed nearby and met the shoemaker. He asked him, "How is your condition? What do you do to support yourself?" "Praised be the Lord," replied the shoemaker, "God provides everyone with his necessities. There are no poor people at all in this town. Everyone lives in a home, enjoys the fruit of his labor, and is content with what he has. And whosoever is content with what he has is a wealthy man."[15]

13. Ziona Cohen, who recorded this tale, adds the following remark: "This is a true story that happened in Jazīrah [her parents' hometown], a village in Turkish Kurdistan [see Ben-Jacob, p. 131]. . . . By the way, I too came from a large family including twelve brothers and sisters, and my father had a pair of donkeys and could hardly support us. However, in contrast to what is told in this story, my father did not stop working, for he did not find any treasure . . . until we grew up and began helping him" (*TEM 1966,* p. 107).

14. See the introduction to tale 2, above.

15. Cf. 'Ab̲ 4:1.

The disguised sultan entered the basement where the shoemaker's family lived, and behold, he saw naked babes lying on the cold, bare floor, and on the table there was not even one crumb of bread. He then turned to the shoemaker's wife, revealed to her who he was, and asked her to send her husband to his palace, adding, "I shall find a way to help him in his distress."

The next day the poor shoemaker put on his clothes, after his wife had mended the patches all night, and appeared before the sultan, who was then sitting in his audience chamber. After a short conversation, the benevolent ruler gave him a fat hen stuffed with two hundred gold dinars.

The shoemaker, of course, did not know about this treasure. When he passed through the corridor, he met the chief butler of the palace who served meals to the sultan every day. The butler asked the shoemaker, "Would you care to sell this hen to me?" The shoemaker, knowing he had nothing else to eat with the hen, agreed to sell it, and the butler gave him two dinars in exchange for it.

The shoemaker thereupon returned home cheerful and happy, and gave the money to his wife, who bought with it some necessary food. They all ate until they were full and blessed the sultan and the Lord. However, at the end of the meal he and his family were again poor, just as they had been before.

Several days later the shoemaker went once more to the sultan, for his wife would not let him rest and pressed him, saying, "Go back to your benefactor and ask for his help." This time the sultan gave the shoemaker a fattened duck with four hundred gold dinars stuffed in its stomach. Once again the poor shoemaker, as he walked upon the big carpet in the corridor, met the butler who had bought the hen several days before, and after a short conversation he sold the duck to the butler for four gold dinars.

As he passed the marketplace, he bought with the money some necessary food that would suffice to nourish his family for a whole week. At the end of the week the shoemaker's wife pressed her husband again to go to the palace. Again he stood before the sultan. This time the shoemaker received from his benefactor a fattened turkey, containing six hundred gold dinars. As he walked bent down under the heavy load, the butler came toward him and asked him to sell the heavy fowl for six dinars.

The shoemaker received the money, bought the necessary food

in the marketplace, and his family lived on it for two weeks. They blessed the Lord and the sultan for this kind deed.

Now, they knew that there was no hope of benefiting from the blessed and generous hand of their benefactor more than three times. When the last bread crumb in the house was gone, the shoemaker's wife sent her husband out to look for his fortune somewhere else.

The shoemaker walked for days and weeks, until he reached a spacious field in which there were deserted wells with a pump attached to each well. The people he met there explained it to him thus: "These wells are the fortunes of human beings. A person's name is written on each pump. You may get closer to them, but if you see a pump in operation you must not touch it."

The shoemaker came closer to the wells and searched diligently until he found his name written on one of them. Behold, only a few drops were dripping from the pump, and it was almost dry. The shoemaker tried to fix the pump to get more water flowing through it, but the result was the opposite — the water stopped flowing altogether. When he asked about the meaning of this, the people explained it to him thus: "This well is your fortune. When you touched the pump while it was operating, your well of fortune dried up." So the shoemaker returned in despair home to his wife and children.

The shoemaker's wife, a woman of valor, now went herself to the sultan's palace. When the sultan peeked through the window, he saw her and immediately sent his servant to bring her in. When she complained about their bad luck, he indignantly demanded to know what her husband had done with the fowls that he had received from him, and the wife told him all that had happened to them. The sultan immediately summoned the butler and ordered him to return to the shoemaker all the gold dinars that he had found inside the fowls.

The butler did so, but as the shoemaker, loaded with the great treasure, was going down the staircase of the palace, he suddenly collapsed and fell to the ground. By the time people came up to see what had happened, he was dead.

One of the shoemaker's hands was tightly clenched, and none of the servants was able to open it; but then the sultan himself came along and succeeded in unclenching it. In it he found a piece of parchment upon which was written, "One cannot change the fate of a person born without luck."[16]

7. The Happy Carpenter[17]

Hebrew text: Avitsuk, no. 16, pp. 62–65 (IFA 3943); notes, pp. 161 (Hebrew), 179–80 (English).[18] Recorded by J. Avitsuk from Mordecai Joseph, born 1919 in Kirkuk, Iraqi Kurdistan, who in turn heard it from his mother, born in Tbilisi (Tiflis), Georgia (Transcaucasia), who spoke Neo-Aramaic, Turkish, and Russian. The motif of the wily old woman (K 2293) is combined with the motif of the disguised king and his vizier (K 1812, N 467, P 14.19), who examine the true nature of their subjects (H 500).

One day the king and his counselor went hunting. On their way they passed the town market and observed the people there. Behold, they saw a carpenter sitting quite calmly, with his legs crossed, and shaving his head with a very sharp ax while at the same time doing his regular work. The king and his counselor watched the carpenter very carefully and saw that he was indeed shaving his head without hurting himself[19] with the sharp ax.

The king said, "This carpenter must be an excellent craftsman — look how he does not hurt himself." The counselor replied, "No, he is not a superior carpenter. He does not hurt himself because he is always content, cheerful, and happy. If he were discontented and unhappy, he would certainly hurt himself." But the king did not agree with the counselor.

At nighttime they returned from hunting, but the carpenter was still on their minds. The next day the counselor went back to the marketplace and saw the carpenter again sitting and shaving his head with the sharp ax. He asked some people, "Where does this

16. A rhyme in the original Hebrew:

אין לשנות הגורל
לאדם שנולד בלי מזל.

17. The original title in Hebrew is "(Right) on the Hair."

18. An abridged Hebrew version in *Noy-SMYK*, no. 4, pp. 26–31; notes, p. 57, entitled "By Virtue of Domestic Peace."

19. In the original Hebrew the words "head," "foot," and "body," are used interchangeably. In the translation I have retained "head" or "himself" for the sake of consistency.

carpenter live?", and when they gave him the address he hired an old woman to go to the carpenter's house and incite his wife against him.

The old woman went to the happy carpenter's house and knocked on the door. A voice from inside asked, "Who is there?", and the old woman replied, "I want to ask you something." As the carpenter's wife opened the door, the old woman noticed that the house was orderly, clean, and well kept, and that the wife was comely and was just then cooking some delicious dishes. The old woman realized that the carpenter loved his wife and that she in turn loved him.

Then the old woman asked, "Where is your husband?" "He is now in the marketplace," replied the wife; "in the evening he comes home with his day's earnings, and we both are glad and happy." "When does he come home?", asked the old woman. "In the evening," was the reply. "You should know," whispered the old woman, "that your husband goes to . . . I really should not tell you anything, but well, not everything is as it seems."

The carpenter's wife saw that the old woman was trying to say something but instead mumbled and hesitated. She therefore pressed her, "You must tell me everything. Where does he go? Where does my husband go?" The old woman made it seem as if she had a deep secret to tell her and continued mumbling, "I saw him once or twice entering some house; but I really am telling you nothing. No, I refuse to tell you. Why should I ruin your life?"

At this the carpenter's wife said bitterly, "Now I know why he always comes home happy, singing, and cheerful. Let him come home this evening — he will get what he deserves." The old woman asked the wife not to tell her husband who had revealed his secret, and she promised to keep it to herself.

In the evening the carpenter knocked on the door of his home, but no one answered; he knocked again and again, but there was no response. "What has happened to my wife?" he asked himself, "she always comes out quickly when she hears my knock on the door, and opens it affectionately. We both sing as we eat the already prepared meal, and are happy. But now, what is happening here?"

He knocked again and again, and finally, extremely worried about his wife, he split the door with the ax and entered his home. What did he see? His wife was lying in bed, fully dressed, weeping and sobbing. Frightened, the carpenter asked her, "Wife, what has happened to you? Why are you crying?"

The wife jumped up from the bed and screamed at him, "You still dare to ask why I cry? You go to another woman, and then you come back to me to eat and drink and make fun of me? Get out of here! Get out this instant!"

"What has happened to you, wife?" asked the astonished husband, but the wife continued screaming, "Do you think that I do not know that you have another woman, and that you visit her daily? Get out of my house!" The carpenter departed and walked aimlessly in the streets all night, weeping and grieving.

The next day he arrived as usual at the marketplace and again began shaving his hair with his sharp ax. The king and his counselor now saw him sitting and weeping, with copious blood running down from him, and without noticing that he was hurting himself. The counselor said to the king, "Do you see, O king, my master? I told you that the man is not a very skilled carpenter. When his heart is glad and contented, he works so well that he does not hurt himself with the ax. But now that his heart is sad and pained, he fails to do so."

The king asked the counselor, "How do you know this?", and the counselor explained how he had hired the old woman and why the carpenter was weeping. The king then ordered the counselor, "Tell the old woman to go back right now to the carpenter's house and restore peace therein."

So the old woman went to the carpenter's house, told the wife the truth, and there was again peace between husband and wife. Once more the carpenter sat in the marketplace and shaved his head with the sharp ax without hurting himself. His mouth was again full with songs and hymns, and his heart was contented and happy.[20]

8. The Luck of a Child

Hebrew text: Avitsuk, no. 20, pp. 80–81 (IFA 2556); notes, pp. 163–64 (Hebrew), 178–79 (English). Recorded by J. Avitsuk from Sasson Joseph, born 1910 in Merivan,[21] Iraqi Kurdistan. He told the tale in "Kurdish" (probably meaning Neo-Aramaic), and his sons translated it into Hebrew.

20. That a man's success and well-being depend on his wife is a common motif in folk literature; cf. Gen. Rabbah 17 about the wicked wife who turned her pious husband into a wicked man, and the pious wife who turned her wicked husband into a pious man, because "all depends on the wife." See chap. XX, proverb 258, below; Mizraḥi, note to tale no. 25.

21. "An Arab village with only five Jewish families" (Avitsuk, p. 179). No locality with this exact spelling is mentioned in Ben-Jacob. Perhaps the same as Mirava, where "in recent times there were a few Jews who worked in agriculture" (Ben-Jacob, p. 116).

The beginning of the tale is derived from the aggadic motif about the prophet Elijah, who appeared before Rabbi ʿAḳiba and his wife; see B. Nĕḏ 50a. Cf. the brief Neo-Aramaic version with English translation in Garbell, pp. 117–18. See chap. IX, n. 1, above. However, the turning of the straw into gold as a reward for a good deed (motif D 475.1.20) occurs only in this version.

Once upon a time there lived a husband and wife who were very poor and had nothing at all in their house. The wife, who was pregnant, gave birth to a son at ten o'clock at night, but she had nothing with which to wrap the tender babe. The poor father groaned and cried, "We have no clothes, not even some wool, to cover the babe, and he may die by morning."

Suddenly a man appeared, stood at the entrance to the room, and said, "Peace be upon you! Do you have some straw to lend me? My wife has just given birth, and we have nothing to lay the child on. He may die of the cold." The couple replied, "We are very poor, but we do have some straw. If you want it, please take it."

The man took his cloak,[22] filled it with straw, thanked the couple, and went off. As he stepped outside he threw the straw down next to the door, but the couple did not notice.

After the stranger had left, the husband said to his wife, "Look how rich we are! There are people who do not have even straw, and we are rich compared with them."

In the morning the husband got up, went outside, and found there many silver and gold dinars. He called his wife and said to her, "Look how much silver and gold we have behind the door!" They realized then that the man who came at night to ask for straw was none other than the prophet Elijah, of blessed memory, and that the straw had turned into silver and gold.

The husband went to the marketplace and bought the necessities for his home, and the rest of the money he hid away in a vessel, saying to his wife, "Let us flee from this town, for its people are wicked and jealous. If they learn that we have become rich, they will slay us."

So they fled to a town where no one knew them, and there they

22. The Hebrew word is *ṭalliṯ*, "prayer shawl" or "cloak."

asked, "Is it possible to build here a fine, good house?" A man replied, "I have such a fine, good house. If you like it, well and good; if not, do not buy it."

The couple decided to buy the house. In the evening they went to look at it. As they walked through the rooms, they noticed a bulge in one of the walls. The wife touched it with her finger, and behold, the stone moved from its place and revealed an opening in the wall full of silver and gold. The husband said to his wife, "Look, God has granted us even more than before."

The next day the couple were about to talk to the landlord, but he said to them, "I am the same man to whom you gave straw, and I changed it into gold. That gold was the good luck of your son. This house is your[23] own good luck, and the bulge in the wall is your wife's good luck. May you live in happiness and good fortune — please know that I, the prophet Elijah, am blessing you." Having finished his statement, the prophet Elijah ascended in flight to heaven.

9. One Gram More, One Gram Less

Hebrew text: Marcus, no. 14, pp. 68–69 (IFA 4839); notes, pp. 167 (Hebrew), 206 (English). The Hebrew text is a combination of four types, of which only the first two are retained in this translation. Recorded by Jonathan Danieli from his mother Śimḥah, born 1918 in Sanandaj,[24] Persian Kurdistan.

AT 920*E(IFA): "King learns from children playing in the courtyard how to solve complicated judicial problem." IFA has recorded 11 versions; cf. *Noy-Tunisia,* no. 10; Avitsuk, no. 27 (Iraqi Kurdistan). *AT* 926 C–*D (IFA): "Cases solved in a manner worthy of King Solomon." Cf. *Noy-Morocco,* no. 7; *Noy-Iraq,* no. 24; *TEM 1972,* no. 4 (Syria); according to the note by O. Schnitzler (*TEM 1972,* pp. 107–08), the motif of "a pound of flesh" (J 1161.2) is known from Shakespeare's *The Merchant of Venice,* as well as from older Roman and medieval literary and legal sources.

In a certain town there lived two neighbors, one rich, the other poor. One day the poor man became completely destitute. With

23. Meaning the husband's. However, it was previously stated that they both had decided to buy the house, probably at a very low price.

24. On this place and its Jewish community see Ben-Jacob, pp. 148–49; p. xxiv, above.

what would he buy food for his starving children? What could he do? He went to the rich man and asked him for a loan. The rich man readily agreed to lend him one thousand pounds, but on one condition, namely, "If you repay the loan to me in one year, well and good; if not, I will cut one hundred grams out of your flesh."

The poor man thought to himself, "God's deeds are great — He will help me to repay the loan within a year." He left the rich man's home joyful and happy, with the thousand pounds in his pocket.

However, when the year was over the poor man once more had not even one penny in his pocket. He thought to himself, "What shall I do now? The rich man will now surely cut one hundred grams out of my flesh."

While he was thinking, the door opened and the rich man stood at the entrance to his house, demanding, "Pay me back the thousand pounds that I lent you." The poor man confessed that he did not have a single penny, but he suggested, "Do not cut anything out of my flesh. Let us rather go to the king and have him pass judgment between us." The rich man agreed, for he knew that the law was on his side.

So they came to the king and told him the whole story, but the king was perplexed, as he did not know how to decide the case. What did he do? He postponed his decision for thirty days.

The two neighbors returned home while the king called his most eminent adviser, the vizier, and told him about the case, adding, "You must solve this problem. If you find no solution within thirty days, you shall die."

The vizier went off to roam in the land, thinking to himself, "Perhaps I shall find the solution among the common people." Twenty-nine days passed, and still there was no solution. On the thirtieth day, as the vizier was walking around in a remote village and thinking about his approaching death, he heard a voice saying, "Mine is yours, a gram less or a gram more." The vizier thought at first that he was dreaming, but when he looked closely he saw two children playing.

He decided to listen further, in the hope of benefiting by their talk. Behold, one of the children said to the other, "You be the poor man, and I the rich man." "I agree," said the other in the course of the game, "you may cut off some of my flesh, but only under one condition: if you cut off one gram more than I owe you or one gram less, I shall kill you." The other child thought for a moment and then announced, "In that case, I want neither your money nor your flesh."

The conversation over, the vizier hurried back to the king's palace, burst in without paying any attention to the people around, and shouted, "I have the solution!" Although the king was very anxious to know what the solution was, the vizier refused to reveal it until the day of the trial.

On the day of the trial a multitude of people gathered to hear the king's judgment, while the poor man and the rich man stood facing each other. The vizier began by saying to the rich man, "We have decided that you may cut off some of the poor man's flesh, but not one gram more or one gram less than the hundred grams on which you have both agreed. If you cut otherwise, your sentence is death." At this the rich man declared, "I renounce my claim to the poor man's flesh," and left the court mourning and grieving.[25]

10. Ḥamdullāh, Nisan, and Iyyar

Hebrew text: Marcus, no. 15, pp. 72–76 (IFA 5060); notes, pp. 168 (Hebrew), 205–06 (English). Told by Esther Raḥmānī, a native of Persian Kurdistan, to her nephew Jonathan Danieli. Combination of five types: *AT* 1542, "The clever boy"; *AT* 1540, "The student from paradise"; *AT* 1384, "The husband hunts three persons as stupid as his wife"; *AT* 1541, "For the long winter"; *AT* 1450, "Clever Elsie." Cf. Weinstein, no. 6; *Noy-Schwili,* nos. 113, 114, 129.

In one of the towns of Persia there lived a husband and wife. One day the husband, whose name was Ḥamdullāh,[26] asked his wife to hold two cans of cooking oil, one for Nisan and one for Iyyar,[27] and then went out for a walk. Some time after he left, two men, one named Nisan, and the other Iyyar, one riding a donkey and the other a horse, passed through the town. Nisan called out to Iyyar, "Iyyar, come and help me load this bag onto the horse." "I am coming right away, Nisan," replied Iyyar.

25. The Hebrew phrase is borrowed from Esther 6:12, *mourning and having his head covered,* said of Haman, after his plot against Mordecai was defeated, very much as in this story.

26. Meaning in Arabic "Praise to God," generally not used as a proper name.

27. Names of months in the Jewish calendar (April and May), but Nisan is also commonly used as a proper name among the Persian Jews.

When the wife heard this, she ran to them with the two cans of oil in her hands and begged them, "Do me a favor and take your cans of oil with you." The two did not understand what she was talking about but decided, "Why not take what is given to us as a gift?" They therefore took the cans and continued on their way.

When Ḥamdullāh came home and asked about the cans of oil, his wife told him that Nisan and Iyyar had arrived and that she had given them the cans, as he had commanded her. The husband screamed, struck his wife, and then explained to her, "I meant the months of Nisan and Iyyar, not people with these names." Then he left his home, saying to himself, "I shall not return home until I find a woman who is even more stupid than my wife."

After about two months Ḥamdullāh arrived at one of the wealthy villages in the country. He was exhausted and grimy and his clothes had become rags. A local woman who passed by asked him, "What is your business here, grimy fellow? Where have you come from?" Ḥamdullah replied, "From hell."

The woman, thinking that his mouth had spoken the truth, ran to the house of a widow whose husband had died a short while before, entered it in a hurry, and called out, "Madam, a man from hell has just come to our village. He is over there."

At this the widow ran to Ḥamdullāh and asked him, "Have you seen my husband Ḥājj Jābir in hell?" Ḥamdullāh replied, "Yes indeed, I met your poor husband. He was selling matches in hell, and he requested me to go to his wife and ask her for his money and his belongings."

The widow ran back home, filled bags with silver and gold, and even invited Ḥamdullāh to dine with her. He enjoyed the good meal and took the bags with him. As he was leaving, the widow turned to him, holding a big gold watch in her hand, and said, "I beg of you, do me a favor and take also this watch to my husband." "Why not? I am always at your service," replied Ḥamdullāh, and he left the place as quickly as he could.

After about two hours a relative of the widow came by for a visit, and she told him about all the events of the day. The man realized that some deception had occurred, so he mounted his horse and pursued Ḥamdullāh. When Ḥamdullāh, who was resting under a tree, saw the approaching horseman, he realized what this was about, so he ran to the nearby mill and shouted to the miller, "Listen, this horseman is coming to skin your head, to make a drum therewith for the wedding of the king's son."

The miller shouted back, "What shall I do?" Ḥamdullāh suggested that he make some excuse to the horseman, then himself climbed to the top of a tall tree, from which he could see all that was happening.

When the horseman arrived at the place, the miller began to explain to him that his head was covered with sores and his skin was not appropriate material for a drum. While they were talking, Ḥamdullāh leaped onto the widow's relative's horse, rode speedily away, and disappeared from sight.

The widow's relative returned home without telling anyone about his failure. When the widow asked him what had really happened, he replied, "I gave my horse to the man from hell, so that he should not be late in arriving there, for as is well known, the gates of hell close at three o'clock."

Meanwhile Ḥamdullāh continued his journey. In one of the villages he happened to come near a farmer's house. "Do you take in guests?" asked Ḥamdullāh. The farmer, the head of the family, replied kindly, "Why not? Come in, please."

So Ḥamdullāh entered the house and enjoyed a good meal. After the meal the father asked the older of his two daughters to brew a glass of tea for the guest, and as she was brewing the tea in the kitchen she reflected in her heart, "Surely this guest has come to ask for me to be his wife. He will take me with him far away, and I will bear him a son. One day, while I am gone to the marketplace, my son may well climb up to the roof, fall down, and be killed." As she reflected about this, she burst into bitter weeping.

The father, unaware of what was going on, sent his younger daughter to brew the tea and see what happened to her sister. When she saw her sister weeping she asked her to tell her the reason, but when she heard the story she too began weeping bitterly.

When the father saw that half an hour had passed and there were still no daughters and no tea in sight, he sent his wife to the kitchen. When the mother heard about the sad event that may well befall her grandson, who might fall down from the roof, she in turn burst into bitter tears. Finally, the father himself went into the kitchen, and when he heard about what might befall his grandson, he too joined the mourners.

Meanwhile, the heart of the honorable guest, that is to say, our friend Ḥamdullāh, was seized with great worry. What did he do? He too went into the kitchen, and when he heard the reason for the weeping he laughed in his heart, but with his mouth he said (angrily), "You killed my son! It is because of you that he fell down from the roof. Therefore I shall sue you in court."

The father now appealed to Ḥamdullāh, imploring him, "I beg of you, do not bring on the police. We will give you anything you wish, but please do not accuse us before the police." So Ḥamdullāh took from them silver and gold and all kinds of goods, and then continued on his journey.

One of the neighbors who heard the story realized that Ḥamdullāh had tricked the farmer and set out to pursue him. But Ḥamdullāh, who was now aware that he might be pursued, acquired a carriage for himself and drove it as fast as possible. As he approached his home, he saw that the widow's relative and the farmer's neighbor were speedily overtaking him. What did he do? He locked himself inside his house, where his wife welcomed him with great joy.

The two men who were pursuing Ḥamdullāh met on their way and told each other about his misdeeds. When they reached his house they pounded on the door and demanded to be let in, and Ḥamdullāh, pretending innocence, ushered them in and invited them to have a meal. Afterward they asked him to let them sleep in his house just one night, and Ḥamdullāh agreed, but explained to them, "My mother, who is unwell, is here in the house. You must not cough, because any coughing at all will cause her death. I will kill anyone who coughs," Ḥamdullāh warned them.

The guests agreed to this strange request, and Ḥamdullāh went to his room to sleep. The two men agreed to kill their host at midnight and regain for themselves all that he had stolen. But just before they could execute their plan they heard Ḥamdullāh's voice lamenting, "O mother, why did you pass away so untimely? I wish you were still living so that I could talk to you."

At this one of the guests said to the other, "You must have coughed and caused his mother to die," but the other replied, "It is you who is the culprit." Both of them noticed a window in their room and escaped through it, whereupon one of them came close to the window of Ḥamdullāh's room and peeked in, for they wanted to make sure that his mother had died. Noticing him, Ḥamdullāh said to his wife, "Look, there is a pumpkin in the window. Cut a piece out of it and cook it for me, for I have wept a lot for my mother." The wife took a sharp knife in her hand and cut off the head of the man who stood at the window.

After this the happy couple celebrated their victory over their enemies, and Ḥamdullāh, realizing that there were indeed people even more stupid than his wife, decided to continue having a good life with his wife and never quarreled with her again.

11. The Power of Man

Hebrew text: Marcus, no. 16, pp. 78–80 (IFA 5206); notes, pp. 168 (Hebrew), 205 (English). Told by Zion Ḥakīmzādeh, born 1910 in Kermanshah, Persian Kurdistan, to his daughter, Orah. *AT* 157 A: "The lion searches for man." In this version the lion is replaced by a young elephant. As for man's ingratitude and cruelty toward animals, IFA has several versions: cf. *Noy-Tunisia,* no. 14; *Noy-Iraq,* no. 107; Marcus, no. 32 (Iraqi Kurdistan); *Noy-JAT,* Nos. 16, 30 (see *Noy-JAT,* pp. 222–23, for several other sources); Gaster (1924), no. 441; Schwarzbaum, pp. 274 ff.

A goose and a duck lived peacefully on a river bank, and often said to each other, "How good and how pleasant is our place! No one will ever catch us here."

One day they saw from a distance a gazelle running quickly toward them. When she arrived they asked her, "Gazelle, why are you running?" She replied, "How is it that you are sitting here so calmly? Behold, an animal called man is approaching, and he has an instrument called gun which brings much slaughter and bloodshed upon us."

The birds did not believe her and asked, "What has come over you? Who is this man?" But before they could finish their conversation, behold, a man approached. The gazelle slipped away and fled like an arrow (shot) from a bow, but the man pointed his gun at the goose and killed him.

The duck, however, managed to escape behind the rocks on the river bank, and later reached a young elephant who was sitting on a hill. The elephant asked the duck, "Who are you? Why have you come here in such terror?" The duck replied, "My name is duck. I have come here because there is an animal named man who kills us with a gun that he carries in his hand." The elephant said, "Sit next to me. I shall show this man how powerful I am. I shall teach him a lesson."

While they were still talking, behold, a donkey reached the place. The elephant asked him his name and added, "And why have you come running here?" The donkey replied, "Cruel man puts a saddle upon me and on top of it heavy bags, and he makes me carry them to faraway places. I cannot do this any longer." The elephant said, "You too sit down here. I shall show this man how strong I am."

After a short while a galloping horse arrived, and after introducing himself spoke of what man had perpetrated against him: "He puts a big saddle upon my back, he curbs my head with a bridle, and behind me he hitches a wagon. Moreover, he lashes me with a whip to make me run faster. But now," the horse concluded, "I have escaped from man's tortures and have come here." The elephant said to him, "You, too, please sit with us. I shall show this man how strong I am."

While they were sitting, a camel came running by and said, "A creature named man loads upon me twenty bags full of potatoes, and then tells a little child to lead me. And when I stop to rest for a little while, the child beats me with his stick without mercy, urging me to move fast. My strength and my patience cannot sustain me any longer. I have escaped and have come here."

So the camel joined the duck, the donkey, the horse, and the elephant. Now behold, a man, a carpenter by trade, arrived there. The elephant asked him, "Who are you?" "I am a carpenter," replied the man. The elephant asked him, "And why have you come here?" "I have to make a large box for your father to sleep in at night," replied the carpenter.

The young elephant cried, "No, and again no! Do not make this box for my father; make it for me." But the carpenter refused, saying, "I must make it for your father, for he is the king of the elephants." The young elephant replied, "If you do not make the box for me, I will strike you with my long trunk."

The carpenter pretended to be frightened and agreed to make the box for the young elephant, who was very joyful over his victory.

When the carpenter finished making the box, he called the young elephant and asked him to lie in it, in order to make sure that it was a good fit. The innocent young elephant did so, and the carpenter closed the box and secured it with nails, and then set it on fire.

The horse, the donkey, the camel, and the duck were frightened and fled, running far away, while the man's voice accompanied them all the time, crying, "I will show you how powerful man is!" In this way did the animals learn to recognize the power of man.

12. The Ewe, the Goat, and the Lion

Hebrew text: *Noy-JAT*, no. 8, pp. 29–33 (IFA 2230). Recorded by Abraham Nisan from his grandfather, a native of Iraqi Kurdistan. *AT* 43: "Bear builds house of wood; fox, of ice";[28] *AT* 123: "Wolf in disguise eats up kids";[29] *AT* 1861 A: "Judge is partial to whomsoever gives him a larger bribe."

There were once a ewe and a goat. The ewe was very fond of the goat and the goat was likewise fond of the ewe. One day the ewe said to the goat, "Let us build a house for ourselves. Rainy days will come soon, and without a shelter we will have no place to hide ourselves from the rains."

The goat would not listen to the ewe and rejected her suggestion. The ewe then appealed to another goat, but was again rebuffed. What could the ewe do? She began to build the house relying on herself alone. However, during the construction she appealed again to the goat, "Let us build a common house for ourselves." But her suggestion was once more rejected.

The ewe continued her work alone until it was successfully finished. A few days later the rainy season began. One day, as torrential rain was pouring down, the goat came by and pleaded with the ewe, "Please let me sleep one night with you in the shelter." But the ewe rejected his plea, and the goat had to spend the night outdoors. The next day the ewe came out of her house, and behold, the goat was lying outside dead and lifeless.

28. See *Noy-JAT*, p. 249.
29. Ibid., p. 232.

The ewe decided to use the goat's carcass to build a new and stronger house. His hide served as a tent cloth, his legs as columns, and so forth. All in all, the house was very beautiful.

When spring arrived the ewe gave birth to two lambs and named them Anjula and Banjula. Whenever the ewe went outside to graze she would lock the lambs indoors, and only in the evening, when she returned home, would she call out, "Anjula, Banjula, open the door! Your mother is back and has a lot of milk for you." The lambs would then open the door, and the ewe would feed them her milk.

This continued for a month or two, until one day the lion noticed it and decided to kill and eat the lambs. But how was he to do it? How should he carry out his evil plan? Finally he found a solution: he decided to disguise himself as the ewe, approach the house, and ask the lambs to open the door for him. The lambs would think that this time their mother had returned early and would open the door.

So the lion went to the ewe's house and called out, "Anjula, Banjula, open the door! Your mother is back and has a lot of milk for you." The lambs replied, "Our mother does not return so early," and the lion retorted, "Today there was a lot of herbage, and I managed to eat quickly." The lambs replied, "Our mother has long ears, small legs, and is white, whereas you are very strange looking."

So the lion went away, dyed himself with a white dye, and returned to the lambs, but this time too the lambs refused to open the door. What did the lion do? He broke the door open and killed and ate both lambs.

In the evening the mother returned home and called, "Anjula, Banjula, open the door! Your mother is back and has a lot of milk for you." No answer and no response. The ewe repeated her call two and three times, but there was still no response. She then pushed the door open, and what did she see? The house was empty. The ewe did not know what to do.

She went to the fox's house and cried out, "Fox, fox, come out and fight me! Why did you take my sons?" The fox came out, saying, "I did not take your sons, ewe — I have no reason to fight you."

The ewe then went to the chicken coop, and the chickens woke up and began clucking out of fear of the ewe. The ewe called out to them, "You have taken my lambs. Come out and fight me!" The chickens replied, "We did not take your lambs — we have no reason to fight you."

The ewe then came down the chicken coop's roof to the dog's lair, and the dog came out, asking, "What do you want from me, ewe?" The ewe said, "You have taken my two lambs from me. Come out now and fight me!" The dog replied, "I have not taken your lambs, ewe — I am not going to fight you."

Finally, the ewe went to the lion's den, and he came out and roared, "Who is it that wakes me up from my slumber? Who is disturbing my sleep?" The ewe replied, "It is I who am disturbing you, and I shall continue to do so. Why did you kill my lambs? Come out now and fight me!" The lion replied, "I have indeed killed your children, but I will not fight you until we go to the judge and hear his decision."

The ewe consented, and both of them agreed on a date for the trial. The ewe prepared a bowl of white, fresh, and wholesome milk as a gift for the judge. The lion, too, took a large balloon,[30] painted it nicely, put in it four seeds of wheat, inflated it, and took it to the judge's house to give to him as a gift.

The lion and the ewe entered the judge's house and greeted him, and the judge returned their greetings. All three sat down. The ewe handed the judge the milk bowl, saying, "This is all I can give you," while the lion gave the balloon to the judge's wife, saying, "This is all I could bring you."

The curious woman could not restrain her desire to know what was inside the balloon, and as she began opening it, a seed was suddenly blown out and struck the judge's eyes with such force that he was blinded. The next seed struck the wife's eyes and she too was blinded. The third seed struck the wall and made a hole in it, and the fourth one struck the door and made a hole in it too.

What did the judge do? He fetched a pair of pincers and pulled out all the lion's teeth. He then sharpened the ewe's horns until they were as sharp as lances. Then he turned to both contestants and announced to them, "My sentence is that you must contend in battle with each other."

So first the lion bit the ewe, but his bite was weak, for he no longer had his teeth. When it was the ewe's turn, she gored the lion in his stomach, for her horns were now very sharp. And behold, out of the lion's belly came forth the two lambs, Anjula and Banjula, alive and well.

30. Balloons were made from an animals's bladder. The lion's strange gift suggests his predatory nature as well as his stupidity.

So the ewe brought both her children back home and continued raising them in health and soundness.

13. The Fox as Tailor and Weaver

Hebrew text: *Noy-JAT*, no. 18, pp. 52–53 (IFA 7011); notes, p. 236 (English). Recorded by Shīrīn Jonah from her nephew, born in Persian Kurdistan. *AT* 102: "Dog (fox) as wolf's shoemaker (tailor), eats up the 'raw material' furnished to him by the wolf."

Once upon a time there lived a wolf and a fox. One day they met in the forest, and the wolf asked the fox, "What is your occupation and what do you do for a living?" The fox replied, "I sew garments and weave cloth." The wolf said, "I need a fine garment — sew me one." The fox said, "Very well, provided that you bring me twenty-five lambs. I shall make you a very fine garment out of their wool."

The wolf agreed, and the fox assured him that the garment would be ready in a month. The next day the wolf brought the promised lambs to the fox, but the fox did not even start work on the garment. Instead, he and his family greedily ate the lambs and stuffed themselves with great pleasure.

About a month later the wolf came by and asked the fox for his garment. Frightened, the fox said, "Oh yes, I have sewn it, and the trousers are ready, but there was not enough wool for the coat. I need another twenty lambs, and a month from now the entire garment will be ready."

The wolf agreed and brought the fox twenty more lambs. Once more the fox greedily ate them, enjoying himself for another month.

At the end of the second month the wolf came by to ask for his garment. The fox was again very frightened, for he really did not know at all how to weave and sew. What would he tell the wolf now? So he said to his little children and to his wife, "When the wolf comes by, we shall all come out of our lair to welcome him. Then I shall send you, my little son, to fetch the garment for our uncle wolf. You will enter our lair but not come out. Then I shall tell you, my second son, to go in and fetch the garment for our uncle wolf. You too will enter but not come out. Then I shall tell you, my wife vixen, to go and fetch the garment. You too will enter the lair but not come out. Then I myself will go to fetch the garment, and I too will hide in the lair."

And so it happened. When the wolf saw that the entire family of the fox had disappeared, that is to say, had all entered the lair but had not come out again, he became very frightened, for he thought that a giant voracious beast dwelt in the lair, and if he too should enter it the beast would devour him as well. What did he do? He left the place and returned home without the garment.

As for the fox and his family, they had a great feast.

14. The Raven, the Fox, and the Rabbit[31]

Hebrew text: *Noy-JAT*, no. 124, pp. 124–25 (IFA 6081); English notes, pp. 205–06. Recorded by Marcella Noah from Salmān Abraham, born in Iraqi Kurdistan. *AT* 244: "Raven as foolish imitator." Cf. Ginzberg, *1*, 39.

There was once a raven who lived in a little nest. Whenever a storm would come and winds would blow, he shivered from cold and fright. One day he flew into the forest and fell asleep there. While he was sleeping all the animals laughed at him, so he asked himself, "What did I do to these animals that they are laughing at me?"

One day he gathered enough courage to approach a bird and ask her, "Why am I laughed at?" She replied, "Because you sleep with your head on." He asked, "How is it possible to sleep without my head on? Does not everyone sleep with his head on?" The bird explained to him, "All birds put their heads under their wings when they sleep, but you do not do so."

The raven thought to himself, "It seems that at night the other birds cut their heads off and in daytime fasten them back to their bodies." For a long time he sought advice on how to cut off his head, but all his efforts were fruitless.

One day he met the fox on his way and appealed to him, saying, "Fox, fox, tell me, how do the birds manage to sleep without their heads?" The fox laughed and said, "I cut their heads off for them and put them in a good and secure place, where no one can take them away. Would you like me to cut off your head for you?" "Yes," said the raven.

31. The original title is "The Fox, the Raven, and the Rabbit." I have changed the order because the main character is the raven.

Suddenly a rabbit came up and said to the fox, "Do not cut off the raven's head. The birds were just teasing him." Then he explained to the raven, "The birds do not cut off their heads — they merely hide them under their wings. That is why you do not see their heads. And this way they sleep better."

From that day on, the raven slept with his head under his wings. He told his story to his children, grandchildren, and great-grandchildren, and advised them all to put their heads under their wings whenever they fell asleep. And so they do down to the present day, just as they were told by their forefather, the raven. By this virtue — their obedience to their forefather — they live a life of happiness, peace, and tranquillity.[32]

15. The Serpent and the Poor Man

Hebrew text: *TEM 1974–1975*, no. 17, pp. 73–74 (IFA 10585); notes, pp. 198–202 (Hebrew), 248 (English). Recorded by Zipporah Levin from Israel Shomer, born 1912 in Köy-Sanjaq,[33] Iraqi Kurdistan, who spoke Neo-Aramaic, Kurdish, and Turkish. He heard his stories from Arab, Jewish, and Kurdish merchants.

AT 285 D: "Serpent rewards poor man but kills his disobedient son." IFA has 18 parallel versions, six of which are from Iraqi Kurdistan; the others are from Greece (1), Turkey (1), Yemen (2), Iraq (3), Iran (1), Bukhara (1), Afghanistan (2), and Romania (1). Cf. *Noy-JAT*, pp. 197–200 (English notes). Cf. below, no. 16.

There was a very poor man who had no luck at all. He went from one place to another looking for work, but wherever he went he was always rejected: "Who are you? We have no work for you. Go away from here."

One day, when he had not even a crust of bread to eat, he became quite desperate, saying, "O God, what kind of life is this? What have I done wrong?" So he left the town, sat down in a desolate place, and began weeping. After weeping for a while, he took out of his pocket a flute made of reeds and began playing it. In Kurdistan

32. The story was most probably told by parents to children, hence the somewhat repetitious didactic message at the end.

33. *TEM* 1974–1975, pp. 134–35; on the town and its Jewish community see Ben-Jacob, pp. 101–03.

they used to play such a flute in times of mourning as well as in times of joy.

Hearing the sound of the flute, a serpent emerged from his pit, listened to it, and began dancing. When the serpent grew tired of dancing he returned to his pit, and about five minutes later he came out with a diamond in his mouth. He put the diamond down next to the poor man and returned to his pit.

The man took the diamond home, knowing that a diamond was an object of value, and went to a jeweler and sold it to him. With the money he received for it, he bought goods for the house: cupboards, tables, chairs, fine beds, food, and drink. Each day he went to play the flute for the serpent, and each day the serpent gave him a diamond.

One day the man said to his son, "You go today to such and such a place, and play the flute there until you see a serpent coming out of his pit and dancing. Let him dance until he grows tired. Then he will go and bring you a diamond. Take the diamond, but do not touch the serpent,[34] and come back to me. From this day on you will play daily for the serpent, and the diamonds will be for you."

The son said, "Very well, father." He took the flute and went off. He played the flute and the serpent saw that he was not the same man, but he thought to himself, "This one must be the poor man's son, and his father must have sent him."

So the serpent danced until he grew tired, then he returned to his pit and brought out the diamond. The son returned home with the diamond, and the father said to him, "You have done well. Each day you will go there and play the flute."

But the son thought to himself, "Why do I have to go every day?" The next day, when the serpent finished dancing and returned with the diamond, the son seized his tail, and the serpent immediately leaped at him and killed him.[35]

16. The Pain from a Blow Heals, the Pain from a Word Does Not

The Neo-Aramaic text and an English translation, reproduced here with

34. Apparently this was requested by the serpent; see further on.

35. According to the recorder, the abrupt end, lacking a more detailed description of the son's behavior and the serpent's reaction, is due to the fact that the informant told the story when he was very tired, after having been interviewed for several hours about the traditions of his community.

minor changes, appeared in an article by I. Avinery (*JAOS* 98 [1978]: 92–96), told to him by S. Levy, born in Zakho,[36] Iraqi Kurdistan. For a bibliography and parallel versions of this tale type (*AT* 285 D) see no. 15, above. Here the serpent is replaced by the lion, who is offended by the poor man's wife. The moral of the story is that physical pain is much less severe than spiritual pain: the former can be cured, the latter is quite incurable.

There were once a man and a woman who had small children. The man was a woodcutter, and each day from morning till dark he would stay in the woods, but he would come home empty-handed, although there were also days when he would earn one or two pounds per day. They led, therefore, a difficult life. Each day this man's wife would quarrel with him about the living expenses and would curse him, until he despaired of his life.

One day he went to a field far away and said to himself, "Let me stay here — perhaps a lion or some other beast of prey will come by and devour me, so that I will have some rest." He finally arrived in front of a cave, and just as he looked into it a lion came out, his eyes quite red, and stood at the cave opening. The man felt very happy, saying in his heart, "Here now is this lion — he will devour me, and I shall have rest."

As he looked on, the lion opened his mouth and said to him, "O man, you, what are you doing here? Why are you not afraid of me? How is it that you are standing here like this in front of me instead of running away? Have you by any chance despaired of your life?"

Our man answered the lion, saying, "As for me, O lion, my soul is truly filled with despair. I have small children and a wife. I go out each day from morning till dark to cut wood, but I do not earn more than one pound or two. And many a day I come back home with my hands and feet bare. My wife quarrels with me each day and says to me, 'The children are hungry and naked. I cannot endure this sort of life any longer.' She curses me thus and so. I therefore said to myself, 'Let me go into a field, perhaps a lion will devour me.' Well, here I am. Devour me!"

The lion, however, was an understanding one. He took out a

36. On which see Ben-Jacob, pp. 58–62.

pound and gave it to the man, saying, "My good man, here is this gold pound — take it to your children. And each day, at this time, come here in front of this cave, and I will give you another pound."

The man was very happy and kept on invoking a blessing upon the lion. Then he went happily to his home. When he arrived, his wife saw that her husband was in high spirits and said to him, "Well, let us see what you have brought today." He told her, "Do not worry. This is what happened between me and a lion. From now on we shall have one gold pound every day."

The days went by, the man receiving his pound regularly, so that the couple's life became comfortable. One day the man's wife took hold of her husband and said to him, "You must invite this lion to our house, so that I too can see what kind of a lion he is." Whatever her husband told her — "Look here, we cannot invite him. He is a lion. How can he enter the town without frightening small children? There are pregnant women here who might miscarry out of sheer fright" — whatever he tried to tell her had no effect on her.

So he invited the lion. No matter what the lion said to this man — "Look here, I cannot come. I am a lion, a beast of prey. How can I come into town among people?" — the man would not give up. The lion finally said, "Very well, I will come at two o'clock after midnight."

At two o'clock at night the man went out and brought the lion indoors. He seated him at the table and put before him all sorts of food. The lion ate his fill and drank, until just before sunrise. Then he got up and said that he had to leave. He bade them farewell and told the man that he could continue coming each day to receive his pound. Then he said goodbye and left.

The wife praised him highly and added, "He really is a nice lion, but it is a pity that he has bad breath." Her husband, very angry, said to her, "Look here, be quiet, lest he should hear you. He may not have gone yet." The wife said, "Oh no, does he know our language?" Her husband replied, "Of course he understands it. Is he not the king of all beasts?"

The next day the man went to the lion, and when he arrived there the lion came out, but instead of giving him a pound he said to him, "Take this ax and strike my head with it with all your strength, until you split it in two." The man stood there astonished, and said to the lion, "Sir lion, what are you saying? How can I do this, after all the kindness with which you treated me all these years? How can I repay you with evil?"

The lion replied, "It cannot be otherwise. You have no choice but to strike my head with this ax." The man said to him, "But why?" "I will tell you afterward," replied the lion. So he forced the man to strike his head with the ax, and he did so. Thereupon the lion took a rope and tied it tightly around his head. Then he said to the man, "Well, now you may go your way, and come back after two weeks."

Two weeks later the man came back to the lion and saw that his head had healed completely. The lion said to him, "You see how my head has healed. The pain from a blow heals, but the pain from a word does not."[37]

17. The Child Whose Shirt Stuck to His Skin

Hebrew text: *TEM 1974–1975*, no. 4, pp. 36–42 (IFA 10120); notes, pp. 144–57 (Hebrew), 256–57 (English). Recorded by Jacqueline Allon[38] and Charles Meehan from Naomi Ella, who heard it from ḥakam Joshua, a native of Iraqi Kurdistan.

AT 930, "Prophecy of child's future greatness," and *AT* 730* A (IFA), "Miraculous rescue of Jewish community." The tale has several other motifs, which include the child's maturity and the conflict between parents and children. The detailed analysis by Yafa Kamer includes a comparison between motifs in this tale and in the Biblical story of Exodus,[39] the prototype of the rescue of the Jewish community from danger.

Once there was a great ḥakam[40] who was visited by women unable to become pregnant. He would bless them and write amulets for them, and they would conceive. He himself had a wife, but they had no children.

37. That is to say, the lion was still suffering from the insulting words of the man's wife. This quotation is a proverb; cf. below, chap. XX, proverb 108 (cf. proverb 174).

38. Mrs. Allon very kindly provided me with the original Neo-Aramaic text, which I used for making some minor additions and corrections in my English translation.

39. E.g., the magic acts performed by Moses and Aaron at the court of Pharaoh, and the magic acts performed by the youth in the king's palace; the drowning of Pharaoh in the Red Sea, and the sinking of the king into the ground. Some of the motifs are similar to the story of Samson, e.g., the barrenness of the mother and Samson's hair versus the boy's shirt as the divinely appointed secret symbol of their strength.

40. The Hebrew words *ḥakam* and *rab*, both meaning rabbi, are used interchangeably throughout the story, but I have retained the word rabbi for the sake of consistency.

One day a woman came to his house and asked his wife, "Where is the rabbi?" The wife asked, "What do you need him for?" She replied, "For several years I have been unable to conceive. I have been told that when the rabbi recites a blessing over a barren woman and writes an amulet for her, she becomes pregnant."

The rabbi's wife, after hearing this request, said to her husband, "I too have been unable to become pregnant. A woman told me that you can heal women like me. Why should not we too have a child?" He replied, "I know that it is impossible for you to have a child, for if you give birth to a boy he will get into trouble or cause trouble to himself and to all the Jews. If the child is a girl, it will be even worse. That is why I have not prepared an amulet for you."

But his wife kept begging him, "Bless me, so that I too may have a child." Feeling sorry for her, he blessed her. Nine months later a baby boy was born, and they washed him and brought clothes to dress him. But when they put a white shirt on him it stuck to his body, and it was impossible to take off. The boy grew up with that shirt, and it expanded with him just like his own skin.

When he was about three years old, his father engaged a teacher to teach him. The teacher began by saying, "This is the letter *alef*." The boy replied, "Yes, I know that this is *alef*, but why does it have four legs?" The teacher replied, "Well, I do not know why it has four legs. I was never taught anything about this. All I know is that this is *alef*."

Then the teacher continued, "This is the letter *beṯ*." The boy said, "I know that this is *beṯ*, but why is it shaped like an oven?"[41] The teacher replied, "Let us leave *beṯ* alone and move to the letter *gimel*." The boy asked, "Why does the *gimel* have a tail?" The teacher now grew angry and said to the boy's parents, "I cannot teach your son." They then engaged four more teachers, but he did the same thing to each one of them, and they all left him. Finally his parents gave up teaching him.

41. The cooking ovens in Kurdistan, made of clay or stones, have the shape of the square letter *beṯ*. On the local custom of teaching the letters to small children with such picturesque explanations of their shape, see Brauer, pp. 200–01: "*Alef* has four heads; *beṯ* is like an oven; *gimel* has a tail; *daleṯ* is like a door [sickle]; *he*ʾ has her son in her bosom; *waw* is like [the teacher's] stick; *zayin* has a turban; *ḥeṯ* is like a home garden; *ṭeṯ* has her hand in her breast pocket; *yoḏ* is small like you; . . . *nun* — her head is up but her foot is down; . . . ʿ*ayin* has two heads; *pe* — her head is bent in like a snake; *ṣaḏe* looks like eyes, nose, and mouth; *ḳof* stands on one foot; . . . *taw* — her foot is crooked" (my own translation, modified to incorporate Brauer's footnote to "stick" and a mistranslation of the Neo-Aramaic text for "home garden").

The boy grew up. When he was six or nine years old he used to play outside with other children, but he often seized them and beat them because they used to laugh at the dirty shirt that was stuck to his body.

One day the king's son was also playing with the children, and as soon as he began to talk against the rabbi's son, the latter beat him so badly that he almost died. The king's son was taken to a hospital, and the king came to the rabbi and asked him, "Why does your son beat my son and the other children? This time I will forgive you, even if my son should die from his injuries. But if your son beats the children one more time, I shall destroy the whole Jewish community."

The rabbi came home weeping. When his wife asked him what happened, he replied, "The king warned me that if our son beats the children one more time, he will destroy the entire Jewish community." His wife said, "What shall we do? This is terrible."

After debating for a while they decided, "We will lock the door and pretend we are asleep, and when our son knocks on the door we will not open it. He will understand that we do not want him any longer. Let him go whithersoever he wishes." They agreed on this and did so. The boy came home, knocked on the door several times, but they did not open it. The boy then said to himself, "It seems that my parents do not want me to be with them any longer. From now on I shall follow my own way and wander in the world."

He wandered off far away, until he reached another town, and in the evening he entered the local synagogue. The beadle saw how dirty and grimy his shirt was and asked him, "Who are you and what do you want?" He replied, "I am a stranger and have no place to sleep. I would like to sleep here in the synagogue." The beadle felt sorry for him and let him sleep there on a floor mat, and also brought him some food to eat. Then the boy covered himself with his robe and fell asleep.

Very early in the morning, much before the rest of the congregation, the son of the local rabbi and the son of a mystic rabbi[42] entered the synagogue, because they had been unable to sleep that night. While they waited for the others to come along they began talking, and the boy listened to them.

The son of the local rabbi said, "I am in love with a certain girl. I

42. The Hebrew word here is *mĕḳubbal,* "one learned in Kabbalah (Jewish mysticism)."

wish I could kiss her, spend at least half an hour with her, and then die." His friend said, "I too love a certain girl. I wish I could kiss her, spend one night with her, and then die."

At this the boy stood up and said to them, "Are you not ashamed of yourselves talking like this in the synagogue?" They replied, "What can we do? Love has completely consumed our hearts, and we are ready to die for our love." He said to them, "If this is so, I shall bring the two girls here, but you must not touch them. You may only talk to them for half an hour. Whosoever touches them will dry up like stone."

They promised him not to touch the girls, whereupon the two young girls were immediately presented before them, and the young men began talking to them. The rabbi's son was so much in love that he forgot himself and kissed the girl, and at that very moment he dried up and became like stone. The girls went home, and his friend ran away.

When the other people came to the synagogue for the morning prayer, they saw that the rabbi's son looked stiff like stone. The rabbi whose son had turned into stone asked the beadle, "What happened?" The beadle replied, "I do not know. There is a youth who sleeps here in the synagogue, and it seems that he has caused all this." So the rabbi called the youth and asked him, "Do you know why my son has turned into stone?" The youth replied, "Yes, I know. I caused it."

"You caused it?" said the rabbi, "I demand of you that you bring my son back to life right now." "I too demand of you — give me your daughter to wife," said the youth. The rabbi said, "I cannot promise you this — I must first ask the mother and the daughter, and then I shall give you an answer."

The rabbi asked his wife and his daughter, saying, "There is a grimy-looking youngster in the synagogue who has turned our only son into stone, and he wants our daughter in payment for bringing him back to life. What do you suggest?" They debated for a while and finally decided, "Very well — the main thing is to free our son."

So the rabbi returned to the youth and said, "Very well, I will give you my daughter to wife." He signed a statement of agreement, and the youngster released his son from his petrified state.

The rabbi then brought the youth home, and behold, he was so grimy that it was impossible to look at him. The rabbi invited only ten[43] men to the wedding and married off his daughter to this grimy-looking young man.

The daughter took a big knife and put it under her pillow, saying to herself, "Tonight, when he falls asleep, I will slay him." When the bridegroom entered the room he said to his bride, "Before we go to sleep, let us have something sweet. There is under the pillow a bar of chocolate — let us eat it." The wife pretended she had not heard him, and he repeated his words twice and even three times, until the wife was compelled to respond. She looked under the pillow, and behold, instead of the knife she saw a large bar of chocolate. She was stunned.

They both ate the chocolate, and then the bridegroom said, "The wedding that your father arranged for us was not worth much. Soon angels, ten righteous ones, will appear and recite over us the seven wedding benedictions.[44] This will be our true wedding."

The bride was frightened, but behold, there came King David, peace be upon him, the prophet Elijah, of blessed memory, and others like him, who made arrangements for the wedding and recited the seven benedictions. They also brought new angelic clothes for the bridegroom, removed his grimy shirt, and dressed him in the new clothes. Then a festive meal was prepared, and all ate and drank and sang songs and hymns.

Before dawn the guests said to the bridegroom, "This is a deep secret, and the entire matter must not become known to anyone else before the right time, as God may will it." The bride overheard everything they said and realized that her husband was not an ordinary person. After the guests had left he said to her, "Did you hear? All this is a secret. If you reveal it you shall die," and she replied, "Very well." Then he put on his grimy shirt, which stuck to his skin as before,[45] and they slept until morning.

Early in the morning the bride's mother knocked on the door, for she had agreed with her daughter to help her get rid of her husband's body after she had slain him. The mother said, "My daugh-

43. The statutory quorum (*minyan*) for public prayer at a wedding; he was ashamed to have his daughter publicly marry this disreputable-looking youngster.

44. The seven benedictions forming part of the wedding ritual: (1) over wine; (2) over all creation; (3) over the creation of man; (4) over procreation; (5) over gathering in Zion; (6) over bridegroom and bride; (7) over all Israel, including the bridal couple. See, e.g., *Daily Prayer Book*, ed. P. Birnbaum (New York, 1949), pp. 753–55; *EJ*, *11*: 1038–40.

45. This important detail is omitted in the Hebrew translation, although without it the story does not make sense; see further on.

ter, where is his body? Give it to me, and I will go and cast it into the sea." The daughter replied, "Mother, he is my husband — I could not do this to him. I love him and am satisfied with what God has bestowed upon me." The mother then said, "My daughter, that is very good. If you are content, why should I worry?" Thereupon she left.

The next morning the bridegroom said to his bride, "I shall not leave this room at all. You will bring me food three times a day and such books as I may need." The bride agreed, and brought him daily his food and his books, and he did not leave the room but studied all the time.

One day an eminent and famous rabbi died. The Jewish cemetery was far from the city, on the other side of the sea, and the Jews had to use a boat in order to bury their dead. Ten persons came to the funeral and boarded the boat that was to carry the coffin to the other side of the sea, but the boat would not move and remained where it was. How did this happen?

When the king of that city learned that the dead man was a famous rabbi, he said in his heart, "Now I will have a good reason to exterminate the Jews." What did he do? He cast a spell on the boat so that it could not be moved from its place. Then he announced to the local rabbi, "Your boat is blocking other boats. If you do not move it within three days, I shall put all the Jews to death."

The rabbi returned home weeping, gathered all the sage men, and told them about the king's threat. The Jews wept and fasted, and the next day, when the bride went to bring food for her groom, she saw her father and mother weeping and their eyes swollen. She asked them, "Why are you weeping?", and when she heard the story she too sat down and wept, but after half an hour she remembered that she had to bring food for her husband.

So she returned home with her eyes still swollen, and the bridegroom asked her, "What is wrong?" She told him all that had happened, whereupon he said to her, "Go and tell your father to give the king an affirmative answer. You may sleep in peace — I will go to the king and take care of this matter. Tell your father to bring with him a hammer and a long nail."

She went to her father and told him all this, and he said, "How can this youngster go before the king in his grimy shirt? Is it not enough that there is a decree against us? Do we now need the king to make a mockery of us as well?" But all the other sage men said,

"We are doomed in any case. Whatever happens, for better or for worse, let it happen. Take him with you." So the rabbi agreed and said to his daughter, "Very well. Tell him that I will do as he says."

They brought with them a hammer and a long nail, and the youth said to the rabbi, "When we reach the palace and the king asks you, 'Have you brought me an answer?', say 'yes' and point to me, that is to say, I will give him the answer."

So it was done, and the king grew very angry and said, "Are you making fun of me? Is this mere youngster to answer me?" The youth stood up and said, "Yes, I will answer you, my lord the king. Look out the window and see if the Jewish boat is still in its place. It is no longer there — it is gone." The king was amazed and was at a loss for words. The young man then said to him, "Well, answer me! You ought to realize now that you do not know how to do magic tricks, and that there are others who know how to better than you." So spoke the youth to the king, while all his viziers were sitting by and listening.

Then the young man added, "You have performed one magic trick, but I can do more and better." He took the nail and with one blow of the hammer drove it into the ground. As he hit the nail, behold, the king too sank into the ground up to his knees, whereupon he shouted, "I beg of you, release me. I am willing to serve as a slave to the Jews." But the young man hit the nail once more, and the king sank further into the ground, up to his waist, to the onlookers' great astonishment. Finally, as he hit the nail a third time, the king sank into the ground up to his neck.

The young man then turned to the viziers, saying, "What do you say? Are you going to exempt the Jews from your decrees and from all the heavy taxes, or would you prefer to be buried alive in the ground like your king?" They all agreed to leave the Jews alone and signed a pledge to this effect. Then he hit the nail once more, and the king sank completely into the ground.

The bridegroom then returned home with his father-in-law, the rabbi, who was stunned by the wonders performed by the youth. He said to the rabbi, "I was born especially to avert this decree against the Jews and to redeem them. As for my grimy shirt, it is the divine secret that brought about this redemption. Now that the evil decree is annulled, I can take off the shirt and wear good clothes instead." Later on the youth brought his parents to that town, and all the

Jews had a great celebration. May God annul the evil decrees against Jews in our days as well.

18. The Righteous Man, the Black Man, and Our Master Moses

Hebrew text: Marcus, no. 17, pp. 81–83 (IFA 5615); notes, pp. 168–69 (Hebrew), 205 (English). Recorded by Orah Ḥakīmzādeh from her father, Zion Ḥakīmzādeh,[46] a native of Persian Kurdistan. *AT* 759, "God's justice vindicated at the end (theodicy)." Other motifs include race prejudice and true faith versus performance of religious duties out of sheer habit. IFA has 24 versions of this type, some of which have been published; see *TEM 1961,* nos. 1 (Iraqi Kurdistan), 6 (Egypt); Baharav, no. 56 (Morocco); *Noy-Schwili,* no. 51; Weinstein, no. 7.

There was once a very righteous man who lived alone in a cave in the forest. He studied Torah and Talmud day and night and stood up in prayer so long that his hands and feet ached. For this he was granted a great favor by God, who provided him with food day after day.

One day our master Moses went to visit this righteous man, and on that day two portions of food were sent down from heaven,one for the righteous man and one for his guest, our master Moses.

The righteous man welcomed his guest and brought him into his cave, but when he took out his food to share it with the guest he noticed a miraculous thing — two portions of food had been sent down from heaven instead of the usual one. The righteous man thought to himself, "One portion should be enough for me and my guest. I shall keep the second portion for myself, to eat at another time."

So he brought out one portion and shared it with our master Moses. They both began eating, and when Moses finished eating he took leave of the righteous man, after thanking him, and continued on his way.

Later on, Moses came to another little cave, went inside, and at the entrance saw the owner, a black man. Behold now this miracle — the black man, too, received his portion of food from God every day. The black man welcomed Moses and went to fetch his portion

46. Cf. the introduction to tale 11, above.

of food in order to divide it into two halves, but suddenly he saw in front of him two portions of food. So the black man said in his heart, "Surely God has sent one portion for me and one for my guest." What did he do? He took both portions and served them at his table.

As they were about to eat, our master Moses looked around and saw that in the black man's cave there were cups and plates made of gold. (One must remember that in those days people did not eat with forks and spoons, because they ate with their hands. There were therefore no knives, spoons, and forks.)[47] What did the black man do? He put both portions on one plate, which he served to Moses, and waited until Moses had extended his hand and taken as much food as he wanted. Only then did he extend his own hand and take what food was left. This was how the black man treated the man of God who had appeared before him. Moses finished his meal, thanked the black man for his kind hospitality, and left the cave.

After he had gone a few steps, he heard a great noise from inside the cave. He returned to the cave and saw the black man breaking the golden plates and cups to bits. Moses was puzzled and asked the black man what he was doing, to which he replied, "Today I had a very important guest, and yet God has sent me just an ordinary meal, nothing special."[48]

So Moses continued on his way, thinking to himself, "Behold this black man, who does not even know how to pray yet receives from heaven food which is better than that of the righteous man; whereas the righteous man, who prays and studies day and night, receives poorer food than the black man. Is that possible?"

When Moses returned to heaven he addressed God, saying, "If I ask Thee a question, wilt Thou agree to answer it?" God agreed, and Moses asked, "The black man in whose cave I was a guest received a portion of food better and larger than that of the righteous man, who prays to Thee and occupies himself with Thy Torah day and night. Yet the black man is a simple man, who does not even know how to pray. Why didst Thou prefer him to the righteous man?"

God replied, "I shall open to you here the hearts of both men, and let us see whose heart is cleaner and purer, the heart of the righteous man or the heart of the black man." So God showed Moses the heart

47. The parenthetic remark appears in the Hebrew text.

48. That is to say, he was sorry that he could not serve his guest a more sumptuous meal. Cf. the various proverbs on hospitality, chap. XX, proverbs 92–101, below.

of the black man, and behold, it was shining in its cleanness and purer than any pure thing. Then he showed him the heart of the righteous man, and behold, it was darker than any dark thing, more impure than any impure thing.

God asked Moses, "To whom now should I grant a better portion of food, to the righteous man or to the black man? Behold, today I gave both of them double portions of food. The righteous man set aside for himself one portion and shared with you only the second portion. What good are his Torah and his prayers so long as he behaves like this and so long as his heart is tainted? The black man did not behave like this, for his heart is pure and clean, full of truth and faith. And if he does not know how to pray, it is not his fault."

19. The Donkey Who Gave Advice, the Ox Who Became Sick, and the Rooster Who Was Clever

Hebrew text: Marcus, no. 21, pp. 90–92 (IFA 6951); notes, pp. 170–71 (Hebrew), 204–05 (English). Recorded by Raḥamim Ḥakīmzādeh from his father, Sulaymān Ḥakīmzādeh, born in Kermanshah, Persian Kurdistan. It was originally told in Neo-Aramaic, and was translated into Hebrew by the son.[49]
AT 207 A, "Ass induces overworked bullock to feign sickness," and *AT* 670, "The animal languages." IFA has several versions, some of which were published; cf. *TEM 1961,* no. 5 (Eastern Europe); Baharav, no. 17 (Libya); *Noy-Iraq,* no. 28; *Noy-Libya,* no. 40; *Noy-JAT,* nos. 40, 41.[50]

There was once a man who, like King Solomon in his time,[51] knew all the languages of the world. However, all he owned was just a pair of oxen, a donkey, a dog, and a rooster.

One day the donkey asked the oxen, "Tell me, what kind of work do you do?" They replied, "We plow the land from morning till night. When we return home we receive some straw to eat, and the next day we go back to our work." The donkey burst into laughter, "Ha-ha-ha, hee-hee-hee! . . . As for me, only once a month am I

49. For this and other biographical notes, see Marcus, pp. 77–78. Kermanshah is not listed by Ben-Jacob among the localities of Persian Kurdistan, but it is mentioned as a town with a Neo-Aramaic speaking Jewish community in his introduction, p. 22.

50. For additional old and new references for these types see *Noy-JAT,* pp. 213–14. Humorous elements are characteristic of most of the versions.

51. See Ginzberg, *6,* 287–88, n. 34.

taken to town carrying no more than one bag of barley. That is all the work I have to do."

The oxen then asked, "What should we do in order not to work so hard?", and the donkey advised them thus: "Let one of you taste none of the food put in front of him. In the morning your master will think that he is sick and will not take him to work."

The oxen gladly agreed to follow the donkey's advice, but their master, who knew the languages of all living creatures and had understood their conversation, laughed to himself. His wife asked him, "Why are you laughing?", and he replied, "If I explain the reason to you, I shall die." The wife said, "What do I care if you die? Why did you laugh? I must know." The master thought it over and then replied, "Let me think about it for three days, and then I shall reveal my secret to you."

The next day the master entered the barn and saw just what he had expected to see after the animals' conversation the night before. What did he do? He approached the donkey who had given advice and took him to work instead of the "sick" ox.

That day the donkey suffered a great deal, and in the evening he returned to the barn tired and exhausted. The "sick" ox turned to him and asked, "How are you? How did you spend the day?" The donkey shrewdly replied, "I do not understand at all the meaning of your complaint. Your work is perfectly easy — you merely pull the plow as you walk; you carry no load on your back." And he added, "Today I heard the master talking to the butcher, and he offered him a sick ox for slaughter. Hurry therefore and get well, and eat the food in front of you."

The master overheard this conversation also and again burst into laughter, and his wife once more asked him why he laughed, but he refused to answer her.

Three days later the master announced to all the residents of the town that the next day would be his last in this world. Many people began mourning for the one who was to pass on the next day, and even his loyal dog stood aside and shed tears. Only the rooster continued to rejoice, laugh, sing, and dance. So the dog asked him, "Why are you happy and laughing when our beloved master is about to pass on?"

The rooster replied, "Our master has gone mad. Does he have to commit suicide because of a foolish demand by his wife? I have twenty wives — hens — and yet every day I give them a writ of divorcement (*geṭ*) and marry new ones."

This conversation, too, was overheard by the master, and he immediately stopped the mourning and approached his wife holding two white-hot iron bars in his hands. His wife was just about to say to him angrily, "Tell me immediately why you laughed"; but when she saw the white-hot iron bars in his hands and realized that he meant to touch them to her legs, she changed her tone of voice and said, "I beg your pardon. I was wrong. Please forgive me. You may laugh as much as you wish, and I shall never again ask you questions about it."

Thus mourning was turned into celebration, and from that day on both of them lived a life of happiness, trust, and mutual understanding.

20. The Prince Who Became a Pauper

Hebrew text: Marcus, no. 22, pp. 93–94 (IFA 5692); notes, pp. 171 (Hebrew), 204 (English). Recorded by Ephraim Ḥanukkah from his mother, Miriam, born in the village of Gazna,[52] Iraqi Kurdistan. *AT* 1533, "The wise carving of the fowl." Cf. *Noy-Iraq,* no. 8; Marcus, no. 14; Gaster (1924), no. 303 (several literary versions are listed in Gaster, p. 235); Lam. Rabbah 1:4. Other motifs are: poor and grimy but wise and generous versus rich and clean but spoiled and insensitive; tears open the heavenly gates of mercy.[53]

In a faraway land there lived a king, a queen, and their only son, who was a good child but very spoiled. The young prince was always clean, because he liked cleanliness and orderliness in his surroundings, but he had a friend, a poor and grimy boy, whose clothes were in rags and whose feet were always bare. But this poor boy, whose name was Elijah, was clever, kindhearted, and very devoted to his old and poor mother.

One day, as Elijah was walking in a green field, he saw a little bird flying about. He quickly caught it and ran home with it. "Mother," he said, "I have caught a little bird. Please hurry and roast it for me in a pan." The mother roasted the bird in the pan,

52. Ben-Jacob, p. 97: "In the year 1947 there were [only] 16 Jews who were farmers, growing mainly wheat, barley, and vegetables. They all [later] emigrated to the State of Israel." The village is situated in the region of Arbil.

53. See chap. 1, n. 25, above.

and Elijah took it but did not eat it himself. Instead he hurried to his friend the prince to share it with him. The prince looked at the thin and scrawny bird, and refused even to touch it. Moreover, he laughed at Elijah for bringing such a tiny bird as a gift.

Elijah was hurt and offended. He went home saddened, with tears running down his cheeks, and asked himself, "Why did my friend laugh at me, and why did he refuse to accept my gift, even though it is a modest one?"

God saw the poor boy's tears and felt pity for him. As the boy stood by the side of the road with the roasted bird in his hands, the king and the queen passed by in their chariot. When they saw the boy, they invited him to eat with them and asked him to give them the roasted bird as a gift. All of them — the king, the queen, their spoiled son, and the poor Elijah — then sat down to eat.

"Let us divide the roasted bird and give each one of us his share," suggested the king. The queen, too, smiled, but the prince made a sour face and turned his nose up. So Elijah divided the bird in this way: he gave the head to the king, the stomach and legs to the queen, and the wings to the prince.

"Why did you divide the bird in this way?" they asked him, puzzled as they were. "The king is the head of the family, therefore I gave him the bird's head," replied the clever boy. "The queen is a woman and mother, and will yet bear many sons; therefore I gave her the stomach and the legs. The little prince will grow up and become a man, will grow wings, and will wander a great deal in the world."[54]

The king and the queen wondered at the child's wisdom, and felt ashamed of their spoiled son who laughed at him and mocked him. They thereupon drove their son from the house and made the poor Elijah and his mother very rich.

Thus the rich and spoiled prince became a wandering pauper, while the poor child became rich, respected, and loved by all.

21. The Letter to God

Hebrew text: Marcus, no. 42, pp. 153–54 (IFA 4477); notes, pp. 176–77 (Hebrew), 201 (English). Recorded by Judah Kalīmī from his father,

54. In an oral version of this type from Zakho, the guest gives the legs to the sons, because they are the pillars of the family, and the wings to the daughters, because they will get married and "fly away" from the family. Cf. Gaster (1924), p. 113 (English summary).

Nisan Kalīmī, born 1900 in Kermanshah, Persian Kurdistan. *AT* 841* A (IFA), "Poor man miraculously helped, and rewarded for his sincere deed." This is a very common type in Jewish folktales, the time of plot being usually the eve of Passover or of Sabbath. IFA has recorded 22 versions, some of which have been published; cf. *Noy-Folktales,* no. 35; *Noy-Tunisia,* no. 70; *Noy-Iraq,* no. 41; chap. XX, proverb 102, below.

In a certain town there lived a man who was extremely poor. As the Passover holiday approached, the poor man had neither food nor clothing for his children, who were clad in rags. He felt entirely at a loss, and asked himself, "What shall I do?" Finally he decided, "I shall write a letter to Almighty God and ask Him to provide me with all that I need for the holiday."

So the poor man wrote the letter, mentioning all the things that he and his family needed, and let it fly up into the air. In his heart he felt confident that the letter would find its way to heaven.

The letter flew along on the wings of the wind until it landed near the king's palace. The vizier found it, read its contents, and wondered, "Who is it that sends a letter to God?" So he took the letter and showed it to the king. The king read it and said, "Surely the Jew had in mind the god on earth, that is to say, me, the king." He was very pleased that the Jew honored him so much as to call him god.

What did the king do? He filled a cart with all the good things for Passover, adding twice as much as the Jew had requested, and the fully loaded wagon reached the poor man's house just in time. That year he and his family celebrated the Passover holiday quite properly, and rejoiced in it as they never did before. Such is the reward for trust in God.

22. The Carpenter, the Tailor, and the Rabbi

Hebrew text: Marcus, no. 43, pp. 154–55 (IFA 4478); notes, pp. 177 (Hebrew), 201 (English). Recorded by Judah Kalīmī from his father, Nisan Kalīmī, a native of Persian Kurdistan.[55]

AT 945/II, "To whom does the wooden doll belong?" In other versions the question is "Who will take her to wife?" while in this version the question

55. Cf. tale 21, above.

is "Who will adopt her as a daughter?" Cf. *Noy-Morocco,* nos. 1, 25; *Noy-Tunisia,* no. 27; *Noy-Schwili,* no. 29.

There were once three friends — a carpenter, a tailor, and a rabbi. They used to go out together to various localities to earn their living. One evening, as they were traveling, they reached a large orchard. Since it was getting dark they decided, "Let us sleep here tonight."

They also agreed that each one should stand watch for four hours. They cast lots, and the carpenter drew the first watch. The tailor and the rabbi fell asleep, while the carpenter stood guard. He walked around doing nothing else and became bored, so he decided, "I must do something to relieve my boredom." What did the carpenter do? He cut off a piece of wood, shaped it into the likeness of a little girl, and decorated it with all the necessary details. When his shift was over, the wooden doll was finished.

Now it was the tailor's turn to stand guard. As he walked aimlessly here and there, he noticed the large wooden doll made by the carpenter. In order not to feel lonesome, he decided to continue working on the doll. What did he do? During the four hours of his shift he sewed some magnificent clothes for the doll and dressed it with them. When he finished his work, the second watch was over. He awakened the rabbi, whose shift had now come.

The rabbi took up his watch, grew bored with it, and suddenly saw the beautiful doll clad in magnificent clothes. He realized that this was the handiwork of his friends, the carpenter and the tailor. So he said to himself, "I will pray for the breath of life to enter this doll." He prayed, and his prayer was heard, that is to say, it was accepted and fulfilled, and the rabbi began talking with the girl, who was now no different from any other girl.

In the morning each of the three friends claimed, "The girl belongs to me." The carpenter said, "Had I not decided to form her out of wood, she would not have existed at all, and you two could not have dressed her and brought her to life." The tailor said, "Had I not dressed her, she would have been just a scarecrow." The rabbi said, "Had I not prayed to the Holy One, blessed be He, to blow the breath of life into her, there would have been no dispute among us, for she would have been thrown away like a mere piece of wood."

Finally they cast lots.[56] The rabbi was the fortunate one to win her, because, after all, he had brought her to life. The rabbi took her home, adopted her as his daughter, and she proved to be no different from the rest of his children.

23. The Sword of Redemption

Translated from the abridged Hebrew version in *Noy-SMYK,* no. 8, pp. 44–47 (IFA 6602); notes, pp. 59–60. Recorded by Zvi Chaimovitz from Zion Sayda, a native of Iraqi Kurdistan. The story expresses the longing of this Jewish community for redemption through heroic acts by messianic leaders such as David Alroy.[57]

The Jews who lived in the northern part of Iraqi Kurdistan believed that the sword of our master Moses was buried in one of the mountains of their region. They also believed that whosoever found it would bring salvation to his people and return them to the Land of Israel.[58] They ardently longed for redemption, and therefore many of them tried to find the sword. Unfortunately, the sword was never found, and many of those who searched for it were killed on their way by bandits.

Once three friends decided to set out to find the sword in spite of the dangers involved. They said, "Great is the suffering of our people, and the time of redemption is surely at hand."

So they traveled for a long time until they reached a village built on top of a lofty mountain. The village headman, the agha, was blind — he had eyes but could not see. He grew very angry at these Jews, for he knew of the legend about the sword, and he did not like this idea of Israel's redemption.

When he heard that three foreign Jews had arrived in the neighborhood of the village, he realized what they were searching for. So he summoned three of his servants and ordered them, "Take an old, broken, and rusty sword and bury it at night, not too far from where

56. Because they could not come to an agreement otherwise. It seems that the rabbi won because he was the most likely to bring her up properly.

57. See the legend about him, chap. XIII, above.

58. The legend about the sword of Moses is derived from the legend about the sword of Methuselah, with which he used to fight demons and perform miracles. This sword later came into the possession of Abraham, Isaac, and Jacob and eventually passed to Moses; see Ginzberg, *1,* 141; *5,* 165–66, n. 63; *Noy-SMYK,* p. 60.

the Jews will be sleeping. Do this quietly, so that the Jews will not notice. Then come back to me, and I will tell you what to do next."

The servants of the agha fulfilled his command, buried the sword, and then returned to their master's house. "Now," said the agha, "go out again to the same area. Find a hiding place for yourselves where the Jews cannot see you, and wait there. When you see the three Jews retrieving the sword out of the ground, seize them and bring them to me."

Early next morning the three friends went out to search for the sword. They saw a place between two rocks and began digging in it, and behold, they found an old and broken sword. Before they had time to touch it, the agha's men jumped up from their hiding place, tied their arms, and brought them to the agha's house.

"What were you looking for, and what did you find in my land?" asked the agha angrily. The Jews saw that everything was known and revealed, and that it was no use lying, so one of them replied, "According to an old legend, the sword of the prophet Moses is to be found in the mountains of Kurdistan. We searched for it, but we found only an old piece of sheet metal."

"Aha!" cried the agha, "I know that you are really looking for the sword with which you mean to rule over us and even kill all of us. Is this the way to repay us, evil for good? Here in Kurdistan you are free people. What do you lack? What redemption are you looking for? But tell me one thing," continued the agha in a low voice, "what about me? Do you plan to kill me too at the time of your redemption?"

One of these Jews was a wise and understanding young man who realized how great was the danger in which they found themselves, and that only an appropriate response would save them. He remembered that *Death and life are in the power of the tongue* (Prov. 18:21), so he began by saying, "O agha, you know the tradition about the sword of the prophet Moses, but not all of it. According to this tradition, one must render great honor, and even more than honor, to the man in whose land the sword is found. O agha, have you not heard about that sheikh in whose field the Jews found red heifers suitable for sacrifice? That sheikh is now a very rich man."[59]

59. Probably referring to the legend about Dima ben Netina, a Gentile from Ashkelon whose reverence for his father was so great that he would not awaken him when he was sleeping upon a chest holding a precious stone wanted by the Jews for the high priest's breastplate. The Jews thinking that he hesitated only because he wished to obtain a higher

"You speak well," said the agha, who understood what the Jew was driving at. "If so, let each one of you pay me twenty silver dinars, and you may continue searching on my land." "O agha," replied the Jew, "we have with us only five dinars. We will give them to you now, and when we find the sword you shall receive the rest." The agha laughed, "I see that you are a wise Jew. I accept your offer."

The three friends then took their work tools and went home. But the desire to find the sword of our master Moses is still burning in their hearts.

24. The Amulet

Hebrew text: Alfiyah,[60] pp. 12–13.[61] The belief in the curing power of amulets was widespread among the Kurdistani Jews. Many physical and psychological disorders were believed to be the result of a demon's touch,[62] and could be cured by an amulet written by a ḥak̲am. This story seems to suggest that the sage realized that the amulet was a kind of placebo, which exercised a positive psychological influence on the patient and his family regardless of its contents.[63]

This is a story about a woman from Zakho[64] whose son had a sudden attack of weeping. He could not stop weeping all day and all night, and nothing could calm him down. The woman was at a loss and finally went to consult the sage Shabbethai ʿAlwān,[65] of blessed memory. The sage entered his room and after a few minutes came out and gave the worried mother an amulet, saying, "Hang this around your son's neck, and he will calm down."

price for it, offered him more and more money. After his father awoke, he sold the stone at the original offering price and later reaped his reward by selling a red heifer (Num. 19:2–9) at a very high price; see Gaster (1924), no. 188, and references, p. 223; B. Ḳid 31a. The legend is well known in Islamic literature as well; see Schwarzbaum, pp. 233 ff.

60. The introduction to Alfiyah's Kabbalistic book includes many anecdotes about miraculous acts performed by the sages of Zakho, the principal town of Iraqi Kurdistan. These anecdotes were collected by the author's son from various informants in Jerusalem.

61. Appeared also in Stahl, pp. 49–50.

62. See Sabar (1962), pp. 27–28.

63. For details on the various written contents of amulets and for photographs of amulets used in Jewish communities in the East and West see *EJ*, s.v. "Amulet," 2, 906–15.

64. See Ben-Jacob, pp. 58–62.

65. "Among the distinguished sages of Zakho were the brothers Shabbethai, Moses, and Joseph ʿAlwān. All three served as *dayyanim* [rabbinic judges] and religious leaders of the Jewish community of Zakho" (Alfiyah, p. 16).

The mother did as he said, and after several hours the child calmed down and fell asleep. When the child grew up and no longer needed the amulet, the mother, out of sheer curiosity, opened it and found a blank piece of paper with nothing written on it. She thought that perhaps the holy letters had flown away or were written in invisible ink.

So she went to the sage Shabbethai and asked him about this mystery. He replied, "Is it important to you whether the paper in the amulet is written on or not? It is sufficient that your son's illness has disappeared, and thank God for that."

25. The Midwife, the Cat, and the Demons

Translated from the Hebrew version in Sabar (1962), p. 28. Originally told in Neo-Aramaic by my mother, Miriam Sabar, born 1922 in Zakho, Iraqi Kurdistan. Parallel versions:[66] (1) *Noy-Folktales,* no. 12 (English), recorded by M. Zehavi from a laundress born in Zakho (an abridged Hebrew version is in *Noy-SMYK,* no. 5; notes, p. 57; IFA 279); (2) Baharav, no. 48 (*Noy-JAT,* no. 29; IFA 4564), told by Jacob Tshaprak, a native of Turkish Kurdistan.
AT 156 *B, "Woman as midwife of snake (of cat, of demon)"; *AT* 476*, "Midwife of demons (or frogs) is rewarded." For several Jewish literary sources (in which the midwife is replaced by a *mohel,* circumciser), see *Noy-Folktales,* pp. 24–25; Baharav, p. 263.

A Jewish family in Zakho[67] was renowned for its wealth, acquired, it was said, through a grandmother who was a midwife.

One night, when she returned home from a busy day of many deliveries, she felt quite exhausted.[68] As she was about to fall asleep, she saw in front of her bed a red-haired cat walking very gingerly and in an advanced stage of pregnancy. The beautiful cat captured her heart, and she instantly expressed a wish, "I wish I could act as midwife for this cat."[69]

66. It seems worthwhile to compare the details of all three versions from Kurdistan, in order to give the reader a general idea of the parallel versions of the story.

67. In Baharav's version the location is given as Diyarbakir, the informant's home in Turkish Kurdistan. In Zakho this story was told about the Moshe Gabbay family, the wealthiest in the town.

68. Noy: "One day she sat outside her house embroidering, being very tired after a hard day's work." Baharav: "Once the midwife passed by a well."

69. Noy: "Suddenly she saw a beautiful cat. . . . My grandmother said to herself, 'If only I were this cat's midwife!'" Baharav: "Suddenly she saw a black, big, and fat cat walking toward

After a few minutes, having just fallen asleep, she was awakened by two men who asked her to follow them. When she asked "What for?" they replied, "A moment ago you expressed a wish — we want to fulfill it for you."

So she went out with them, and they traveled with her for a great distance in a carriage pulled by two goats, until they reached a stone bridge.[70] There she saw a great celebration, with groups of dancers dancing around a very beautiful woman who was about to give birth. They immediately seated her next to that woman and asked her to be in charge of the delivery.

While she was making preparations, she heard the female dancers chanting, "If it is a boy, we shall give her rich gifts; but if it is a girl, we shall put her to death."[71] The midwife understood that they were referring to herself.[72] Fortunately for her, the female demon gave birth to a baby boy, and the joy among the demons was great.[73]

One thing amazed the midwife: she noticed that the clothes worn by the dancers were none other than those belonging to her own family. She recognized them well, but in order to be sure she marked them with bloodstains, so that she might check them when she returned home.[74]

At the end of the celebration she asked them to take her home, and they did so, giving her as a gift a bundle of onions and garlic. Naturally, she was greatly disappointed, but she did not dare to ask any questions or request another gift instead.[75] On the way

---

her. The woman said, 'Had this cat belonged to me, I would have lent her a helping hand, just as I do for human females.'"

70. Noy: "They reached a stone bridge, each stone of which was ten meters square. They entered a huge cave." Baharav: "They carried her a long way until they reached a lonely house in an open field. They climbed many stairs until they reached an attic with lighted windows."

71. Noy: "If the newborn is a son, you will get everything you wish, but if it is a daughter, God forbid it." This threat is missing in Baharav; cf. n. 73, below.

72. In both parallel versions she is offered at this point food and drink, but having been warned earlier by the pregnant demon not to eat anything lest she become a demon herself, she refused the offer, saying, "I am not used to nonkosher food — all my life I have eaten only dishes prepared in my own kitchen" (Baharav).

73. Noy: "What rejoicing broke out in the cave! It reached the heavens." This theme is missing in Baharav. Cf. n. 71, above.

74. Baharav: "Suddenly the midwife noticed that a beautiful female demon was wearing a dress belonging to her daughter-in-law. . . . She marked it with her hand which was smeared with oil." The theme is missing in Noy.

75. According to Noy, she was asked to name any gift she wished, but she refused at first, saying, "The reward for a good deed is the deed itself." But having been told that she must

home she threw away the garlic and the onions, one piece after another.

When she arrived home, all she had left in her hand was one onion, which she threw down on the hall floor. The next morning, when she got up from her bed and went into the hall, she was stunned to find that the onion had turned into gold. She realized then that she had made a grave error in throwing away the rest of the onions and garlic.[76] Nevertheless, the single remaining onion brought this family great wealth, and they lived in abundance for many years to come.

The midwife also checked the clothes and found that they were indeed stained with blood, as she had marked them. This shows that demons do often use our clothes when we are sunk in deep sleep.

---

choose something because that was the demons' custom, which could not be disregarded, she asked for a bunch of garlic that she noticed lying in a corner of the room. See the next note.

76. Baharav: "When she passed the bridge, she thought in her heart, 'What will I do with these garlic skins? I had better throw them into the river.' To her great surprise, she saw that the flowing water was now carrying silver coins. . . . Thus she was left with only one coin." According to Noy she brought all the garlic home, and "the next morning her grandchild woke her up, saying, 'Whence did you bring so much gold, Grandma?' . . . She then distributed the gold among her children, grandchildren, and the rest of her family. . . . And so each one of us has kept until this day a piece of the golden garlic, the reward of our grandmother, the midwife, and her gift to us."

XVIII

Nursery Rhymes

Among the Kurdistani Jews children are the center of family life. They are loved and cherished, and constitute a source of inspiration and pleasure for their parents and relatives. The more children the parents have, the prouder they are. Their love and concern for their children are often expressed in nursery rhymes and special greetings and incantations. Since the rate of child mortality was high,[1] many rhymes express wishes and blessings for good health and long life and contain incantations against the evil eye and illness, as well as wishes that the child may be fortunate enough to study Torah, marry, and perform good deeds. They are recited or chanted in the course of daily activities such as having breakfast, entering the room, bathing, wearing a new garment, or going to bed. Some rhymes are simple teasing and joking songs, others describe the child's beauty, especially if it is a girl. Most of the rhymes are quatrains. They are terse, occasionally with no more than two words in each line, yet expressive and imaginative.

BIBLIOGRAPHY
Sabar (1974c).

"Good Morning" Rhyme

(May) your mornings (be) blessed,
(May) your life (be) long,
(May) your enemies[2] (be) shrouded, dead,
(May) your (hot) breakfasts (be) poured, cooled.[3]

1. My own family is a typical example. My mother had twelve pregnancies, but only six of her children survived. The other six died in infancy or early childhood. Cf. also the chapter "Birth and Infancy" in Brauer, pp. 126–46. See also chap. XX, proverbs 33, 34, 65, 70, 253, below; Sabar (1980), p. 294.

2. The enemies are either human beings who cast the evil eye on the baby boy or demons and evil spirits; cf. Brauer, pp. 133, 144–45; and Welcoming Rhymes and Incantation against the Evil Eye, below.

3. That is, may they be always ready to eat.

Feeding Rhymes

1

What will your meals be?
Bread, rice, and halvah,
And manna[4] sprinkled all over.

2

(May your meal be) health and life,
May there be a multitude (of people)[5] at your wedding,
Half of them from ʿAḳra and half from Shosh.[6]
May your father-in-law cut out (garments) for you to wear,
May your mother-in-law sew (garments) for you to wear.

Bath Rhyme

May (the bath) bring health to you.
May you have seven sons,
May the smallest of them all strike you.[7]
(*Variant*: May the smallest of them all kiss your hand.)

Welcoming Rhymes

1

Welcome to this lad!
May he be guarded by the moon and the sun.[8]
May he grow up and become a king.
(May) the luck of his enemies (be) black.

4. That is, honeydew, a secretion collected from leaves of trees, which is very common in Kurdistan; cf. Introduction, n. 86. A drink prepared with it was considered to have medicinal value for women in difficult labor, and nursing mothers drank a lot of sweetened drinks made with grapes, dates, figs, and tea, "to increase their milk." Cf. Brauer, p. 131.

5. Blessings for a wedding at this early age were quite common, and their purpose was to wish that the child may reach a mature age. Cf. Bath Rhyme (having sons), Welcoming Rhyme 1 (becoming a king), 2, Good Wishes and Blessings 1, 2, and n. 17, below.

6. Both are towns in the district of Mosul; see Ben-Jacob, pp. 81–86.

7. The idea is that if one is fortunate enough to have seven sons, it does not matter even if the youngest one strikes his father. However, some prefer the variant line, which expresses obedience to, and reverence for, the father. In any case, the rhyme is not meant to be taken seriously.

8. The wish to be guarded by the moon and the sun is not necessarily a residue of paganism; rather, it may refer to being protected by God day and night, or it may be part of an old magical formula. However, it was believed that pregnant women should not go outside the house during the eclipse of the moon, for fear that the parts of the embryo facing the moon would become covered with red and pink spots. Cf. Brauer, p. 129.

2

Welcome, welcome!
(May you become) the owner of slaves and servants,
May those who hate you lose their eyesight and go blind.

Rhyme for a New Piece of Clothing

(May) your (new) shirt (be) blessed.
This one short,
The next one long.

Lullaby

Go to sleep, go to sleep, go to sleep.
I wish you peaceful sleep and long life,
By the life of those far away from home,
Those who are in strange lands.[9]

Incantation against the Evil Eye

Whosoever dislikes you in this place,[10]
May his head be carried away by a hawk.
Whosoever dislikes you in this neighborhood,
May he be afflicted with leprosy.
Whosoever dislikes you in this house,
May his head be pecked by a hen.

Good Wishes and Blessings

1

(May I be) a sacrifice for this little one.[11]
May he be protected by the Torah.
May he grow up and become a big fellow.

2

Dear to his father is this (boy's) head.
May no ailment ever touch him,
May he be a simple and humble fellow.[12]

9. Probably members of the family, such as the husband, who are away from home in search of livelihood. Swearing by the life or the head of a beloved person is a common practice in Near Eastern societies. Cf. the lullaby in chap. X, I(B) 4, above.

10. Hating someone is the same as casting the evil eye on him; see n. 2, above. Note the gradual punishment expressed in the curse — the closer one is to the family, the lighter the punishment.

11. An endearing wish common in Near Eastern languages.

12. Literally, "a servant of God and a dervish." Note that in this rhyme humility and piety

3

Tiny round one (rolling) under tables,
Nuts and raisins in his lap,
May everyone eat at his ceremonial meals.[13]

4

Good things I wish him,
Long life I ask for him,
This little son, for Torah I raise him.

Teasing Rhyme

May a hen peck at his buttocks,
May she give him a roasted egg,
May she place him in a high corner,[14]
May she feed him bread and chicken.

Rhymes of Praise for Baby Girls[15]

1

Lips (as delicate as thin) paper,
Nose (like) a hazelnut.
(May I be) a sacrifice (for her) to her Creator.[16]

2

Nursling, nursling,
Fresh, pretty, youthful!
This nursling, whose daughter is she?
To the market of Mosul take her,
Garments and ornaments buy for her![17]

---

are stressed, whereas in Welcoming Rhyme 1 the wish is that the child may become a king, and in Good Wishes and Blessings 1, a big fellow.

13. At his Bar-Mitzvah, wedding, etc., when many people will be invited to attend.

14. That is, an elevated and cozy place, where hens and chickens, the most common pets in the house, used to roost. Here the hen is personified as the child's devoted nurse.

15. Out of the sixteen rhymes I collected, only two are specifically for girls, which may reflect the greater affection given to boys. The rhymes for boys mainly bestow blessings and good wishes, while those for girls praise their beauty.

16. See n. 11, above. This line is a form of praise to God for having created such a beautiful child. This terse and imaginative rhyme is reminiscent of the style of the Song of Songs, where lips are compared to scarlet thread (see Song of Solomon 4:3, 7:3–5).

17. That is, for her trousseau. Taking the girl to the market of the metropolitan city of Mosul is a poetic indication that she is so pretty that already at this early age she should be supplied with a trousseau, since she may be betrothed any day. Cf. n. 5, above.

XIX

Folk Songs

BIBLIOGRAPHY

Garbell, pp. 273–79.

Song 1
I shall write a letter with the tips of scissors.[1]
You were a merchant (but) have become a peddler.
(May) I be ransom for you, for your soldier's uniform.
I shall come to meet you in a taxicab.
May God in heaven grant your desire.
(But) now I am dying because of your reticence.

Song 2

I went up to the roof to mix sesame seeds.[2]
Your letter came, I was ready to fly at once (with joy).
I did not know where you were.
You have gone to a wedding.
God grant that it be blessed for you!

Song 3
He went up to the mountain,
He swore (by) the Scroll of Torah.[3]

Song 4
I am velvet, (though) I have no nap;

1. This and the following four songs were recorded from Tamar Cohen (in Neo-Aramaic), born in Ushnuye (Shino), Persian Kurdistan, on which see Ben-Jacob, p. 144. This song is addressed by a mother to her soldier son. Since most women were illiterate, she "writes" the letter with scissors, a woman's common tool. For other "writing" tools see chap. X, I(B) 3, above. The last line is a mild complaint by the mother about her son's failure to write her a letter, thus causing her to worry.

2. The speaker is a woman.

3. The meaning of the song is not clear. Perhaps it refers to Moses.

I am a flower, (for) I have a husband.
(By the) face of mother dear![4]

Song 5

O mother, mother, do not let them take me away.
(My ravisher) is a Gentile,[5] a Kurd, so they tell me.
If you have no room (for me), put me into the stable,
If you have no stuffed leaves[6] (for me), let me eat donkey's dung.
O mother, mother, do not let them take me away.
(My ravisher) is a Gentile, a Kurd, so they tell me.

Song 6

The sun has risen, the moon has set,
A cloud has covered the sky;
A young lad
Has fallen in love with a girl:
"I am in love with you, my dear,
I would not exchange you for the (entire) world.
You are my only star,
Like the sun[7] (shining) over the world."
(*Variant of the last three lines*:[8]
"I am very fond of you;
For the entire world
I would not exchange you")

Song 7

Take your pitcher,
Go to the fountain,
Go slowly, slowly;
I, too, will come (there).
Give me a kiss,
So I will no longer have to die.
Hold (me) with (your) arm, come inside.

4. The last line is obscure and perhaps meant as an oath.

5. Hebrew *goyim* (used as singular; the plural is *goyme*).

6. Known as *yaprakh* or *dolma* (Turkish), a popular dish in the Near East. The grape leaves are usually stuffed with rice, onions, salt, pepper, and raisins or meat, and mixed with oil. For a complete recipe see Garbell, pp. 269–70.

7. The first three words, missing in Garbell's translation, appear in the Neo-Aramaic text.

8. Recorded from Miriam Ben-Shalom, born in Solduz (Naghade), Persian Kurdistan, on which see Ben-Jacob, p. 147.

Come, come, my life, my soul!
"I will not come, by God!"[9]

Song 8
Look at this clear night,
How bright are the stars!
My heart is thinking of you,[10]
(But) no one will bring (me) news of you.
Where are you,[11] who give (me) heart (courage, solace),
Who take (captive) the hearts of your lovers,
Who leave (*or*: make [them] leave) the ways of God,
Who run away from love?[8]

Song 9
I[12] did not want, while I was falling in love,
This inheritance of love.
Your love has caused me much torment,
(But) has later let me attain the inheritance (of happiness).

Song 10
Again I saw my love coming from the mountains —
She had a nosegay of flowers in her hand —
With two (other) girls.
I said to her, "My true love, let me smell those flowers."
She said, "Leave me, go away, do not importune me,
My heart is full of pain."

Song 11
Their roof (was) back of ours.
It was the house of Sheikh[13] Raḥamim.
The wide trousers of my beloved Jochebed
(Were) of sky-blue calico.
I said, "Give me a kiss."
(But just then her father) Sheikh Raḥamim came along.[8]

9. Recorded from several informants. The last line is spoken by the woman.
10. "You" is the woman.
11. Here "you" is plural.
12. "I" is masculine.
13. Among the Jews of Zakho this Muslim title was used only to refer to a member of the Jewish burial society (the *Ḥeḇrah Ḳaddišah*).

Song 12

The plane tree is tall,
(But) there is no fruit on it.
God in heaven is merciful,
There is none like Him.
The stature of my true love is handsome,
There is none like it.
"Come, come, let me see you[10] once more, my true love!
Perhaps I shall go (and) not come back again.
Come, let me see you once more!"[8]

Song 13

"Your[14] dress is long,
May it be blessed,
My dear, my true love!
You have tied your belt,
(But) have not pulled it tight,
My dear, my true love!"
"My belt will be a gift to you,[15]
And I myself will be your ransom,
My dear, my true love!
Your suit is long,
May it be blessed,
My dear, my true love!"[8]

Song 14

May it be blessed, may it be blessed,
May Joseph's wedding be blessed.
May his mother's dress
Be long.[16]

Song 15

"Mother, mother, I am going
To Sarafand[17] to serve in the army."
"Do not go, my son, you must not go,

14. Referring to the woman.

15. Here "you" is masculine.

16. Heard at a wedding.

17. A military training camp south of Tel-Aviv, now called Ṣĕrifin. The song was composed in Jerusalem during World War II. Recorded from Rivka Mizraḥi, of Urmia, Persian Kurdistan, on which see Ben-Jacob, p. 144.

(For) you will fall a victim to the enemy."
"No, mother, I will go
To Sarafand to serve in the army.
May God kindle a fire
In the midst of the enemy's land."
"Do not go, my son, you must not go,
(For) you will fall a victim to the enemy."
"No, mother, I will go
(And) encamp in the enemy's land."

XX

Proverbs and Sayings

BIBLIOGRAPHY

Rivlin, Y. Y. "Pitgamim bi-Lĕšon Targum." *Rĕšumot,* n.s., *1* (1945): 207–15; 2 (1946): 209–14 (Neo-Aramaic with Hebrew translation).

Sabar (1978a).

Segal, J. B. "Neo-Aramaic Proverbs of the Jews of Zakho." *JNES 14* (1955): 251–70.[1]

The letter(s) and number following each proverb indicate the serial number of the proverb in the references, as follows: R = Rivlin; Sa = Sabar; Se = Segal; U = unpublished proverb in my own collection.

Ailments and Misfortunes[2]

1. "The (same) God who gives illness gives its cure." Said to encourage the sick. (Sa 7)
2. "The snow falls upon the mountains." Great persons are usually exposed to more afflictions and difficulties than ordinary people are. (Sa 131)
3. "The sun sets, but troubles linger on." As long as one lives, one should expect troubles. (Sa 147).
4. "The rope follows the bucket (into the well)." Various interpretations are: one loss usually follows another (cf. chap. III, n. 27, above); once the essential thing is lost, what remains is of little use; a wife should follow her husband's wishes rather than insist on her own. (Sa 150)
5. "Whatever the burglar left behind had to be paid to the fortune-teller (called in to trace the burglar by reading omens)." (Sa 89)

1. In a few cases the original English translation of the proverb has been changed slightly to produce more idiomatic English or a closer rendering.

2. The classification of the proverbs by subject is somewhat arbitrary, as one proverb may belong to more than one subject. The reader is therefore advised to look up other related subjects as well, e.g., proverbs about *Children* may be found also under *Family Relations*.

6. "Go where they make you cry, rather than where they make you laugh." Cf. Eccles. 7:2. (Sa 113)
7. "Where there is celebration, be fearful." Every joyful event (even birth) ends with sorrow or death. (R 54)

Ambition

8. "The horse is being shod, so the crab also lifts its foot." Said when an inferior person apes a superior one. (Se 1)
9. "The camel asked for horns, so even its ears were cut short." (Se 2)
10. "Can ravens also fly like doves?" (Se 3)
11. "Whet the appetite of a dog, but do not whet the appetite of men." A dog remains faithful, but an ambitious man cannot be trusted. (Se 4; Sa 134)
12. "A dog is (happy) among dogs, a donkey among donkeys." Be yourself, and join your equals. Said in sarcasm to ambitious inferiors. (Sa 68)
13. "The donkey has ceased breaking wind." Said when an inferior person has been removed from a high position. (Sa 75)
14. "A flea carries a (heavy) load." Said sarcastically of a person who embarks upon tasks that are beyond his ability. (Sa 103)
15. "A human being is a bird, but has no wings." People have many desires and ambitions, but their ability to fulfill them is limited. (U)

Authority

16. "No blood flows from a head cut off by the government." Even serious crimes and murders committed by government officials are accounted as "clean" and lawful, whereas minor crimes of ordinary citizens are punished; or, official execution does not lead to a blood feud. (Se 5)
17. "The mullah's donkey brays more pleasingly." (Se 6)
18. "The servant of the qadi is the same as the qadi." He is equally important, because he controls the access to the qadi (the Islamic judge). (Se 49)
19. "Break my mouth, but do as I say." Freedom of speech — yes, freedom of action — no. (Sa 133)

Avarice

20. "The beard of the avaricious person is in the rump of the

bankrupt person." An avaricious person, even if now wealthy, will end up bankrupt. (Sa 110)

Bragging

21. "He cannot (take them on) one by one, yet he says, 'Let them come two at a time to (fight) me.'" (Se 7). *Variant*: "Come against me six at a time." (R 47)
22. "Breaking wind in the (noisy) coppersmiths' market goes unnoticed." Said of one who brags that he can compete with experts. (Sa 24)
23. "A Turkish bath cannot be heated by flatulent wind (alone)." *Variant*: "Eggs cannot be fried by . . ." Said of the bragging of lazy people. (Sa 58)
24. "'Get up from under me, lest I crush you,' said the gnat to the elephant." Said of a weakling threatening a powerful person. (Sa 108)
25. "A dog is brave in front of his own door." Said of people who are brave at home but cowardly elsewhere. (Sa 114)
26. "You may get to see your backside, (but) that one you will never see." Said to a braggart who speaks about events that are unlikely to take place. (Sa 126)
27. "Wind-breaker, why did you go? Flatulent one, why did you come back?" Said by women of a person who brags before setting out on a mission but returns without having accomplished it. (Sa 135)

Children

28. "We planted wheat, but coarse corn sprouted up." Said of ungrateful children. (Se 15)
29. "The father has come home from the millstones, and the son angrily reviles him." Said of children who are ashamed of their father's occupation, although it provides them with their livelihood. (Se 16)
30. "One maintains ten, but ten will not maintain one." Said of children who refuse to support their father in his old age. (Se 17)
31. "From a rose (comes) a thorn, and from a thorn a rose." Said of bad children born to good parents, and vice versa. Said also in

the sense that good is rarely unmixed with bad, and vice versa. (Se 37)

32. "A dog learns to bark from his sire." Said of children who learn bad manners from their parents. (R 99)
33. "He who loses a firstborn son loses a treasure." (Sa 8)
34. "Spend a hundred (dinars), but do not let your child spend the night in the streets." *Variant*: "The Jew spent a hundred piasters, so that his son might not sleep even one night away from home." Originally this probably referred to ransoming a person from military service or from prison. (Sa 56)
35. "Raising children makes the eyes white," i.e., is a difficult and wearisome task. Usually said by women. (Sa 90)
36. "My mouth is closer (to me) than my mother's." Said by mothers of the selfishness of grown-up children. (Sa 105)
37. "The judge of the children hanged himself," because he was unable to decide which one was guilty. Said humorously of children's noisy and endless disputes (Sa 106)
38. "From (the same) mother and father (come children of) a thousand colors." Do not expect all your children to be the same in appearance or character. (Sa 151)
39. "(Whatever) an adult says at home, a child will tell (even) to the trees." Said in warning against telling secrets in front of children. Cf. B. Suk 56b, "The child's talk in the market-place is either the father's or the mother's (talk at home)." (U)

Contentment

40. "So long as a man does not walk on his hands, he does not appreciate his feet." (Se 18)
41. "Stretch your feet (only) to the size of your rug." Be content with what you have. (Sa 95)

Dreams

42. "A night's dream is vain." Said to comfort one who had a bad dream. Cf. Zech. 10:2. (Sa 142)
43. "Daytime fantasies appear to him in night's dream." Said to explain children's bad dreams. (Sa 30)
44. "Do not sleep in a deep ravine, and you will not have bad dreams." Do not involve yourself in matters that will cause you worry. (Se 141)

Egoism and Self-Interest

45. "I love you, but not better than myself." (Se 80)
46. "Everyone weeps for his own dead." (Se 82)
47. "This one says, 'My beard is burning'; that one says, 'Roast my partridge[3] (over it)'" Said of those who try to benefit from other people's troubles. Cf. "Nero fiddles while Rome burns." (Sa 20)
48. "Everyone pulls the (warming) fire in front of himself." (Sa 85)

Ethnic Slurs

49. "The people of Zakho eat yoghurt and mess themselves up," i.e., are uncouth. Originally said by Baghdadis, but now used also by Zakho Jews to denigrate each other. (Sa 3)
50. "(When) a Kurd is asked, 'Where is your right ear?' he stretches his (right) hand behind his left ear (to reach it)." Probably of Arabic origin. (Sa 47)
51. "A Kurd is (as silly as) an ass." Said by Arabs.[4] (Sa 84)
52. "A Jew does not pay his tax until he is flogged." Said by Kurds. (Sa 61)
53. "They are Jews, they are (like) a broken tree, they (will go) to hell." Said by Kurdish ruffians at the sight of a Jewish funeral. (Sa 67)
54. "(As noisy as) the synagogue of the Jews." Said by Kurds. (Sa 69, variant)
55. "(When a Jew is told), 'Jew, let us go to paradise,' (he replies), 'Is it not Sabbath (today)?'" He will not travel on the Sabbath even to paradise. Said mockingly by Kurds about the rigorous nature of the Jewish religion. (U)
56. "Dog does not eat the flesh of dog." Gentiles harm only Jews, not other Gentiles. Or, malicious people do not harm each other. (Sa 71)
57. "A dog does not understand the tongue of (another) dog." Said of a great uproar or dispute among Gentiles. (Sa 69)

3. The partridge is a very common bird in Kurdish folktales. The singeing of the beard, probably near a bonfire, and the roasting of the bird suggest a hunting scene.

4. A common Arabic ethnic insult in Israel was *'anā Kurdī,* "I am (a) Kurdish (Jew)," said of a person who rigidly follows the directions of his superiors without showing any original thinking or discrimination.

Family Relations[5]

58. "Let all the world be my relatives, be they (even) my enemies." It is always good to have relatives — even if they are bad, they are still better than strangers in times of need. (Sa 82)
59. "(Related) bloods boil in each other's presence." Relatives feel kindly toward each other even if they have never met before. (Sa 40)
60. "Do not go to a place where you have no relatives." (Sa 97)
61. "Whosoever lives far from his relatives, his face is (as sad as) the face of a donkey." (U)
62. "A blow from a brother is (more) painful (than one from a stranger)." (Se 31)
63. "A brother is a brother, but business is business." Relatives and friends should not expect any special favors in business. (Sa 34)
64. "Whatever the father or the older brother says, that is it." Obedience to one's elders is essential. (Sa 88)
65. "Everyone has a father and a mother, but it is very difficult to have a (good) brother." Parents love and take care of their children; not so brothers. (R 53)
66. "Those who become two (eventually) become three." When two get married, their number increases by the birth of children. (R 32)
67. "Between the bull and the cow, the calf drops (dead)." When parents quarel, the one who really suffers is the child. (R 55)
68. "When the rope is cut, the bundle is scattered." When parents die, their children are dispersed. (Sa 144)
69. "My heart is (like) the ironsmith's bellows, at rest neither by night nor by day, (because) my son has never achieved his desire." Said by mothers of unmarried sons. (Sa 87)
70. "The mother whose son has been killed is at rest, the one whose son has not been killed is not." The seeming cruelty of this proverb stresses the constant worries and hardships involved in raising children. (Se 30)

Food

71. "Bread (food) is a friend (on long journeys)." It makes them more pleasant and less tedious. (Sa 98)

5. See also under *Children, Sex, Wives.*

72. "Go to bed hungry, and you will get up full (healthy)." Said to discourage eating before bedtime. (U)
73. "(When) food is present, conversation should be absent." Said in disapproval of too much talking at mealtime. Cf. B. Ta 5b, "No talking at meals." (Sa 62)

Fools and Simpletons

74. "He who took away your wits, may he not enjoy them." Said humorously to a simpleton. (Sa 9)
75. "I do not (wish to) know, (so that) I may have peace of mind." Said sarcastically of fools who ignore harsh reality. Cf. "Ignorance is bliss." (Sa 11)
76. "I will pretend to be a madman, and make my life a happy one." People will not hold me responsible for my actions. (Sa 39)
77. "My male organ is smarter than his head." Said of a stupid person. (Sa 15)
78. "When the donkey entered, the singing stopped." (Sa 21)
79. "(It is like) playing the flute[6] for an ox." *Variant*: "They played the flute for the ox, (but) he did not dance." Talking to a fool is useless. (Sa 33; Se 41)
80. "I tell him it is a stone, and he tells me it is cheese." Said of an obstinate fool. (Sa 49)
81. "I tell him the man is a eunuch, and he asks me how many children he has." (Sa 50)
82. "A hundred are worth one, one is worth a hundred." *Variant*: "One is worth a hundred, and a hundred are worth nothing." One wise man is better than a hundred fools.[7] (R 14; Se 97)
83. "The fellow is white but his speech is black." Said of a good-looking fool. (R 42)
84. "The house is empty (of anything useful) but full of refuse." Said of a person who always talks foolishly and never wisely. (R 56)

Generosity versus Stinginess

85. "He who begs (for alms), one side of his face turns black (with shame); he who never gives (alms), both sides of his face turn

6. Segal's translation "drum" is erroneous.

7. This is Rivlin's interpretation; Segal classifies it under *Wealth*, relating it to the difference between the rich and the poor.

black." A person reduced to begging suffers embarrassment only in this life, but a miser suffers in this world as well as in the world to come. (Sa 10; R 1)

86. "Oil poured upon water does not get lost." Generosity eventually brings its reward. Cf. above, chap. XII; below, proverb 91. (Sa 37)
87. "The cat was told, 'Your excrement is (useful as) medicine' — so he hid his excrement." Said of pettiness.[8] (Sa 48)
88. "The cook loses (her own share of the meal)." After serving each member of the family his portion, the cook herself is left with nothing or only a reduced portion. When helping others, one should expect and accept some deprivation. (Sa 67)
89. "(When you return from a journey), bring a present, be it (even) a stone." *Variant*: "People ask not 'What did you eat?' but 'What have you brought?'" (Sa 92; Se 93)
90. "Borrow by the spoonful, give (back) by the ladleful." Reward well those who have helped you even a little. (Sa 137)
91. "Do (good) and set (it) adrift upon the water." Do not expect an immediate reward. Cf. Eccles. 11:1, and above, proverb 86. (Se 54)

Hosts and Guests

92. "Guests are God's guests." Treat them well. (Sa 5)
93. "An uninvited guest is worthless." (Sa 6)
94. "His hand is long, and his face is black." Said of an ill-mannered guest who shamelessly grabs food. (Sa 18)
95. "The home of a (poor) old woman, rather than the home of (rich) emirs." Poor people may be more hospitable than rich people. (Sa 32)
96. "A place is never (too) narrow for (more) people." One can always make room for guests. (Sa 41)
97. "One speaks of the dog, (and) the dog is at the door." Said of an uninvited visitor. (Sa 52)
98. "A precious (man) asks for an inexpensive (thing)." Said as a compliment to a frugal guest. (Sa 54)
99. "A dog will not leave (so long as he sees) a bone." Said of discourteous guests or children who stay on as long as they see

8. Segal has a shorter variant, "The excrement of a cat becomes medicine," (Se 59), which he erroneously explains as "When it is needed, even a vile thing is of some importance."

food on the table. Said also as advice: If you want to get rid of such guests, stop serving more food. (Sa 70)

100. "Guest, would you like to eat or not to eat?" Said of a miserly host who pretends to be polite; it is of course rude to put such a question to a guest. (Sa 93)

101. "(After) the fox is full, he says, 'The grapes were sour.'" Said of a guest who complains about the food after having eaten a lot of it. (Sa 111)

Holidays

102. "The holiday of Moses (i.e., Passover), (God) Himself provides for it." One should not worry about not having enough provisions for holidays — God (or Moses?), who instituted them, will provide for them. Cf. chap. XVII, tale 21, above. (Sa 17)

Home and Community

103. "Damascus is sugar, (but) my hometown is sweeter." There's no place like home. (Sa 125)

104. "A stone is heavier in its (original) place." A person is more appreciated in his own community. (Sa 77)

105. "A little house with a satisfying life is better than a large house with an empty life." (R 57–58)

Honor and Shame

106. "If you wish to be honored, you have to honor others." Cf. ʾAḇ 4:1, "Who is honored? He who honors (other) people." (R 79)

107. "Debt on men, snow on mountains." Just as it is natural for lofty mountains to have snow on their tops, so is it for men to be burdened with debts. Do not be ashamed to borrow money. (Sa 38)[9]

Human Nature and Human Types[10]

108. "The pain from blow heals, (but) the pain from a word does

9. Cf. proverb 2, above. Segal and Rivlin interpret it differently: "Do not be afraid to incur debts — they will melt like winter snow on mountain tops" (Se 125); "People are apt not to repay what they borrow" (R 86).

10. See also *Bragging, Fools*.

not." The pain of insult is lasting. See chap. XVII, tale 16, above. (Sa 42)

109. "Each faithless person needs an impious person (to defeat him)." (Sa 81)

110. "All the fingers of your hand are not the same (length)." People are of diverse characters — variety is part of nature. Cf. B. Pes 112b (same words but in a different sense). (Sa 83)

111. "That which is absorbed with (the mother's) milk is not given up even in old age." Usually said of bad habits. (Sa 146)

112. "Snow does not cease being cold." An evil person will not change. (U)

113. "The dog's tail is put into the press for forty days, and it comes out (still) curled." Same sense as proverb 112. (Se 40)

114. "The good rooster crows (while he is still) in the egg." A good person is easily recognized. (Sa 64)

115. "If it is a cucumber, it is recognizable when it is (still) tiny." A tiny cucumber appears as soon as the flower drops off. (Se 36)

116. "Wind does not tarry in his rump." Said of overenthusiasm. *Variant*: "His wind comes in pairs." (Sa 25)

117. "(She is like) an egg — without a mouth." A compliment paid to a quiet and well-mannered girl. (Sa 31)

118. "When he goes to the well, it dries up." Said of a ne'er-do-well. (Sa 46)

119. "The dirty is clean." Said of women who "clean" one mess by making a greater one, or persist in unnecessary cleaning. Usually said by one woman of another. (Sa 104)

120. "(If) one limb does not resemble (another) limb, it will not join it." Said to explain a bad marriage or a bad companionship. Cf. "Birds of a feather flock together." (Sa 139)

121. "Your fire did not warm me, (but) I was blinded by your smoke." Said of people who cause only suffering. (U)

122. "A hundred (good) people can live together without quarreling, but two dogs (i.e., bad people) in one place will (always) quarrel." (R 17)

123. "He who wishes to find an excuse will make it (even) out of a broom." (R 37)

124. "(Seize) a sheep by the ears, and an ox by the testicles." *Variant*: "(Seize) a woman by the breasts, and a man by the

testicles." Everyone has an Achilles' heel, a vulnerable point. (Se 122–23)

125. "Ten households, (but) twelve landlords." Said when too many persons try to act as leaders. (R 52)
126. "Nothing is as beautiful as the body of the serpent, but its shape is twisted." Said of a good-looking person whose ways are crooked. (R 74)
127. "A shy man is worth a penny, a shy woman is worth a million." Coyness befits women but is a disgrace in men. (R 78)
128. "The man is young and good-looking, but he does not have a male organ." Said of a handsome man who has a weak character. (R 80)
129. "A liar is invited only once." Once people know his true nature, they will not invite him again. (R 89)
130. "No judge can decide the case of two (disputing) madmen." (R 105)

Influence

131. "Since we spent forty days with them, we became like them." People living together influence each other. (R 33)
132. "A man tied to a donkey will start to bray." *Variant*: ". . . learns to break wind (as loudly)." Said of bad influence upon good people. (Sa 99)
133. "The fish's head rots first." Corrupted leaders corrupt the entire community. (Sa 100)
134. "(When) he stings the wall, (even) the roof swells." Said of far-reaching dubious influence. (Sa 53)

Kindness

135. "Kindness comes on your part as well as on mine." It must be reciprocal. (Se 51)
136. "A man's bread in the belly of his friend is a debt." Help others so that they may help you. (Se 53)
137. "An eye is ashamed before (another) eye." If you appear in person to solicit a favor, it will not be refused. (Sa 14; Se 55)
138. "A mountain does not need (another) mountain, but a man needs (another) man." People need each other, and therefore should be kind to each other. (Sa 138; Se 52)
139. "If you eat with a blind man, eat sparingly." Be kind to him

and do not steal his food. Also generally, Do not take advantage of people weaker than you. (Se 89)

Life and Death

140. "The world is (both) death (and) life." (Sa 44)
141. "The world will endure for no one." Said by those who feel deprived, to console themselves: even those who are happy, strong, wealthy, etc., will eventually die. (Sa 45)
142. "A living dog is better than a dead lion." Cf. Eccles. 9:4. (Sa 72)
143. "Death is a golden key." Said when a suffering or senile person dies. (U)
144. "Let it be death, rather than old age." (U)
145. "The dead one is afraid on account of his sins." (Se 20)
146. "If the dead one is not crooked, his grave will not press down upon him." (R 35; Se 21)
147. "If a man knew when he would die, he would prepare his own shroud." One's fate is unknown. (Se 28)
148. "(Only) after death is there no eye disease." Ailments should be expected as long as one lives. Also said in consolation: there is no suffering after death. (Sa 29)

Luck (Good and Bad)

149. "If your luck is with you, watch out for yourself; if it is against you, watch out for your property." A lucky and prosperous person is in personal danger because of the evil eye and because he usually has enemies. An unlucky person should be cautious about his money, for he may easily lose it. (R 38)
150. "(Like) the scroll (of Torah) in its ark, everyone and his luck." Some Torah scrolls are used often, others rarely. If even the Holy Scroll needs a little bit of luck, how much more so people. Based on the Hebrew proverb: *Hak-kol taluy bĕ-mazzal, 'afillu Sefer Torah šebbĕ-hekal* (Zohar, III, 134a), "Everything depends on luck, even the Torah scroll in the hall (of the Temple)." Usually said of a spinster who is comely and wise. (Sa 112)
151. "No bead remains unstrung." Said to encourage unlucky spinsters — they need not lose hope of getting married eventually. (U)
152. "The bride at the wedding does not know who her husband

is." He may turn out to be bad or may die young — her future is still uncertain. (Se 27)

153. "He is asleep, but his luck is awake." Said of people who have more luck than wits. (Se 29)

154. "Whosoever is not warmed by the morning sun will not be warmed by the evening sun." If a person was unlucky in his youth, he will not become lucky in his old age. (Se 124)

Outward Appearance

155. "The apple is red, but inside it is (full of) worms." (Se 61)

156. "People (are judged) by (their) clothes." Appearance brings more respect than virtue. The proverb is somewhat critical of this rule, yet it is used to encourage its acceptance. It is associated with an anecdote about Bahlūl the jester: When he came to the shah's *dīwān* clad in rags, he was kicked out. When later on he came back wearing an impressive robe, he was shown great respect by being chosen the first to be served the traditional coffee. He took it and poured it on his robe, explaining, "I was here before, but I was kicked out. I assume therefore that the coffee is for my robe, since *it* was not here before." (Sa 65)

157. "In the village — your name, on the road — your clothes." In a man's hometown he is appreciated for his good name and virtue, since everybody knows him; in other places he is judged only according to his appearance and clothing. (R 69)

158. "God knew how (evil) the serpent was; He therefore put his feet in his belly." See chap. I, n. 22, above. Said of afflicted people, such as the blind, who behave viciously: people get what they deserve. (Sa 109)

159. "You think he is asleep, but then he acts like a dormant snake." Same sense as proverb 158. (R 44)

160. "The sound of a drum is pleasant (only) from afar." Foreign places are more attractive from a distance than when actually visited. Also, virtues attributed to strangers seldom stand up under closer scrutiny. (Sa 63)

161. "He whose face is black with soot is not necessarily a blacksmith." All that glitters isn't gold. (R 98; Se 63)

Patience

162. "After distress (comes) ease." (Se 66)

163. "From the dropping of a (single) bird rises an immense heap." (Sa 67)
164. "Farthing by farthing the bin grows full." (Se 91)
165. "He who endures patiently will overcome." (R 24)
166. "Go farther, reach sooner." By taking the long but safe route one will reach one's goal sooner than by choosing unsafe or unknown shortcuts. (U)

Poor and Rich

167. "The tree is very beautiful, but it bears no fruit." Said of a wealthy but stingy person. (R 29)
168. "A camel was offered for sale for (only) one piaster, but I did not have the piaster to buy it with." For a penniless pauper even cheap things are expensive. (R 82)
169. "When there is money, halvah is abundant." Cf. Eccles. 10:19, *Money answereth all things*. (Sa 101)
170. "Tall people pick the peaches, while short ones (who cannot reach high enough) slap their own faces and cry." Said about the rich and the poor. (R 92)
171. "When a (poor) man sneezes, they say to him, 'The ten plagues (of Egypt) on you!' When a (rich) man breaks wind, they say, 'God bless you!'" (R 94) *Variant*: "When a rich man breaks wind, they say, '(God's) mercy on you.' When a poor man (so much as) coughs, they say, 'Shame on you!'" (Se 100)
172. "To a rich man (wearing a new garment they say), 'Wear it well!' To a poor man (they say), 'Where did you get it?'" (Se 98)
173. "When a rich man eats a snake's head, they say, 'How clever he is!' When a poor man eats it, they say, 'How voracious he is!'" (Se 99)
174. "No bad breath comes from the mouth of a lion." People flatter the wealthy. Cf. chap. XVII, tale 16, above. (Se 101)
175. "May the lower (class) be as lucky as the upper (class)!" (Se 132)
176. "Your disgrace is in your pocket — once your pocket is empty, your disgrace comes out." Disgrace is the companion of poverty. (Sa 23)
177. "By the time fat (people) grow lean, the lean ones get rotten." During lean years the rich may have less to eat; but the poor die of hunger. (Sa 57)

178. "What does a full stomach know about an empty stomach?" (Sa 76)
179. "(A person) stung by a snake can fall asleep; (one) stung by hunger cannot sleep." (Sa 96)
180. "He whose stomach is empty, as soon as he eats (something) he is satisfied and his desire is subdued; he whose house is empty (i.e., who is indigent), the more he eats the more his eye remains hungry." Indigent people are constantly hungry, their desire never subsides. (Sa 148)

Practical Wisdom

181. "Acorns cannot be tied with a rope." Do not try to do the impossible. (Sa 27)
182. "(When) a jug breaks, it can be replaced; (not so man)." Do not worry about lost material things. (Sa 28)
183. "Expensive is cheap, cheap is expensive." Better to spend more money and buy something of good quality than to save money by buying something cheap and of poor quality. (Sa 51)
184. "If the donkey will not move toward the load, let the load move toward the donkey." One must compromise. (Sa 55)
185. "Short (story or speech) is sweet." (Sa 79)
186. "Whatever is gone, is gone." Do not grieve about lost opportunities. (Sa 128)
187. "A broken loaf does not become whole (again)." Worrying about a loss is useless. (Sa 136)
188. "(Leave) that worry for that time." Do not worry about future troubles. Cf. B. Ber 9b. (Sa 140)
189. "A word that comes out of (just) two lips circulates (in) the entire village." Said of gossiping or revealing secrets. (Sa 141)
190. "God knows His thieves." Do not cheat or steal, thinking that nobody is watching — God is! (Sa 143)
191. "Big-belly, come and carry the loads." Said sarcastically when a task is given to the wrong person. (Sa 149)
192. "Longevity comes to the man who never goes out of his house." In times of war only those who stay home are lucky enough to survive. (Sa 152)
193. "If you have no one (to talk to), talk to the walls." (U)
194. "Three things should not be trusted: water, fire, and a dog." They all can be dangerous. (R 27)

195. "The earth quakes, but is not destroyed." In times of trouble do not give up hope. (R 88)
196. "One child can lead to pasture a thousand beasts." Intelligence is superior to physical strength. (R 93)
197. "A loose tooth is better pulled out." (Se 12)
198. "He who cheats others cheats himelf." (Se 23)
199. "When the iron is cold, do not strike it." (Se 77)
200. "No rumor goes out that is (entirely) false." (Se 119)
201. "The liar's house caught fire, but no one believed him." (Se 126)
202. "To the mouth, pleasant, but to the belly, a black snake." Said of the onion. (Se 130)
203. "Do not despise yourself." (Se 134)
204. "The broth of many (rival) cooks is inedible." (Se 135)

Promise

205. "A promise, even if a person (must) die to (fulfill) it, should not be broken." (Sa 2)
206. "(Whatever) your mouth says, let your ears hear." Practice what you preach — keep your promise. (Sa 4)

Prudence

207. "Better an egg today than a chicken tomorrow." (Se 71)
208. "Kiss the hand that you cannot bite." (Se 72)
209. "After the alarm, go; before the alarm, do not go." Rushing to help others in a burglary or a fight may cost you your life. (Se 73)
210. "Walls have ears." Always discuss secrets in a low voice. Cf. Lev. Rabbah, 32: "Road has ears, wall has ears." (Se 74)
211. "Do not bring out your bread among the hungry." You will feel obliged to feed them, or they may take the bread away from you, perhaps injuring you or even killing you. (Se 75)
212. "He locked the windows and the doors after his house was burglarized." One should be cautious before the damage is done. (R 61)
213. "Do not eat hot food, and you will not burn your mouth." Cf. "If you can't stand the heat, stay out of the kitchen." (R 71)
214. "A bird went guarantor for a starling, but both can fly away."

Said when both the debtor and the guarantor are not to be trusted. (R 72)

215. "If you have lost one eye, guard (well) the other eye." (R 96)

216. "'Guard, come arrest me,' (said the burglar)." Do not complicate your problems unnecessarily. (Sa 60)

217. "(Save) white money for a black day." (Sa 102)

218. "All dishes need salt, (but only) in reasonable (amounts)." Do not exaggerate. (Sa 132)

Sexual Desire

219. "He is dead, but his member is erect." Said of an old man who is still amorous. (Se 58)

220. "He left his saddlebag to follow his member." Said of people who neglect their work and duties to indulge in carnal pleasure. (Sa 129)

221. "Satan has not died and will not die." Sexual desire is everlasting, and marriage is a must. (Sa 115)

222. "Bachelors are blind." They behave irrationally when in love. (Sa 22)

223. "(After the chaste) bride has come out of (her) village, her buttocks are visible more often than her face." Said of women who are shy before marriage but bold after it. (Sa 74)

224. "The old man has (merely) pinched (her), and the old woman (already) feels pleasure." Women's passions are aroused more swiftly than men's. (Se 56)

225. "An old woman, (even if) a hundred years old, when she hears the sound of a drum, her feet begin to move." Women are always frivolous. (Se 57)

226. "When a whore repents, she becomes a procuress." Immorality is not easily curable. (Se 38)

227. "If husband and wife who are quarreling go to bed, the bed covers will make peace between them." Associated with an anecdote: A king asked his courtiers, "What is the best thing in the world?" They could think of no answer. One of them, a Jew, returned home and told his daughter about the king's question. She said, "Tell him, sexual intercourse." He went back to the king and told him so. The king then asked, "From whom did you hear this?" He replied, "From my daughter." The king then asked, "Is she married or unmarried?" He replied, "She is a virgin." Thereupon the king sent

for her and asked her how she knew the answer. She replied, "My father and mother often quarrel until they almost kill each other, but when they finally go to sleep together, behold, they are at peace." (R 20)

Weather and Seasons

228. "Red cloud in the morning, take the tamper and go up to the roof (to tamp the roofing plaster in order to prevent leaks from the rain); red cloud in the evening, get up (the next) morning and find the weather fine." This weather forecast is universal: "Red sky at night, sailors' delight; red sky in the morning, sailors take warning." (Sa 16)
229. "Snow in the evening, rain the next morning." (Sa 26)
230. "Not every windy day is a rainy day." Also in a metaphorical sense: bad does not necessarily lead to worse. (Sa 86)
231. "Not every cloud brings rain." (Se 64)
232. "In the winter do not let yourself be idle, and in the spring do not let yourself get wet." In the winter do not wait for the rain to stop, for it will continue. In the spring wait for the rain to stop, for it is only a passing shower. (Se 105)
233. "Summer is the father of the poor." They do not need as much clothing and shelter as in the winter. (Sa 107)
234. "(In the winter) fire is better than mother and father (to keep one warm)." (Sa 1)
235. "On Sabbath *Wa-ʾeraʾ*[11] winter is (raining) cats and dogs." (Sa 116)
236. "On Sabbath *Boʾ ʾel parʿoh*[12] winter is mixed up." (Sa 117)
237. "On Sabbath *Bĕ-šallaḥ*[13] winter (begins) to shed its snakeskin." (Sa 118)
238. "On Sabbath *Yiṯro*[14] winter's flesh shrinks." (Sa 119)
239. "On Sabbath *Rappoʾ yĕrappeʾ*[15] winter's feet are crushed." (Sa 120)

11. *I appeared* (Exod. 6:3) — about mid-January; the first word of the weekly Biblical lesson read in the synagogue on that Sabbath. In the original proverb the Hebrew word either rhymes with the Neo-Aramaic words or forms a play on words. See nn. 15, 19, below.

12. *Go in unto Pharaoh* (Exod. 10:1) — a week later.

13. *When (Pharaoh) had let (the people) go* (Exod. 13:17) — end of January.

14. *Jethro* (Exod. 18:1) — first week of February.

15. *Shall cause (him) to be thoroughly healed* (Exod. 21:19) — mid-February. The name of the lesson is actually *Mišpaṭim* (Exod. 21:1), but these two Hebrew words are used here for rhyming purposes. See n. 11, above.

240. "On Sabbath *Tĕrumah*[16] winter becomes an orphan." (Sa 121)
241. "On Sabbath *Ki tiśśa'*[17] do not worry about snow." (Sa 122)
242. "On Sabbath *Way-yakhel — Pĕkude*[18] water in water bottles becomes warm." (Sa 123)
243. "On Sabbath *Way-yikra'*[19] winter is uprooted (i.e., gone altogether)." (Sa 124)

Wives and Women

244. "The husband who batters his wife batters his life (literally, 'his luck')." He only causes more trouble for himself eventually. (R 12)
245. "Lend your wife to your friend, but not your beast of burden." The latter is valuable property in a rural society and may be exploited and abused more than a wife, who can take care of herself in such a situation. (R 16)
246. "Whosoever approaches his wife (sexually) against her will, will have insolent children as a result." (R 21)
247. "If you want to marry a woman, you must have a lot of money or a lot of lies." False promises or boasts capture the hearts of women as surely as material wealth. This motif is common in Jewish and Islamic legends. See Ginzberg, 6, 288: "Solomon once overheard a male bird say to its mate, 'If thou desirest it, I shall forthwith destroy the throne upon which Solomon sits.' Astonished at its impudence, the wise king had this bird appear before him, and asked it to explain what it meant by these boasting words. The bird replied, 'O Solomon, where is thy wisdom? Knowest thou not that one utters foolish things to gain the admiration of the woman one loves?'" Cf. Schwarzbaum, pp. 111–15. (R 34)
248. "There are three kinds of women: human, bitch, and she-ass." Associated with an Islamic legend: "It is told that Noah had only one daughter. When he was about to build the ark, a carpenter, a smith, and a plasterer came to him, and each one of them promised to help him in his task if he would give

16. *Offering* (Exod. 25:1) — third week of February.

17. *When thou takest* (Exod. 30:12) — first week of March.

18. *And (Moses) assembled* (Exod. 35:1) and *(These are) the accounts* (Exod. 38:31) — second week of March.

19. *And (the Lord) called* (Lev. 1:1) — third week of March. Weather forecasts such as these are common also in other Jewish communities. See Sabar (1978a), p. 229.

him his daughter to wife. Noah promised each one of them separately that he would give him his daughter. Thereupon they (all) helped him (to build the ark). After they had finished their work, Noah was at a loss. He prayed to God, and an angel came down and turned Noah's bitch and she-ass into women. Thus he gave one woman to each of the three men. Some time later they came to visit Noah, and only the carpenter was happy, for he was fortunate to have the (human) daughter of Noah, whereas the other two were unhappy. The husband of the bitch complained that she talked endlessly, and the husband of the she-ass complained that she was never satiated sexually and was very lustful." (R 41) See Schwarzbaum, pp. 211–16.

249. "An adulteress needs a house with two doors (one in the front and one in the back)," in order to send lovers away safely when her husband comes home unexpectedly. (R 62)

250. "At night the wife is beautiful and pleasing, in daytime she is erratic and irritating." Said of beautiful but stupid wives. (R 63)

251. "The wife is very beautiful, but she has only one eye." Said of a beautiful but evil-minded woman. "The One-Eyed One" in Neo-Aramaic is the nickname of Sammael the angel of death. For the etymology of Sammael as "the blind one" (*samya'*), see Ginzberg, 5, 121.[20] (R 64)

252. "Only after his wife died did he learn to appreciate her." *Variant*: "Only after his beast of burden died did he learn how to take care of it." Said of husbands who do not treat their wives properly while they are living, but speak affectionately of them and miss them greatly after they are dead. (R 65–66)

253. "Only after the wife bears children do people recognize her good qualities." Rearing children is the true test of a good wife. (R 68)

254. A wife is happier when alone with her husband than when surrounded by a whole crowd." Intimacy for women, in contrast to men, is more important than social life. (R 81)

255. "He who listens to his wife will fall off his chair." Do not consult women on important business matters. (Se 108)

256. "If the mother is a stepmother, the (natural) father likewise

20. See also chap. V, §18, above.

becomes a stepfather." An evil stepmother influences her husband to treat his first wife's children cruelly. (Se 115)

257. "Mother is bother, sister is trouble, (but to) a wife (one says), 'Come, get on my back, and I will carry you to the end of the world.'" After marriage, young men neglect their relatives and care only about their wives. Cf. Gen. 2:24. (Sa 36)

258. "Wife makes husband a success, and wife makes husband a failure." Cf. chap. XVII, tale 7, above, and n. 3 ad loc. (Sa 153)

Work and Self-Reliance

259. "(When my) work is done by my friends, my hands rest (but) my heart wears out." Said sarcastically of other people's help, to encourage self-help. (Sa 127)

260. "He who depends on his friends will go to sleep supperless." (Se 32)

261. "Work is man's salt." It enhances the flavor of life. (Se 44)

262. "Leave today's food for tomorrow, but not today's work." (Se 44)

263. "God does not throw (money) in through the window." One must work for a living. (Se 45)

264. "Give with your hand, but seek (also) with your foot." Work for a living with both your hands and your feet — doubly hard. (Se 46)

265. "Movement (i.e., action) is a blessing." Said to encourage idlers or spinsters to go out and meet people. (Sa 59)

266. "Water that remains long in one place begins to stink." (Sa 91)

267. "Eat like a dog, but rise like a lion." Dogs eat quickly, lions rise quickly. (Se 48)

268. "(Even) contention is better than idleness." (See 88)

269. "Toil (goes on) until death." Said with resignation. (Sa 78)

270. "He who catches fish gets his buttocks wet." (Se 47)

271. "Only if you scratch your body with your own hands, will you achieve relief." *Variant*: "If a man does not scratch his body with his own hand, others will not scratch it for him." (R 19; Se 86)

272. "Success in one's work does not depend on the plain or on the mountain." It matters not where you work but how you work. (U)

273. "If the palm of your hand is not dark (from work), you will have no good taste in your mouth." (R 28)

274. "He who is constantly occupied with study will end up a beggar." Cf. ʾAḇ 2:2, "Excellent is study of Torah combined with a worldly occupation." (R 23)

275. "Every sheep is hung up by its own legs." Every person is responsible for his good and bad deeds. (Sa 80)

276. "When a jug is broken by the maid, no sound is heard from its crash." An employee is afraid to report to his employer damage caused by his carelessness. (R 104)

ABBREVIATIONS

EI	*Encyclopaedia of Islam.* 1st edition, 4 vols.; EI^2 — new edition, vols. 1-3 (in progress).
EJ	*Encyclopaedia Judaica* (English). 16 vols. Jerusalem, 1972.
JAOS	*Journal of the American Oriental Society*
JJS	*Jewish Journal of Sociology*
JNES	*Journal of Near Eastern Studies*
JQR	*Jewish Quarterly Review*
PAAJR	*Proceedings of the American Academy for Jewish Research*
YJS	*Yale Judaica Series*

Tractates of Mishnah, Tosefta, and Talmud

Ab̲	ʾAb̲ot̲	Ned̲	Nĕd̲arim
AZ	ʿĂb̲od̲ah Zarah	Pes	Pĕsaḥim
BB	Bab̲a Bat̲ra	Sanh	Sanhed̲rin
Ber	Bĕrak̲ot̲	Shab	Šabbat̲
BM	Bab̲a Mĕṣiʿa	Soṭ	Soṭah
Giṭ	Giṭṭin	Suk	Sukkah
Ḥul	Ḥullin	Ta	Taʿănit̲
Ḳid	Ḳiddušin	Yeb̲	Yĕb̲amot̲
Meḡ	Mĕḡillah		

B. prefixed to the name of a tractate indicates a reference to the Babylonian Talmud; P. indicates a reference to the Palestinian (Jerusalemite) Talmud; and Tos a reference to the Tosefta (ed. Zuckermandel, Pasewalk, 1880; 2d ed., Jerusalem, 1937). Otherwise the reference is to tractates of the Mishnah.

GLOSSARY

Aggadah
that part of Talmudic (and of later rabbinic) literature which does not deal with legal matters

Agha
a Kurdish lord or chieftain

ʿĂmidah
the principal prayer recited at all synagogue services; also called *Šĕmoneh ʿEśreh* (Eighteen [Benedictions])

ʾĂmoraʾim (sing. *ʾĂmora*)
Talmudic authorities who flourished ca. 200–500 C.E. and whose discussions are contained in the Gemara

ʾAzharot
poems listing the 613 Biblical commandments, recited at Pentecost

Bar mitzvah
the ceremony marking the attainment of religious and legal maturity by a boy at the age of thirteen years and one day.

Daršan
a preacher who delivers the sermon (*draša*) in the synagogue

Dayyan
a judge, a member of the rabbinical court

Dinar (Arabic, from the Latin *denarius*)
a monetary unit in Iraq

Dīwān (Persian, "governmental office")
divan, the royal assembly or court

Draša (*daruš*; Hebrew *dĕrašah*)
a homily or sermon delivered by the preacher (*daršan*)

Exilarch
the chief magistrate of the Jewish community in Babylonia (later, Iraq) from at least the Parthian period (ca. 145 C.E.) to the Mongol conquest of Baghdad in the middle of the thirteenth century. Traditionally the exilarchs were of Davidic descent and represented the Jewish community at the caliph's court

Gaon (pl. *Geonim*)
the title borne by the heads of the Babylonian academies that flourished from the seventh to the eleventh centuries

Gemara
the part of the Talmud containing the comments of the ʾĂmoraʾim on the Mishnah

Genizah
a depository for worn-out and discarded books and documents

Geṭ
a bill of divorcement

Habdalah
the benediction of "separation," recited at the close of the Sabbath or holy day

Hafṭarot (sing. *hafṭarah*; "conclusions")
portions from the Prophetical books of the Bible recited on Sabbaths and holy days after the lessons from the Pentateuch

Haggadah
the ritual recited on the first and second Passover nights at the seder table

Ḥakam
the title of the rabbi of a Kurdistani congregation

Halakah
the part of Talmudic (and of later rabbinic) literature dealing with legal matters; in general, rule or legal ordinance

Ḥăliṣah
the ceremony prescribed in Deut. 25:7–10 to mark the refusal of a man to marry his brother's childless widow, thus releasing her to marry any other man

Halvah
a confection made of crushed sesame seeds and sugar

Ḥazzan
the precentor who chants the liturgy and leads the congregation in the synagogue service

Hefḳer
abandoned or ownerless property

Ḳabbalah
Jewish mystical thought and literature

Kašrut
Jewish dietary laws

Ḳinot (sing. *ḳinah*)
dirges recited on the Ninth of Ab and other fast days, as well as on other sad occasions

Maʿăśeh (pl. *maʿăśiyyot*)
a Jewish folktale or legend

Maqāmāt (Arabic, "sessions, meetings")
a genre of medieval Arabic and Hebrew literature written in rhythmic prose

Mĕgillot ("scrolls")
the collective name of five Biblical books: Song of Songs, Ruth, Lamentations, Esther, and Ecclesiastes

Mĕzuzah
literally "doorpost" (Deut. 6:9); a piece of parchment bearing the verses

Deut. 6:4–9, 11:13–21, and the name *Shadday,* encased in a small cylinder and affixed to the right-hand doorpost of a Jewish home

Midrash (pl. Midrashim)
: the homiletic method of interpreting Scripture; the literature consisting of such homilies

Midraš
: prayer house and school

Minḥah
: the afternoon prayer

Minyan (pl. *minyanim*)
: the quorum of ten adult males required for prayer service in the synagogue and for some other religious ceremonies

Mohel
: a person qualified to perform circumcision

Muʿallim (Arabic, "instructor, teacher")
: a title synonymous with *ḥak̲am*

Mukhtār (Arabic, "elected [officeholder]")
: the title of the Jewish official in charge of public records, such as birth and death certificates

Musaf
: an additional prayer recited on the Sabbath and on festivals

Piyyuṭ (pl. *piyyuṭim*)
: a Hebrew liturgical poem

Pizmon (pl. *pizmonim*)
: a poem with a refrain

Šaddar (pl. *šaddarim*)
: an emissary dispatched from the Land of Israel to collect money to support the Jewish community residing there

Sarāy (Persian, "house")
: the headquarters or palace of the (Turkish) governor

Sayyid (Arabic, "master")
: the title of the prophet Muḥammad's direct descendants; a Biblical prophet

Seder ("order, arrangement")
: a ritual observed at the table on the first and second nights of Passover, when the *Hagga̲dah* is recited

Sĕliḥo̲t (sing. *sĕliḥah*)
: penitential prayers

Sheikh (Arabic, "elder")
: a Muslim scholar; the title of an elder member of the Jewish burial society

Shekinah
: the Divine Presence

Shemaʿ {Yiśraʾel}
"Hear, [O Israel]!" (Deut. 6:4), the name of a group of passages from Scripture (Deut. 6:4–9, 11:13–21; Num. 15:37–41) that must be recited daily, morning and evening.

Ṣiṣiṯ
the fringes attached to the corners of men's four-cornered prayer shawls (Num. 15:37–41; Deut. 22:12)

Sukkah
the booth used in the observance of the Festival of Tabernacles

Tafsīr (pl. *tafsīrim*; Arabic, "interpretation")
Neo-Aramaic translations or paraphrases of Biblical or liturgical texts

Taḳḳanoṯ (sing. *taḳḳanah*)
rabbinic ordinances, having the force of law, enacted to govern the internal life of communities and congregations

Targum (pl. *targumim*)
Aramaic translations of the Hebrew Bible

Wālī
a regional Turkish governor or prefect

Yĕḇamah
the widowed sister-in-law subject to levirate marriage

Yeshiva (pl. *yeshivot*)
a traditional Jewish academy devoted primarily to the study of rabbinic law

SELECTED BIBLIOGRAPHY

Note: Most incidental references cited fully in the notes or unique to a certain chapter are not listed here. See also pp. 135–36, above.

Avidani, 'Alwān. *Sefer Ma'áśeh (!) hag-Geḏolim.* 5 vols. Jerusalem, 5732–36 (1972–76).

Badger, George Percy. *The Nestorians and Their Rituals.* 2 vols. London, 1852. Reprint. Farmborough, UK, 1969.

Bates, Daniel G. "Kurds." In *Muslim Peoples: A World Ethnographic Survey,* edited by Richard V. Weekes, pp. 220–26. Westport — London, 1978.

Benayahu, Meir. "Rabbi Šĕmu'el Barzānī Roš Golaṯ Kurdistan." *Sĕfunoṯ* 9 (1965): 23–125.

Ben-Jacob, Abraham. *Ḳĕhillot Yĕhude Kurdistan* [Kurdistani Jewish communities]. Jerusalem, 1961. Reprint. Jerusalem, 1981.

Benjamin of Tudela. *Itinerary.* Edited by M. N. Adler. London, 1907.

Benjamin II, I. J. *Eight Years in Asia and Africa.* Hanover, 1863.

Ben-Zvi, Isaac. "Lost and Regained: They That Were Lost in the Land of Assyria." *Phylon* 16 (1955): 57–63.

———. *The Exiled and the Redeemed.* Philadelphia, 1961.

Bin Gorion, Micha Joseph. *Mim-Mĕḳor Yiśra'el: Classical Jewish Folktales.* 3 vols. Philadelphia, 1976.

Brauer, Erich. *Yĕhude Kurdistan: Mehḵar 'Etnologi* [The Jews of Kurdistan: An ethnological study]. Jerusalem, 1947.

Cohen, Claudine. *Grandir au quartier Kurde: Rapports de générations et modèles culturels d'un groupe d'adolescents Israéliens d'origine Kurde.* Paris, 1975.

D'Beth Hillel, David. *Unknown Jews in Unknown Lands: The Travels of Rabbi David D'Beth Hillel.* Edited by W. J. Fischel. New York, 1973.

Ehrlich, Joseph. *Ha-Hărariyyim* [The mountaineers]. Tel-Aviv, 1961.

Feitelson, Dina. "Aspects of the Social Life of Kurdish Jews." *JJS* 1 (1959):201–16.

Feldman, A. M., and Miller, E. *The Jews of Sandor: An Exhibition Organized by the Maurice Spertus Museum of Judaica.* Chicago, 1975.

Field, Henry. "Jews of Sandur, Iraq." *Asia* 37 (1937): 708–10.

Fischel, Walter J. "The Jews of Kurdistan a Hundred Years Ago: A Traveler's Record." *Jewish Social Studies* 6 (1944): 195–226.

———. "The Jews of Kurdistan: A First-Hand Report on a Near Eastern Mountain Community." *Commentary* 8 (1949): 554–59.

Garbell, Irene. *The Jewish Neo-Aramaic Dialect of Persian Azerbaijan: Linguistic Analysis and Folkloristic Texts.* The Hague, 1965.

Gaster, Moses. *The Exempla of the Rabbis.* London, 1924. Reprint. New York, 1968.

———. *Maʿaśeh Book.* 2 vols. Philadelphia, 1934.

Gerson-Kiwi, Edith. "The Music of Kurdistan Jews: A Synopsis of Their Musical Styles." *Yuval* 2 (1972): 59–72.

Ginzberg, Louis. *The Legends of the Jews.* 6 vols. Index volume by B. Cohen. Philadelphia, 1946.

Grant, Asahel. *The Nestorians, or the Lost Tribes.* London, 1841. Reprint. Amsterdam, 1973.

Hamilton, James. "The Use of Genetic Markers in Oriental Jewish Historical Studies." *JQR* 62 (1972): 288–313.

Hansen, Henny H. *Daughters of Allah: Among Muslim Women in Kurdistan.* London, 1960.

———. *The Kurdish Woman's Life.* Copenhagen, 1961.

al-Ḥarizi, Judah. *Taḥkĕmoni.* Edited by Y. Toporovsky. Tel-Aviv, 1952. English translation by V. E. Reichert. 2 vols. Jerusalem, 1965–73.

Jastrow, Marcus. *A Dictionary of the Targumim, the Talmud Babli and Yerushalmi, and the Midrashic Literature.* 2 vols. New York, 1950.

Laurie, Thomas. *Dr. Grant and the Mountain Nestorians.* Boston, 1853.

Layard, Austen H. *Discoveries in the Ruins of Nineveh and Babylon.* New York, 1853.

Leslau, Wolf. *Falasha Anthology: The Black Jews of Ethiopia. YJS,* vol. 6. New Haven, 1951. Reprint. New York, 1969.

Maclean, Arthur John. *Grammar of the Dialects of Vernacular Syriac.* Cambridge, 1895. Reprint. Amsterdam, 1971.

———. *A Dictionary of the Dialects of Vernacular Syriac.* Oxford, 1901. Reprint. Amsterdam, 1972.

Magnarella, Paul J. "A Note on Aspects of Social Life among the Jewish Kurds of Sanandaj, Iran." *JJS 11* (1969): 51–58.

Mann, Jacob. "Documents concerning the Jews in Mosul and Ḳurdistān." In his *Texts and Studies in Jewish History and Literature, 1,* pp. 477–549. Cincinnati, 1931. Reprint. New York, 1972.

Minorsky, V. "Kurdistan, Kurds." *EI* 2 (1927): 1130–55.

Patai, Raphael. *Society, Culture, and Change in the Middle East.* 3rd ed. Philadelphia, 1971.

Pethahiah of Ratisbon. *Sibbuḇ.* Edited by E. Gruenhut. Frankfurt a. M., 1905. English translation by A. Benisch. London, 1861.

Rivlin, Joseph Joel. *Širaṯ Yĕhuḏe hat-Targum* [The poetry of the Jews of Kurdistan]. Jerusalem, 1959.

Sabar, Yona. "Ha-ʾĔmunah bĕ-Šeḏim uḇĕ-Mazziqin ʾeṣel Yĕhuḏe Kurdistan." *Yeḏaʿ-ʿAm 8/26* (1962): 27–28.

———. "Tafsirim lĕ-Miḳraʾ u-Fiyyuṭim bi-Lĕšonam ha-ʾĂrammiṯ šel Yĕhuḏe Kurdistan." *Sĕfunoṯ 10* (1966): 337–412.

———. "Hay-Yesoḏoṯ ha-ʿIḇriyyim ban-Niḇ ha-ʾĂrammi šebbĕ-Fi Yĕhuḏe Zakho bĕ-Kurdistan." *Lĕšonenu 38* (1974a): 206–19.

————. "First Names, Nicknames, and Family Names among the Jews of Kurdistan." *JQR* 65 (1974b): 43–51.

————. "Nursery Rhymes and Baby Words in the Jewish Neo-Aramaic Dialect of Zakho (Iraq)." *JAOS* 94 (1974c): 329–36.

————. "Hay-Yĕsoḏoṯ ha-ʿIḇriyyim ban-Niḇim ha-ʾĀrammiyyim šel Yĕhuḏe ʾAzerbayjan." *Lĕšonenu* 39 (1975a): 272–94.

————. "The Impact of Israeli Hebrew on the Neo-Aramaic Dialect of the Jews of Zakho in Israel: A Case of Language Shift." *Hebrew Union College Annual* 46 (1975b): 489-508.

————. *Pĕšaṭ Wayhi Bĕšallaḥ, a Neo-Aramaic Midrash on Bĕšallaḥ* (Exodus). Wiesbaden, 1976a (including "A Survey of the Oral and Written Literature of the Kurdish Jews," pp. 161–78).

————. "Lēl-Hūza: Story and History in a Cycle of Lamentations for the Ninth of Ab in the Jewish Neo-Aramaic Dialect of Zakho, Iraqi Kurdistan." *Journal of Semitic Studies* 21 (1976b): 138–62.

————. "Multilingual Proverbs in the Neo-Aramaic Speech of the Jews of Zakho, Iraqi Kurdistan." *International Journal of Middle East Studies* 9 (1978a): 215–35.

————. "From Tel-Kepe in Iraqi Kurdistan to Providence, Rhode Island: The Story of a Chaldean Immigrant to the U.S.A. in 1927." *JAOS* 98 (1978b): 410-15.

————. "Kurdistani Realia and Attitudes in the Midrashic-Aggadic Literature of the Kurdish Jews." In *Studies in Jewish Folklore,* edited by Frank Talmadge, pp. 287–96. Cambridge, Mass., 1980.

————. "Qiṣtit Ḥannah — Sippur Ḥannah wĕ-Šibʿaṯ Baneha ba-ʾArammiṯ šebbe-Fi Yĕhuḏe Kurdistan." In *Pĕʿamim* 7 (1981): 83–99.

————. "The Arabic Elements in the Jewish Neo-Aramaic Texts of Nerwa and ʿAmāḏīya, Iraqi Kurdistan." In *Franz Rosenthal Festschrift,* edited by J. A. Bellamy and J. Lassner, forthcoming.

————. "Legend vs. Reality: An Analysis and Comparison of Folktales about the Rabbis of Kurdistan with Documents Written by Them or Their Contemporaries." *Proceedings of the First International Congress for Study of Heritage of Sephardic and Near Eastern Jewish Communities.* Jerusalem, forthcoming.

————. *Midrašim bĕ-ʾArammiṯ Yĕhuḏe Kurdistan lĕ-Farašiyyoṯ Wayḥi, Bĕšallaḥ wĕ-Yiṯro.* Jerusalem, forthcoming.

————. "Peruš Dĕraši lĕ-Sefer Yonah bĕ-ʾArammiṯ Ḥaḏašah šel Yĕhuḏe Kurdistan." In *Haḡuṯ ʿIḇriṯ bĕ-ʾArṣoṯ ha-ʾIslam,* edited by Menahem Zohori. Jerusalem, forthcoming.

————. *Sefer Bĕrešiṯ ban-Niḇ ha-ʾArammi šel Yĕhuḏe Zako.* Jerusalem (forthcoming).

————. "Tafsir lĕ-Hafṭarah šel Šĕmini dĕ-Fesaḥ (Isa. 10:32–12:6) bĕ-ʾArammiṯ Ḥaḏašah šel Yĕhuḏe Kurdistan." In *Noy lĕ-Dov,*

The Dov Noy Festschrift, edited by B. Z. Fischler, B. Bayer, and I. Ben-Ami. Jerusalem, forthcoming.

Schwartz, Ora. "Jewish Weaving in Kurdistan." *Journal of Jewish Art* 3/4 (1977): 74–89.

Schwarzbaum, Haim. *Mim-Mĕḳor Yiśra'el wĕ-Yišma'el* [The folkloristic aspects of Judaism and Islam]. Tel-Aviv, 1975.

Shai, Donna. *Neighborhood Relations in an Immigrant Quarter: A Social-Anthropological Study.* Jerusalem, 1970.

———. "Wedding Customs among Kurdish Jews in Kurdistan (Zakho) and in Israel (Jerusalem)." *Studies in Marriage Customs, Folklore Research Center Studies* 4 (1974): 253–66.

Stern, Henry A. *Dawnings of Light in the East.* London, 1854.

Weintraub, Dov, et al. *Immigration and Social Change: Agricultural Settlement of New Immigrants in Israel.* Jerusalem, 1971.

Xenophon. *The Persian Expedition [Anabasis].* Translated by Rex Warner. Edinburgh: Penguin Books, 1949.

al-Ẓāhirī, Zechariah (Yaḥyā). *Sefer ham-Musar.* Edited by Y. Ratzaby. Jerusalem, 1965.

Zikmund, M., and Hanzelka, J. *Kurdistan: Country of Insurrections, Legends, and Hope.* Czechoslovakia: Artia, 1962.

GENERAL INDEX

Aaron, 172
ʿAbd Allāh ben Sibar, 101
Abinadab, 47
Abishai, 65
Abraham, xiii, xix, 9, 187
Abraham, Salmān, 167
Abyssinia, Abyssinians, 61–67. *See also* Ethiopia
Adam, xxxvi, 3–10, 107
Adiabene, xvi, 130
Adoni. *See* Barzānī
Afghanistan, 168
Aghas. *See* Kurdish tribal chieftains
Ahijah the Shilonite, 103
Aḥmad Beg, 109
ʿAḳiba, R., 106, 119, 123, 154
ʿAḳra, xxix, 194
Akraziel, 35
Algeria, xviii
Allāh, 61
Allon, Jacqueline, 44, 172
Alphabet, xxx, 114, 173. *See also* Hebrew language
Alqosh, xxvii–xxix
Alroy Settlement, xxxii, 95
ʿAlwān, Joseph, 189
ʿAlwān, Moses, 189
ʿAlwān, Shabbethai, 189–90
Amasa, 43, 53
American missionaries, xx, xxi
ʿAmidah (prayer), 73
Amidya (ʿAmādiya), xvii, xx, xxxiii, xxxiv, xxxix, 79, 96–127
Amram (Moses' father), 24, 26, 39
Amulets, xxxvii, 172–73, 189–90
Anak (Og's father), 39
Angel of death, 136–38, 221. *See also* Sammael
Angels, 66, 69, 99, 113, 176
Aquila, 85
Arabian Nights (Tales of), 62
Arabic-Jewish literature. *See* Islamic-Judaic literature
Arabic language, xxxvii, 72, 139–40
Arabic loanwords in Neo-Aramaic, xxxiv
Arabic music and songs, xxxviii
Arabic proverbs, xxxiii, xxxix
Arabs, xiv, xv, xvii, 21, 116, 153, 206
Aramaic, xvi–xvii, xxvi, xxvii, xxxiv, xxxvi, 72, 84, 86. *See also* Neo-Aramaic
Ararat, xiii, 96
Arbil (Arbela), xvi, xix, xxix, xxxi, xxxvi, 117, 130–34, 183
Armenia, Armenians, xv, xvii
Armilos, 31
Asaph ben Berechiah, 65
Asenath, 11, 14, 15
Ašiṯa, 127
Ashkelon, 188
Ashkenazi, Aaron, 110
Ashkenazi, Rivka, 136
Ashkenazi, Sasson, 136
Asshur, xxx, 113, 115. *See also* Mosul
Assyria, Assyrian, xiii, xvi, xxvi, 130
Assyrian Christians. *See* Christian Assyrians
Astrologers, Astrology, 96, 99, 109, 120, 124
Augury, 109
Avidani, ʿAlwān, xxxix, 110–11, 117, 124–25
Avidani, Benjamin, 110–11, 129
Avidani, Simeon, 111, 129
Avitsuk, J., 151, 153
Azazel (angel), 40
Azerbaijan, xxxiii
ʾAzharoṯ, xxxvi
Azza (angel), 40
Azzael (angel), 40

Babylonia, xvi, xxvi

SCRIPTURAL REFERENCES

RABBINIC REFERENCES

MISHNAH

ʾAḇoṯ 2:2, *223*; 4:1, *148, 210*

TALMUD, PALESTINIAN

Sanheḏrin, 10, 28c, *79*

TALMUD, BABYLONIAN

Bĕrakoṯ, 4b, *69*; 9b, *216*; 32b, *7*; 64b, *103*
Šabbaṯ, 107b, *146*; 151b, *128*
Pĕsaḥim, 112b, *211*
Yoma, 85a, *118*; 87b, *103*
Sukkah, 56b, *205*
Taʿănit, 5b, *208*; 30a, *72*
Mĕḡillah, 3a, *86, 102*
Ḥaḡiḡah, *117*
Yĕḇamoṯ, 16a, *xiii*; 46a–48a, *86*; 77a, *53*
Nĕḏarim, 50a, *154*
Giṭṭin, 56b–57a, *85*; 57b, *80*; 58a, *76*
Soṭah, 12a, *25, 26*; 36b, *13*
Ḳiddušin, 31a, *189*
Baḇa Mĕṣiʿa, 86a, *122*
Baḇa Baṯra, 91a, *xiii*
Sanheḏrin, 19b, *15*
ʿĂḇoḏah Zarah, 11a, *88*
Ḥullin, 91b, *51*

AGGADIC MIDRASHIM

Gen. Rabbah, 17, *153*; 20, *8*
Exod. Rabbah, 4, *137*
Lev. Rabbah, 7:3, *xxxv*; 32, *217*
Song Rabbah, 1, *114*; 3, *103*
Ruth Rabbah, 2:16, 22, *86*
Lam. Rabbah, 1:4, *183*
Eccles. Rabbah, 11:1–3, *89, 90*
Ben Sira, 2 Alphabet of, 21b, *61*
Esther, Targum Šeni, 1:2, *55*
Mĕḵilta, Pisḥa, 11:24 (Lauterbach, *1*, 88), *87*
Sifre Num., §83 (Horovitz, p. 80), *88*
Tanḥuma, ed. Buber, pp. 81–82, *85, 86*
Yalḳuṭ Šimʿoni, 2, §500, *88*
Zohar, 3, 134, *213*; 3, 144a, *102*; 3, 272a, *51*

TALE TYPES, MOTIFS, AND IFA NUMBERS

Tale Types

Type numbers are from Stith Thompson and Antti Aarne, *The Types of the Folktale: A Classification and Bibliography* (Helsinki, 1961). Asterisks indicate classification added by IFA.

Motifs

Motif numbers are from Stith Thompson, *Motif-Index of Folk-Literature,* 6 vols., rev. ed. (Copenhagen and Bloomington, 1955–58). Asterisks indicate numbers in Dov Noy, "Motif-Index of Talmudic-Midrashic Literature" (Ph.D. diss., Indiana University, 1954).

A. *Mythological Motifs*

Motif no.		*Page*
A44	Torah as God's adviser	4
A63.6	Devil in serpent form tempts first woman (man)	6
A106.2.2.2	Serpent's (Satan's) punishment for misleading Adam	7
A182.3	God (angel) speaks to mortal	113
A185.11	God rewards mortal for pious act	114
A1280	First man (woman)	3
A1611.6	Origin of various Near Eastern peoples	xv

B. *Animals*

B291.1	Bird as messenger	57

C. *Tabu*

C631.1	Tabu: journeying on Sabbath	119

D. *Magic*

D151.5	Transformation: man to raven	76
D200	Transformation: man to object (tree)	119
D457.11	Transformation: eye to another object	73
D475.1.20	Transformation: straw to gold	154
D661	Transformation as punishment	119
D1380.1	Waberlohe. Magic fire surrounds and protects	117, 125
D1761	Magic results produced by wishing	114
D1766.1	Magic results produced by prayer	116
D1766.7.1	Magic results produced in name of deity (Ineffable name)	31, 65, 66, 98
D1766.7.3	Magic results produced in name of saint	123
D1812.3	Future revealed in dream ("prophetic dream")	143
D1813	Magic knowledge of events in distant place	65, 115
D2105.2	Provisions provided by messenger from heaven	114

E. *The Dead*

E754.2.2.1	Angels of death fail to bring soul to heaven	38–39

F. *Marvels*

F531.0.1	Biblical character as giant (Goliath)	46